ROADMAP

to

SUCCESS

Insight Publishing
Sevierville, TN

TABLE OF CONTENTS

A Message from the Publisher

I've done a lot of driving in my life and one thing I have been smart enough to have is a dependable Roadmap. If you don't have a good plan to get from where you are to where you want to go, you will get lost.

I've known many people who have started out in business and thought they had a good plan, but did not achieve the success they wanted. A major problem for many of these people was that they had not sought good advice from people who had achieved success. If you don't learn from the experience of others, you might achieve success but you will probably get there the hard way. You might get lost down many side roads before you find the right one.

Roadmap to Success, is a mini-seminar on how to plan for your success. The successful people in this book have the experience that will help you find what you need to create your Roadmap to success. These perceptive businesspeople were fascinating as they unfolded their own personal Roadmaps and told me about their various success journeys.

I invite you to set aside some quiet time and learn from these exceptional authors. I assure you that your time won't be wasted. It's not often that you can access such a large quantity of quality information that will either get you started or help you get further along on your road to success. This book is an investment in your future—your successful future!

Interviews Conducted by:
David E. Wright, President
Insight Publishing & International Speakers Network

ROADMAP *to* SUCCESS

An interview with...

Jim Dillahunty

David Wright (Wright)

We are fortunate to have Dr. Jim Dillahunty as a contributing author for our discussions of life planning and the construction of a personal Roadmap to success. Dr. Dillahunty is one of the few individuals who can speak from front-line, real-world experiences as a scientist, entrepreneur, founder, and former president of a highly successful financial services firm, Fixed Income Securities, Inc. These real-world experiences of "knowing-how to, and "having done it," are backed up with the academic discipline and rigor of a doctorate in the field of organizational leadership.

Dr. Dillahunty, welcome to *Roadmap to Success*. Let's begin our discussion with a skeptical inquiry. How much of life can we really plan anyway?

Jim Dillahunty (Dillahunty)

I've heard it said that *life is all the stuff that really goes on while we are trying to plan for it*. One absolute truth about life is that we will encounter a continuous stream of unpredictable obstacles and opportunities. That said, I think it is a mistake for us to feel that success is just the result of happenstance, our birth right, or luck, and that preparing and planning for a future we cannot foresee is a waste of time. Even though we do not know what the future will hold for us, we can prepare and plan for the unknown. As a result, we can change the outcomes of life's unpredictable situations to get what we want.

Based on my business experiences, the information I gathered from interviewing successful CEOs, and the research I conducted as part of my doctorate, I discovered how high achievers get what they want in life. They are able to minimize the consequences of adverse situations and maximize the benefits from opportunities. They accomplish this by having developed certain *Life Skills* and by having a *Life Plan* that keeps them on course. Success does not just mysteriously show up on the doorsteps of the fortunate few. Success visits those who are prepared to receive it.

Preparation and planning are the two keys that determine our success in life and they vastly increase our ability to transform potential into reality, no matter what situations we encounter. Together these twin pillars are the supporting foundations of our intentions and our skills. Based on them we set out the action plans we need to prosper in unpredictable situations. Just as in athletic competition, we are never 100 percent sure what will happen in a particular game. But we had better show up prepared, with our skills honed, and our game plan well thought out or we are sure to be sent home disappointed and beaten.

Wright

Do we really need a plan to get where we want to go in life?

Dillahunty

The simple answer for many is: no you don't. Getting by in life does not require a plan. However, in the twenty-first century, *"life boils"* with so many distractions and opportunities that we can get by, drifting along, passively latching on to whatever convenient situations happen by us. On the other hand, if you want to do more with your life than simply, "go with the flow," "follow along in the herd," and "stay where you are," then a well-thought-out, and well-executed plan is absolutely essential for maximizing your individual human potential.

Businesses require and use plans, and so should we as individuals. Our businesses are no more important than our own lives. In fact, I would argue that in our individual lives, planning is equally if not more important to success. A business can long outlive its founders and managers. In life, we only get one chance to get it done right. We have one shot at creating the life we want, and we need an effective and realistic way to make visions into realities. We all need a Roadmap to success—a Life Plan. Part of the planning process requires us to take stock of where we are, where we want to go, and the preparation we need to tend to.

Wright

Are you saying that planning and preparation are more important today than in the past?

Dillahunty

We live in a vastly more complicated era than just twenty years ago. Just look at the schedules of most households; everyone is moving at top speed headed in different directions at the same time. If you are leading a family, planning a career, and working in business, you know the definition of the term *frenetic*. And if you own a business, add to that mix the stress of increased competition from a global economy while you work to introduce new products to new markets, turn sales into profits, prospects into customers, managers into leaders, and children into adults. Yahoo published the results of a study just a few months ago that showed just how fast-paced we are today. The study showed that we can do in eight hours what took our parents forty-three hours to complete! No wonder we feel like we are stuck on a permanent spin cycle.

Not only do we live at a faster pace, there is far too much information blasted our way for anyone to cope with: some fifteen exabytes of *new* information in 2008 alone! Fifteen exabytes of new information is equivalent to eighty-six feet of books for each and every one of the 6.3 billion men, women, and children on the planet. Not only are we overwhelmed by new information, much of it is erroneous, fabricated, or just plain wrongheaded!

And there are so many distractions and seductive media sirens telling us that the *best way* to get ahead is to take the *easy way*. The *easy way*, we are told, requires no preparation and no planning, not even "what's for dinner"! This misguided belief that we can get to success by taking the easy path is one of the main reasons that in America we graduate so few engineers and scientists from our universities.

Wright

Is there one mistake that you think keeps many of us from succeeding with the plans we do have?

Dillahunty

I think we put too much emphasis on *vision* and not enough on *action*. Many of the most popular self-help seminars and motivational books give the impression that a clear vision allows us to prevail over all obstacles. Envisioning the intended results and ignoring the pragmatic step-by-step incremental actions needed to bring visions into reality is, I think, a mistake. The vision part is the easy part. Visions are like dreams of perfection and grandeur, but vision is only the first part of the success equation. It takes pragmatic action to bring visionary goals into reality.

I read recently that when Tiger Woods, the professional golfer, first began to play the game as a youngster, he would draw the

> *The Way [Dao] of our intentions is an easy vision; not so the path.*
> Dr. J. Dillahunty,
> homage Confucius

trajectories associated with the various clubs and visualize the rise and travel of the ball; that was the easy part.

But Tiger Woods did not stop at the vision, he would spend hundreds of hours practicing his strokes to obtain the trajectories that each club was designed to produce. The combination of vision and continuous, pragmatic, step-by-step practice, allows him to produce in reality the visions in his mind's eye.

Wright

Is there one single concept that will help us to get on and stay on the path to our success?

Dillahunty

Actually there are three—*preparation, planning* and *engagement*—that put us on and keep us on the path to success. Preparation, planning, and engagement are vitally important in determining our level of success, and the degree to which we convert our *potential* to *bankable results.* Preparation begins with a Strategic Assessment and the development of Life Skills, and Planning requires a written commitment of action. Engagement is what we actually do with what we know how to do.

First let's discuss what we mean by a plan (I'll discuss the Strategic Assessment, Life Skills development, and Engagement later on in this discussion).

A plan is a Roadmap for our lives that we use to help us get from where we are to where we want to go, hence the title of this book, *Roadmap to Success.* In spite of the fact that life is unpredictable, we still need to prepare and plan for it. In my workshops and leadership sessions I emphasize the enormous benefits that result from taking the time to write down our thoughts and intentions into a life plan. In my experience the advantages of distilling our intentions into a written format brings a number of important benefits to us.

A written plan:

a) Organizes our thoughts and provides us with clarity,
b) Takes stock of our assets and liabilities,
c) Shines a spotlight on inconsistencies and problems,

d) Provides for a steady course as we encounter misadventures,

e) Identifies the strengths on which to build,

f) Identifies the weaknesses we need to compensate for,

g) States our intentionality and serves as a convenient way to communicate it to our social network of close advisors, and

h) Serves to marshal our resources for the tasks at hand.

We can certainly carry our plans in our heads. Most of us do. But when they are written down, they take on a life of their own and are much more useful in getting us where we want to go than just keeping them in our heads. Having said that, "a plan should be written" does not mean "written and then put away" on a shelf never to be seen again until the following New Year's Eve session of writing resolutions. Written plans are living documents and serve us best if they are constantly updated and reviewed for progress, opportunities, and problems, and revised accordingly.

Wright

What do we need to do to develop a successful Roadmap to success?

Dillahunty

A Roadmap to success has several elements. First, we need to determine, where we want to go and what we need to get there. This is a Strategic Assessment exercise and I'll show our readers how to do this in just a minute.

Second, we need to develop a specific set of Life Skills. After we discuss the Strategic Assessment process I will outline the Life Skills we need for success in the twenty-first century. A plan without the skills needed to make it happen invariably leads to frustration, failure, and abandonment of the plan.

Third, we need to actually write down and create the plan of action. From the development of our Life Skills we'll move into writing our plan— our Roadmap to success.

On occasion in my workshops some participants are at first skeptical about the value of a written plan, saying that "life is too complex, unpredictable, and changes too fast to write things down." Actually, it is the complexity, pace, and unpredictability of life that gives written plans their value. If we are heading out on a road trip with only the vision of "Let's go west!" a map would be helpful, if not an absolute requirement. The "westward" highway map we can buy gives us the step-by-step turns, indicates the route numbers, and describes some of what we'll see along the way. Not so in life; we travel by our own wits. There are no "off-the-shelf" maps to buy, no GPS systems, no AAA emergency, and no "On Star" services to call if we get lost. And since we'll never know what we'll encounter on our journey into the future, survival, and success depend on the skills we take along and the maps we create.

Our Roadmap to success starts with a Strategic Assessment of where we are, where we want to go, and what we have to work with; it's like packing for any long trip. The assessment begins by thinking through and discussing a few Strategic Questions that will help us prepare and in the end help make visionary dreams into realities.

Wright

How do you go about conducting a Strategic Assessment?

Dillahunty

The construction of an effective Roadmap begins with an assessment of where we are, where we want to go, and the critical issues that they raise. A "Strategic Assessment" sounds complicated but it's easy to do. It's all about answering five questions—the same strategic questions that companies answer when they start writing a business plan. I believe this assessment technique originated in the 1970s from the Boston Consulting Group (www.bcg.com). The issues that we must discuss as preparation for creating our Roadmap to success are:

1. Where am I now?
2. How did I get here?
3. Where am I going?
4. Where should I be going?
5. How will I get there?

Each question should be addressed as a discussion question. The issues brought to the surface by each question provide insights into the situations we find ourselves in. Write out your issues. The objective of the Strategic Assessment is to uncover truths. Don't let the questions intimidate you—think of them as having a conversation with a close friend.

If you do not like to write, there are two techniques that can make it really simple to prepare your responses to the Strategic Assessment: 1) Use a digital voice recorder that can then plug directly into your PC and have your conversation automatically transcribed from voice into print (Google *"Dragonspeak"*) or 2) Use a technique called *Mind Mapping* (Google *"Mind Mapping"*). A *Mind Map*, according to Wikipedia, "is a diagram used to represent words, ideas, tasks or other items . . . used to generate, visualize, structure, and classify ideas, and as an aid in study, organization, problem-solving, decision-making, and writing." At first glance *Mind Mapping* looks like a giant, multi-colored doodle, but it's quite a useful technique, especially if you do not like to write, type, talk into a recorder, or don't have ready access to a computer. Also, I recommend the Mind Mapping technique for readers who learn best through visual representations.

The response to each question has three parts; 1. A critical and truthful discussion of the question. 2. The *Conditioning Factors*; recurring patterns of behavior, life situations, limitations etc. and 3. The *Significance* of 1, 2 as they relate to you. (Note; The reader can download the entire set of Strategic

Questions and response forms at www.NewParadigms.com; click on Forms, then Strategic Assessment.)

The discussions and topics related to the strategic questions are:

1. **Where am I now?** In answering this question, tell yourself the truth because "where you are now" can materially affect where you *can* go. "Where am I now?" should represent a discussion of the emotional, financial, and professional baggage you are carrying around, as well as your strengths, weaknesses, and liabilities accumulated thus far in your life. How would you describe the situations you are in with regards to your personal goals, business plans, and family life?

   Conditioning Factors. From the discussion points of "Where am I now?" assemble a list of Conditioning Factors (CFs). Conditioning factors represent the overarching characteristics of your current situation. For example, many of the participants in my workshops find that they have been conditioned to believe they are not smart enough to get ahead or that they are not attractive enough to find affection from another person. These types of Conditioning Factors act like lead weights and limit the risks we are willing to take and the opportunities we do not engage. You may also have a host of positive CFs as well.

   Significance. The Conditioning Factors you distilled in the above discussion of "Where am I now?" represent either challenges or assets or unrealized potential. If, for example, you are a highly organized person (a CF), but avoid taking on new responsibilities or tasks (another CF), the Significance is that you are greatly underutilized and you are limiting your success potential.

2. **How did I get here?** Write out an accurate listing or discussion of how you got to where you are today.

Conditioning Factors. Assemble a list of the Conditioning Factors that describe how you got to where you are. Include both actual demonstrated strengths and experienced shortcomings.

Significance. Now distill the major significant issues into either challenges or untapped opportunities. In effect you are asked to determine "what are the consequences?" of these Significant elements for my life?"

3. **3. Where am I going?** This is the question that evaluates the results of the choices you have made in your life. Do not be judgmental in your responses, just factual. All of us have developed a certain amount of momentum that keeps us in our groves (or ruts). What are the elements of your momentum?

    Conditioning Factors. What habits, traits, behaviors, and characteristics are influencing your decisions that keep you on the path you are on? Are they assets to be developed or baggage to be gotten rid of?

    Significance. What are the Significant elements that describe the conflicts and opportunities in "Where am I going"? Is your momentum carrying you where you want to go?

4. **4. Where should I be going?** This is the question that when answered, separates and highlights your potential from your reality. Most people feel that they have untapped potential waiting to be realized. This is your assessment of that potential, especially in light of the discussion centered on "Where am I now?"

    Conditioning Factors. How much of the difference between "Where should I be going?" And "Where am I going?" is due to the influence of others. Do you associate with a group of non-performers, content to just get by? Does your social network consist of high performers that inspire you? Answer this question truthfully to assess *where you should be going*, given your intentions and desires.

Significance. What are the Significant elements that describe the conflicts between where you are going and where you feel your talents can take you?

1. **How will I get there?** This is the *big* question. If answered truthfully and takes into account the answers to the previous four strategic questions, this will form the basis for your Roadmap to success—your Life Plan. The answers should represent honest evaluations of what you think it takes to get *you* where *you* want to go. This section should also include the critically important element of timing. Great intentions come to naught if they are not held to account with a timescale of anticipated accomplishments and actual milestones.

   Conditioning Factors. The conditioning factors associated with "How will I get there" should take into account your past plans and outcomes. Do you plan well but execute poorly? Do you concentrate too much on vision and not enough on day-to-day action? Are you resilient in the face of adversity? What do you need to stop doing? Who do you need to avoid in your life? How have your behaviors conditioned you into accepting limitations?

   Significance. Describe the most significant elements that are either limitations or untapped potential.

When you have completed this exercise, put the questions, answers, and conditioning factors into one document to review. This review will give you a much clearer picture of the intentions, assets, and liabilities that form the framework of your Life Plan or Roadmap to success.

Wright

Now that we have our strategic assessment, what are the Life Skills we need to prepare for our life's journey?

Dillahunty

The good news is that there is only a handful of Life Skills needed to master our environment and bring our highest potential into the realm of reality. More good news: the skills I will outline are the critical skills needed for success in life and leadership and they are learnable skills, learnable at any age. Sometimes we fall victim to the false belief that as we get older, we are not capable of learning new skills or acquiring new beliefs. Freudian psychology tries to convince us that our brains are hardwired by the time we are eight years old. That assertion is false. During our entire lives, our brains are constantly forming new synaptic connections. To help this process along we all need to continually build new synaptic pathways by learning and improving.

The five Life Skills that I will outline for the readers work together, interacting and reacting with one another to produce results that are not foreseeable in the beginning. The metaphor that I use to describe how these five essential Life Skills work together is that of *baking bread*. To create the end result—bread—we combine five essential ingredients: water, flour, salt, leaven, and heat. The result is *bread*, which comes from the interaction and reactions of the ingredients. The bread we get does not resemble any of the individual ingredients—one cannot find a grain of salt or the cup of water or the heat we added in the end result. They have been transformed. But all five ingredients were absolutely essential to get the end result we wanted. It's the same for the Life Skills that I will describe. The end results of developing our

Life Skills can be seen in our courage, character, tenacity, intuition, temperament, integrity, etc., but these qualities are results, not ingredients!

Life Skill Number 1: The first essential *Life Skill* is represented by one of our basic human needs, the desire to associate with others of like kind—humans are social animals. I call this skill *Social Capital.* It is a skill in that the people we surround ourselves with should be chosen and not limited to those who just show up in our lives.

Social Capital is the investment account of our human relationships. It begins with the friendships we develop in grade school, and should continue as a lifelong process to seek the company of those who will contribute to the success of our lives. Social Capital is our network of personal and professional relationships that we rely on for advice, counsel, influence, favors, criticism, intelligence, and serves us as a sounding board for our ideas and problems.

Social Capital does not mean being the life of the party or the most popular person. Social Capital is developed by conscientiously seeking relationships with those who will make positive, encouraging, and valuable contributions to our lives.

Life Skill Number 2: The second *Life Skill* represents our ability to recover from life's adversities. I call this skill *buoyancy.* It allows us to recover quickly from upsets and adversities.

> *Experience is not what happens to the mind or the heart, but what the mind and the heart do with the experience.*
> —J. Milton

Buoyancy is a learned skill that allows us to bounce back from adversity and to learn from it. Bouncing back is not the skill; bouncing back wiser because of what you have learned. All of us encounter unpredictable upsets in our lives that we do not deserve.

If Failure knew what a wonderful person you are, it would never visit you. But it doesn't, so it sprinkles disasters about like magical pixie dust! In fact, the more we try to bend circumstance to our will and carve out success for our lives, the more we fail. And if you're not failing, you're not trying.

Trying and engaging always lead to failure. The only people who never fail are those who never try. We call these "never-try-anything-new" people *bureaucrats*. Their only mission in life is to never make a mistake that can be blamed on them! So they hide in organizations and shoot down every good idea that comes along, but never take the risk to engage for fear of public failure.

Life Skill Number 3: This skill set is the most extensive Life Skill and can be summed up in one word: *Kaizen*. *Kaizen* is a Japanese word meaning *continuous improvement* that I have adapted to mean *continuous improvement and learning in life*. In the twenty-first century all of us face a  considerable challenge to just keep up with the fast pace of change. The rate at which we are asked to adapt to new realities is so rapid that if we don't conscientiously devote time to continually upgrading and improving our own sets of brainware, we run the risk of becoming technically obsolete. If you have a computer that's over six years old, chances are you are using it for a door stop because it cannot run most of the software available today.

The same processes apply to our own cranial computers (i.e., our brains). Just like our PCs, our brains require continual upgrading of our operating systems for us to deal effectively with the changes and complexities of today's environment. The processes of *Kaizen*—of developing a program of continuous learning—up-grades your internal operating system and keeps it current. Keeping on a program of *Kaizen* represents the most extensive of all the Five Life Skills, but it is not difficult to do. (You can find more detail about the nature of Kaizen at www.NewParadigms.com, or just Google "Kaizen Processes.")

Life Skill Number 4: This skill represents our ability to integrate *Facts and Values* into our decision-making. We live in a complex environment and quantitative skills are required to sift through mountains of information, much of it misleading, and interpret what it means to us. But too often we rely only on quantitative facts to make our decisions. Facts of themselves contain no value. If you read a newspaper headline: *"Ten People Died Last Night,"* the statement in itself is a fact, but it has no value—no meaning. Is the fact that ten people died good or bad? The story might go on: *"Ten People Died Last Night. All were 105 years old and died in their sleep at base camp **after** their successful ascent of Mt. Everest."* This explanation adds value to the headline, and I suspect most readers would think to themselves, "Wow, I should be so lucky!"

Many who get in trouble by following the latest financial scheme to riches fail to integrate the facts of the deal with their values. For example, those who recently got

> *Values give facts their meaning, and values with-out facts are unsupportable beliefs.*
> —Dr. J. Dillahunty

into trouble by over committing to real estate speculation let the quantitative facts get ahead of their value system. The fact was "real estate keeps going up," and people wanted to get in on this easy way to riches. But the questions related to personal values, questions like: "Is it wise to risk our entire nest egg in one asset class?" and "Do I really understand the details of real estate investing?" were never addressed. Not integrating the hard number facts with the soft values proved a recipe for disaster.

Life Skill Number 5: Engagement. If you are able to master all the Life Skills outlined in this discussion you are still short of achieving any success in life unless you actually do something with the skills you have. You must engage in the tasks of life.

The processes of engagement are like the heat we add to baking. Without the heat of engagement you will be left with a lot of non-functional ingredients—ingredients that show great potential but continually fall short. Have you ever met people and come away thinking, "Wow, they have such great potential?" Many of these high potential people never amount to anything or never achieve all that they are capable of because they fail to engage. Engagement means taking risks, and risks can result in failure. As I indicated earlier, if you are not failing, you are not engaging. The only way to avoid failure is to never engage.

One of the most effective methods of structuring engagements as learning experiences comes though the processes of mentoring. We can mentor others and we can also mentor ourselves.

> *Good decisions come from experience—Experience comes from bad decisions.*

Mentoring encourages engagement and provides the safety net to help us review our failures and interpret them for what they are—learning

experiences (painful and unpleasant perhaps), not a personal indictment of inadequacy. Mentoring processes incorporate all of the Life Skills in an environment of counsel and encouragement. Mentors act as guides who support and assist us

through failure, critique our behavior, and act as a sounding board for problem resolution and the assessment of opportunities. Most people in my workshops can remember and vividly describe the life-changing influence of one individual in their past. Often, however, mentors are the invisible hands that, like a catalyst in chemical reactions, help us transform without being a visible part of the reaction itself.

The Five Life Skills I've discussed are the essential ingredients for success derived from my years of operating my own successful company and from the research conducted during my doctoral research with leaders and highly successful

> *When we are afraid to engage and stop at the vision of a thing, we remain safe in an autistic retreat where there are no consequences.*
> *—G. Vaillant*

individuals. The good news is that the Five Life Skills are learnable at any age; you do not have to be born smart or rich or in the right circumstances to master them and you do not have to copy anybody else's behaviors to acquire them. The degree to which you develop the Five Life Skills is up to you—they represent conscious choices.

Before we discuss how to build our Roadmap to success let me summarize the concepts of the Life Skills: When combined, the five core Life Skills interact to produce results that could not be envisioned beforehand. Just like in the baking metaphor, we cannot see the end result (bread) by examining the flour, water, salt, leavening, and heat. Bread is a result of the interaction of the right ingredients—*the right stuff*. If you put the right stuff into your inventory of Life Skills you will experience transformational change and success that you cannot envision beforehand!

Many people in my seminars ask "where does *courage* come from?" and "Where does *character* come from?" As I have indicated, they are the results of the interactions of the Life Skills. You cannot be courageous by just acting courageous, nor can you build character by acting as though you had it. These qualities emerge from the mix—you can't simply glue them on any more than you can glue on feathers and expect to fly.

So before we discuss how to construct a Roadmap to success, let's review the essential Life Skills required for "Top of the Mark" success in the twenty-first century:

1. **Social Capital**: the network of people that surround and support us
2. **Buoyancy**: the ability to learn from and bounce back from adversity
3. **Kaizen**: continually upgrading and improving our abilities through self-reflection, listening, systems thinking, self-discipline, time management, and learning
4. **Facts and Values**: integrating hard facts with soft values for better decisions

5. **Engagement**: getting out and doing; nothing comes from our skills unless they are engaged in the world about us

Wright

So where do we start to build our own unique Roadmap to success?

Dillahunty

We start with a plan and the plan is a logical sequence of events in transforming our visions and our intentions into realities we can take to the bank. The planning formula for the Roadmap to success has several key elements as are depicted in the illustration:

> ### The Planning Cycle
>
> 1.) Write the Plan
> 2.) Communicate it to your Social Network
> 3.) Engage the action steps
> 4.) Reflect on the results
> 5.) Re-write the plan based on what you learn

Step 1 in the Roadmap is to prepare a *Written* plan that is based on "where you want to go" and "how you plan to get there." Some would argue that only businesses need written plans, but I take issue with that thinking. Earlier in our discussion I mentioned that I think this is erroneous thinking. To get the results we want of our one and only life, write a plan. The benefit of taking our visions and putting them down in writing is that it brings us a sense of clarity in an often confusing and inconsistent world of problems and opportunities.

The reader can begin the planning cycle by using discussion notes from the responses generated in answering the five strategic planning questions. In this initial step the emphasis should be on "Where I want to go," and, "How will I get there?" Start your life plan with a general narrative that describes what you want to accomplish and the methods you'll use to reach those accomplishments.

Step 2 is to *Communicate* the plan to your network of supporting friends and associates, your mastermind group—your Social Capital account. Your network of Social Capital is composed of individuals who will provide you with advice, criticism, influence, intelligence, and can serve you as a sounding board to assess problems and opportunities. All corporations have a board of directors whose job is to be mindful of the intentions and actions of the firm's officers. In your Life Plan you have a similar need for the supporting structure of individuals that can help guide and mentor you.

I suggest quarterly meetings with key people in your Social Capital account. These meetings can be formal or you can meet one-on-one to discuss your plans, progress, actions, and outcomes. The role of your Social Capital network is to provide accurate and insightful criticisms and feedbacks of your plan. It's not to be used as a social group.

Step 3 in the planning process is to *Engage* the action items contained in your plan. As I mentioned earlier in this discussion, all the skills, all the planning, and all the visions are a waste of time if they are not actually engaged in the real world. The purpose of Engagement is that it produces the results and provides valuable feedback on what works and what does not work in getting you where you are going. Few, if any, plans actually work as we think they will. Engagement provides us the feedback about how to refine and change our methods so that we can get where we want to go.

Step 4 is to take the time to *Reflect* on our actions, results, and the progress we are making (or not making) toward our intended outcome. What did we learn from the actions taken? What advice did our social network provide? What new actions should we take?

What can we learn from the failures and difficulties we encountered? These are among the questions that need to be asked as we self-reflect. Self-reflection also provides us the opportunity to think through our intentions and reassert that they in fact represent where we want to go and the methods we are using to get there.

Step 5 is to *Re-write* the plan based on what we have learned. Another advantage of having a written plan is that it provides a basis of review in the face of reality and progress. Few plans ever progress as they were initially designed. All plans need to be revised and updated to take into account new assets, new liabilities, new realities, and changes in the environment. Not even the multi-billion-dollar rockets we send into space travel with a fixed plan exempt from revision. Along the trajectory's path the onboard computer systems are updated, new calculations made, and revisions incorporated into the flight plan. As you can see in the illustration of the life-planning sequence, it is in fact a cycle. A plan once written, communicated, engaged, and reflected upon needs to be re-written, re-communicated, re-engaged, re-reflected, and yes, re-written yet again. The longer the time horizon of your Roadmap to success, the more revisions will be needed. The future *will* present unforeseen obstacles and opportunities for us to consider and react to.

Wright

Dr. Dillahunty, how would you summarize the methods you have outlined for preparing a Roadmap to success?

Dillahunty

Some things in life are predictable. We will all encounter a continuous series of unpredictable opportunities and problems. Our preparation and

Life Skills will determine if we will overcome the obstacles and seize upon the opportunities.

Preparing a Roadmap to success sets out our intentions, takes stock of our situation, and gives us an effective method for getting where we intend to go. A Roadmap to success does not have to be long and complicated—a small three-ring binder will do quite well.  But for best results it should be written, communicated, engaged, reflected on, and re-written in a continuous cycle.

As I think about what we have discussed today, I am reminded of a poem I learned forty years ago about the importance of knowing where you are going and communicating it to others:

"A burro once, sent by express,
His shipping ticket on his bridle,
Ate up his name and address,
And in some warehouse, standing idle,
He waited 'til he like to died.
The moral hardly needs the showing:
Don't keep things locked up inside—
Say who you are and where you are going"
(*W. Gibson*)

If readers would like to download forms to construct their Roadmaps or for more discussion on Life Skills or where to find Gibson's poem please visit www.NewParadigms.com and contact me directly.

About the Author

Dr. Dillahunty has thirty years of experience as a highly successful CEO, entrepreneur, sales and customer service trainer, and public speaker. Dr. Dillahunty brings his front-line experience in customer service and leadership development together with his academic research and storytelling to delight and inform audiences around the world through, keynotes, workshops, teleconferences, podcasts, and consulting. This unique combination of experience and academic rigor makes Dr. Dillahunty uniquely qualified to bridge the gap between *"Knowing and Doing."*

Books by Dr. Dillahunty:

1. *Blueprint for Success*. Co-authored by Dr. Dillahunty with Drs. Stephen Covey and Ken Blanchard. A collection of the nation's best minds; defining what it takes to be successful. Insight Publishing: Sevierville, TN, April 2008.
2. *Roadmap to Success*. Co-authored by Dr. Dillahunty with Drs. Stephen Covey and Ken Blanchard. A collection of essays from the world's top experts on transforming our ideas and visions reality. Insight Publishing: Sevierville, TN, projected publication date, as July 2008.
3. *Leadership 4.0*. Authored by Dr. Dillahunty. A definitive work that uncovers the fatal flaws and stumbling blocks that plague personal and professional development programs. Publication, June 2008.
4. *Customer Service 4.0*. Authored by Dr. Dillahunty. A bright and insightful work that begins with the concept that Customer Service does *not* begin after the sale. Publication, August 2008.

Dr. Dillahunty is an international speaker on the topics of **Leadership Development, Customer Service,** and **Life Skills.**

Dr. Jim Dillahunty
NewParadigms, LLC
7220 Trade St, Suite 310
San Diego, CA 92121
www.NewParadigms.com
jdillahunty@msn.com
Please visit www.NewParadigms.com for a free gift.

ROADMAP to SUCCESS 2

An interview with...

Dr. Stephen Covey

David E. Wright (Wright)

We're talking today with Dr. Stephen R. Covey, cofounder and vice-chairman of Franklin Covey Company, the largest management company and leadership development organization in the world. Dr. Covey is perhaps best known as author of *The 7 Habits of Highly Effective People*, which is ranked as a number one best-seller by the New York Times, having sold more than fourteen million copies in thirty-eight languages throughout the world. Dr. Covey is an internationally respected leadership authority, family expert, teacher, and organizational consultant. He has made teaching principle-centered living and principle-centered leadership his life's work. Dr. Covey is the recipient of the Thomas More College Medallion for Continuing Service to Humanity and has been awarded four honorary doctorate degrees. Other awards given Dr. Covey include the Sikh's 1989 International Man of Peace award, the 1994 International Entrepreneur of the Year award, Inc. magazine's Services Entrepreneur of the Year award, and in 1996 the National Entrepreneur of the Year Lifetime Achievement award for Entrepreneurial leadership. He has also been recognized as one of Time magazine's twenty-five most influential Americans and one of Sales and Marketing Management's top twenty-five power brokers. As the father of nine and grandfather of forty-four, Dr. Covey received the 2003 National Fatherhood Award, which he says is the most meaningful award he has ever received. Dr. Covey earned his undergraduate degree from the University of Utah, his MBA from Harvard, and completed his doctorate at Brigham Young University. While at Brigham Young he served as assistant to the President and was also a professor of Business Management and Organizational Behavior.

Dr. Covey, welcome to *Roadmap to Success*.

Dr. Stephen Covey (Covey)

Thank you.

Wright

Dr. Covey, most companies make decisions and filter them down through their organization. You, however, state that no company can succeed until individuals within it succeed. Are the goals of the company the result of the combined goals of the individuals?

Covey

Absolutely—if people aren't on the same page, they're going to be pulling in different directions. To teach this concept, I frequently ask large audiences to close their eyes and point north, and then to keep pointing and open their eyes. They find themselves pointing all over the place. I say to them, "Tomorrow morning if you want a similar experience, ask the first ten people you meet in your organization what the purpose of your organization is and you'll find it's a very similar experience. They'll point all over the place." When people have a different sense of purpose and values, every decision that is made from then on is governed by those. There's no question that this is one of the fundamental causes of misalignment, low trust, interpersonal conflict, interdepartmental rivalry, people operating on personal agendas, and so forth.

Wright

Is that primarily a result of an inability to communicate from the top?

Covey

That's one aspect, but I think it's more fundamental. There's an inability to involve people—an unwillingness. Leaders may communicate what their mission and their strategy is, but that doesn't mean there's any emotional connection to it. Mission statements that are rushed and then announced are soon forgotten. They become nothing more than just a bunch of platitudes on the wall that mean essentially nothing and even create a source of cynicism and a sense of hypocrisy inside the culture of an organization.

Wright

How do companies ensure survival and prosperity in these tumultuous times of technological advances, mergers, downsizing, and change?

Covey

I think that it takes a lot of high trust in a culture that has something that doesn't change—principles—at its core. There are principles that people agree upon that are valued. It gives a sense of stability. Then you have the power to adapt and be flexible when you experience these kinds of disruptive new economic models or technologies that come in and sideswipe you. You don't know how to handle them unless you have something you can depend upon.

If people have not agreed to a common set of principles that guide them and a common purpose, then they get their security from the outside and they tend to freeze the structure, systems, and processes inside and they cease becoming adaptable. They don't change with the changing realities of the new marketplace out there and gradually they become obsolete.

Wright

I was interested in one portion of your book, The 7 Habits of Highly Effective People, where you talk about behaviors. How does an individual go about the process of replacing ineffective behaviors with effective ones?

Covey

I think that for most people it usually requires a crisis that humbles them to become aware of their ineffective behaviors. If there's not a crisis the tendency is to perpetuate those behaviors and not change.

You don't have to wait until the marketplace creates the crisis for you. Have everyone accountable on a 360-degree basis to everyone else they interact with—with feedback either formal or informal—where they are getting data as to what's happening. They will then start to realize that the consequences of their ineffective behavior require them to be humble enough to look at that behavior and to adopt new, more effective ways of doing things.

Sometimes people can be stirred up to this if you just appeal to their conscience—to their inward sense of what is right and wrong. A lot of people sometimes know inwardly they're doing wrong, but the culture doesn't necessarily discourage them from continuing that. They either need feedback from people or they need feedback from the marketplace or they need feedback from their conscience. Then they can begin to develop a step-by-step process of replacing old habits with new, better habits.

Wright

It's almost like saying, "Let's make all the mistakes in the laboratory before we put this thing in the air."

Covey

Right; and I also think what is necessary is a paradigm shift, which is analogous to having a correct map, say of a city or of a country. If people have an inaccurate paradigm of life, of other people, and of themselves it really doesn't make much difference what their behavior or habits or attitudes are. What they need is a correct paradigm—a correct map—that describes what's going on.

For instance, in the Middle Ages they used to heal people through bloodletting. It wasn't until Samuel Weiss and Pasteur and other empirical scientists discovered the germ theory that they realized for the first time they weren't dealing with the real issue. They realized why women preferred to use midwives who washed rather than doctors who didn't wash. They gradually got a new paradigm. Once you've got a new paradigm then your behavior and your attitude flow directly from it. If you have a bad paradigm or a bad map, let's say of a city, there's no way, no matter what your behavior or your habits or your attitudes are—how positive they are—you'll never be able to find the location you're looking for. This is why I believe that to change paradigms is far more fundamental than to work on attitude and behavior.

Wright

One of your seven habits of highly effective people is to "begin with the end in mind." If circumstances change and hardships or miscalculations occur, how does one view the end with clarity?

Covey

Many people think to begin with the end in mind means that you have some fixed definition of a goal that's accomplished and if changes come about you're not going to adapt to them. Instead, the "end in mind" you begin with is that you are going to create a flexible culture of high trust so that no matter what comes along you are going to do whatever it takes to accommodate that new change or that new reality and maintain a culture of high performance and high trust. You're talking more in terms of values and overall purposes that don't change, rather than specific strategies or programs that will have to change to accommodate the changing realities in the marketplace.

Wright

In this time of mistrust among people, corporations, and nations, for that matter, how do we create high levels of trust?

Covey

That's a great question and it's complicated because there are so many elements that go into the creating of a culture of trust. Obviously the most fundamental one is just to have trustworthy people. But that is not sufficient because what if the organization itself is misaligned?

For instance, what if you say you value cooperation but you really reward people for internal competition? Then you have a systemic or a structure problem that creates low trust inside the culture even though the people themselves are trustworthy. This is one of the insights of Edward Demming and the work he did. That's why he said that most problems are not personal—they're systemic. They're common caused. That's why you have to work on structure, systems, and processes to make sure that they institutionalize principle-centered values. Otherwise you could have good people with bad systems and you'll get bad results.

When it comes to developing interpersonal trust between people, it is made up of many, many elements such as taking the time to listen to other people, to understand them, and to see what is important to them. What we think is important to another may only be important to us, not to another. It takes empathy. You have to make and keep promises to them. You have to treat people with kindness and courtesy. You have to be completely honest and open. You have to live up to your commitments. You can't betray people behind their back. You can't badmouth them behind their back and sweet-talk them to their face. That will send out vibes of hypocrisy and it will be detected.

You have to learn to apologize when you make mistakes, to admit mistakes, and to also get feedback going in every direction as much as possible. It doesn't necessarily require formal forums—it requires trust between people who will be open with each other and give each other feedback.

Wright

My mother told me to do a lot of what you're saying now, but it seems that when I got in business I simply forgot.

Covey

Sometimes we forget, but sometimes culture doesn't nurture it. That's why I say unless you work with the institutionalizing—that means formalizing into structure, systems, and processing the values—you will not have a nurturing culture. You have to constantly work on that.

This is one of the big mistakes organizations make. They think trust is simply a function of being honest. That's only one small aspect. It's an important aspect, obviously, but there are so many other elements that go into the creation of a high-trust culture.

Wright

"Seek first to understand then to be understood" is another of your seven habits. Do you find that people try to communicate without really understanding what other people want?

Covey

Absolutely. The tendency is to project out of our own autobiography— our own life, our own value system—onto other people, thinking we know what they want. So we don't really listen to them. We pretend to listen, but we really don't listen from within their frame of reference. We listen from within our own frame of reference and we're really preparing our reply rather than seeking to understand. This is a very common thing. In fact, very few people have had any training in seriously listening. They're trained in how to read, write, and speak, but not to listen.

Reading, writing, speaking, and listening are the four modes of communication and they represent about two-thirds to three-fourths of our waking hours. About half of that time is spent listening, but it's the one skill people have not been trained in. People have had all this training in the other forms of communication. In a large audience of 1,000 people you wouldn't have more than twenty people who have had more than two weeks of training in listening. Listening is more than a skill or technique; you must listen within another's frame of reference. It takes tremendous courage to listen because you're at risk when you listen. You don't know what's going to happen; you're vulnerable.

Wright

Sales gurus always tell me that the number one skill in selling is listening.

Covey

Yes—listening from within the customer's frame of reference. That is so true. You can see that it takes some security to do that because you don't know what's going to happen.

Wright

With this book we're trying to encourage people to be better, to live better, and be more fulfilled by listening to the examples of our guest authors. Is there anything or anyone in your life that has made a difference for you and helped you to become a better person?

Covey

I think the most influential people in my life have been my parents. I think that what they modeled was not to make comparisons and harbor jealousy or to seek recognition. They were humble people.

I remember one time when my mother and I were going up in an elevator and the most prominent person in the state was also in the elevator. She knew him, but she spent her time talking to the elevator operator. I was just a little kid and I was so awed by the famous person. I said to her, "Why didn't you talk to the important person?" She said, "I was. I had never met him."

My parents were really humble, modest people who were focused on service and other people rather than on themselves. I think they were very inspiring models to me.

Wright

In almost every research paper I've ever read, those who write about people who have influenced their lives include three teachers in their top-five picks. My seventh-grade English teacher was the greatest teacher I ever had and she influenced me to no end.

Covey

Would it be correct to say that she saw in you probably some qualities of greatness you didn't even see in yourself?

Wright

Absolutely.

Covey

That's been my general experience—the key aspect of a mentor or a teacher is someone who sees in you potential that you don't even see in yourself. Those teachers/mentors treat you accordingly and eventually you come to see it in yourself. That's my definition of leadership or influence—communicating people's worth and potential so clearly that they are inspired to see it in themselves.

Wright

Most of my teachers treated me as a student, but she treated me with much more respect than that. As a matter of fact, she called me Mr. Wright, and I was in the seventh grade at the time. I'd never been addressed by anything but a nickname. I stood a little taller; she just made a tremendous difference.

Do you think there are other characteristics that mentors seem to have in common?

Covey

I think they are first of all good examples in their own personal lives. Their personal lives and their family lives are not all messed up—they come from a base of good character. They also are usually very confident and they take the time to do what your teacher did to you—to treat you with uncommon respect and courtesy.

They also, I think, explicitly teach principles rather than practices so that rules don't take the place of human judgment. You gradually come to have faith in your own judgment in making decisions because of the affirmation of such a mentor. Good mentors care about you—you can feel the sincerity of their caring. It's like the expression, "I don't care how much you know until I know how much you care."

Wright

Most people are fascinated with the new television shows about being a survivor. What has been the greatest comeback that you've made from adversity in your career or your life?

Covey

When I was in grade school I experienced a disease in my legs. It caused me to use crutches for a while. I tried to get off them fast and get back. The disease wasn't corrected yet so I went back on crutches for another year. The disease went to the other leg and I went on for another year. It essentially took me out of my favorite thing—athletics—and it took me more into being a student. So that was a life-defining experience, which at the time seemed very negative, but has proven to be the basis on which I've focused my life—being more of a learner.

Wright

Principle-centered learning is basically what you do that's different from anybody I've read or listened to.

Covey

The concept is embodied in the Far Eastern expression, "Give a man a fish, you feed him for the day; teach him how to fish, you feed him for a lifetime." When you teach principles that are universal and timeless, they don't belong to just any one person's religion or to a particular culture or geography. They seem to be timeless and universal like the ones we've been talking about here: trustworthiness, honesty, caring, service, growth, and development. These are universal principles. If you focus on these things, then little by little people become independent of you and then they start to believe in themselves and their own judgment becomes better. You don't need as many rules. You don't need as much bureaucracy and as many controls and you can empower people.

The problem in most business operations today—and not just business but non-business—is that they're using the industrial model in an information age. Arnold Toynbee, the great historian, said, "You can pretty well summarize all of history in four words: nothing fails like success." The industrial model was based on the asset of the machine. The information model is based on the asset of the person—the knowledge worker. It's an altogether different model. But the machine model was the main asset of the twentieth century. It enabled productivity to increase fifty times. The new asset is intellectual and social capital—the qualities of people and the quality of the relationship they have with each other. Like Toynbee said, "Nothing fails like success." The industrial model does not work in an information age. It requires a focus on the new wealth, not capital and material things.

A good illustration that demonstrates how much we were into the industrial model, and still are, is to notice where people are on the balance sheet. They're not found there. Machines are found there. Machines become investments. People are on the profit-and-loss statement and people are expenses. Think of that—if that isn't bloodletting.

Wright

It sure is.

When you consider the choices you've made down through the years, has faith played an important role in your life?

Covey

It has played an extremely important role. I believe deeply that we should put principles at the center of our lives, but I believe that God is the source of those principles. I did not invent them. I get credit sometimes for some of the Seven Habits material and some of the other things I've done, but it's really all based on principles that have been given by God to all of His children from the beginning of time. You'll find that you can teach these same principles from the sacred texts and the wisdom literature of almost any tradition. I think the ultimate source of that is God and that is one thing you can absolutely depend upon—"in God we trust."

Wright

If you could have a platform and tell our audience something you feel would help them or encourage them, what would you say?

Covey

I think I would say to put God at the center of your life and then prioritize your family. No one on their deathbed ever wished they had spent more time at the office.

Wright

That's right. We have come down to the end of our program and I know you're a busy person. I could talk with you all day, Dr. Covey.

Covey

It's good to talk with you as well and to be a part of this program. It looks like an excellent one that you've got going on here.

Wright

Thank you.

We have been talking today with Dr. Stephen R. Covey, cofounder and vice-chairman of Franklin Covey Company. He's also the author of The 7 Habits of Highly Effective People, which has been ranked as a number one bestseller by the New York Times, selling more than fourteen million copies in thirty-eight languages.

Dr. Covey, thank you so much for being with us today.

Covey

Thank you for the honor of participating.

About the Author

Stephen R. Covey was recognized in 1996 as one of Time magazine's twenty-five most influential Americans and one of Sales and Marketing Management's top twenty-five power brokers. Dr. Covey is the author of several acclaimed books, including the international bestseller, The 7 Habits of Highly Effective People, named the number one Most Influential Business Book of the Twentieth Century, and other best sellers that include First Things First, Principle-Centered Leadership, (with sales exceeding one million) and The 7 Habits of Highly Effective Families.

Dr. Covey's newest book, The 8th Habit: From Effectiveness to Greatness, which was released in November 2004, rose to the top of several bestseller lists, including New York Times, Wall Street Journal, USA Today, Money, Business Week, Amazon.com, and Barnes & Noble.

Dr. Covey earned his undergraduate degree from the University of Utah, his MBA from Harvard, and completed his doctorate at Brigham Young University. While at Brigham Young University, he served as assistant to the President and was also a professor of Business Management and Organizational Behavior. He received the National Fatherhood Award in 2003, which, as the father of nine and grandfather of forty-four, he says is the most meaningful award he has ever received.

Dr. Covey currently serves on the board of directors for the Points of Light Foundation. Based in Washington, D.C., the Foundation, through its partnership with the Volunteer Center National Network, engages and mobilizes millions of volunteers from all walks of life—businesses, nonprofits, faith-based organizations, low-income communities, families, youth, and older adults—to help solve serious social problems in thousands of communities.

To Contact Dr. Stephen R. Covey...
Visit www.stephencovey.com...

ROADMAP *to* SUCCESS 3

An interview with...

Krista Moore

David Wright (Wright)

Today, we are talking with Krista Moore. Krista has established an international reputation as an inspirational leader and results-oriented executive coach. As President of K. Coaching, LLC, an executive and team coaching practice, Krista works with highly successful CEOs, presidents, and sales executives helping them reach their highest level of achievement. She brings more than twenty-five years of sales leadership experience, business knowledge, and business coaching certification to ignite the potential of her coaching clients. As a sales executive, Krista frequently entered new markets to establish name recognition, create market share, and revamp organizations. Her leadership was highly effective in creating sales strategies and building "ships"—relationships and partnerships. Krista's "ship-building" is a holistic coaching approach designed to help clients attain business goals and exceed professional expectations while cultivating strong personal and business relationships and partnerships. Krista helps clients build solid "ships" that include empathy, integrity, balance, and purpose.

Krista, welcome to *Roadmap to Success.*

Krista Moore (Moore)

Thank you, I'm glad to be here.

Wright

I'm curious about your shipbuilding concept. Where did it come from?

Moore

I spend a lot of time delivering one-on-one coaching to business owners, sales leaders, and executives. This concept emerged from one of my coaching engagements, and it's an interesting story.

I was working with a great client, a sales executive who needed to improve both his business partnerships and his sales leadership skills. His sales reps were reluctant to take him on calls because he would talk too much, take over the sales call, and really wasn't very effective.

Developing his sales reps to close more business, and being more effective himself in front of the customer was a big part of his responsibility. Another coaching objective for us was to ensure that he was building key relationships with business partners and high level clients. He was the executive sponsor in those relationships, so to speak, and he needed to carve out time to develop them.

We'd been working together on these areas for about three months, and one day he called me.

"Krista, I have the perfect client that I'm going to practice some of this learning on," he said. He told me the client's name and it was someone I knew. I also recognized what a great new client opportunity it was for him.

"Are you sure this is the guy you want to start with for practicing these skills?" I asked. I was concerned that this individual—we'll call him Grumpy—was going to be a bit of a challenge. But my client said yes, he was ready, he wanted to do it.

So he went along with the sales rep on the call. During the call, he sat back and didn't say a word. He let his sales rep run the meeting. The rep asked great open-ended questions, discovered the client's needs, really applied solutions, and was getting ready to close the account. My client just sat there being very professional, very supportive, and let the sales rep lead the presentation.

All of a sudden Grumpy turns to my client and says, "So . . . what do you do anyhow?"

My client froze for a minute and sat up in his chair. On the wall behind Grumpy was a large photograph, a blow-up of Grumpy standing in front of a big fishing boat. He was grinning from ear to ear. His arms were outstretched; he was holding a string of fish and smiling. My client was locked on that photograph, trying to think of how to respond. He then said, "I build ships!"

Grumpy said, "Whadaya mean ya 'build ships'?"

"I build ships—I build partnerships and I build relationships."

Well, it was at that point when Grumpy and the client started building their ship together.

When my client called me and told me the story, I thought, "This is great! This is borderline brilliant stuff; we could have a lot of fun with shipbuilding." So I took that concept and I really started to think about it. I put pen to paper, and that's where the whole shipbuilding idea came from.

At first I thought, this is pretty cool stuff. What can we do with this? Then I realized that helping people build their ships is what I do every day.

Wright

As you said, the shipbuilding concept can have a lot of analogies. Explore some of those with us.

Moore

I began thinking about what my ship looks like and what should a ship look like? At first I thought, "I want a big ship—I want a big, beautiful ship, like the Titanic." And then I thought, "Well, maybe size really doesn't matter. I mean, look at the Titanic, it sank, right?" Then I realized that it wasn't so much about the size of the ship or what the ship looked like, it was more about the purpose of that ship—a ship is built with a purpose in mind—and one thing for sure is that a ship needs to be solid or it will sink.

I thought about companies like Enron and how they didn't make it. They sank—they went out of business. I asked myself, "Were they working on their ships? Were they taking care of their customers and their business partners? How were they treating their internal employees? Were they building ships that were solid, purposeful, and that would last a lifetime? If these companies and many others would have concentrated on building their ships, would their business outcomes be different?

I'd like to put a stake in the ground and say that if your partnerships aren't solid or your relationships don't feel right, you feel uncomfortable, a bit out of balance; your ship—your personal ship—is not solid and it's not purposeful. So you need to do something about that.

Everyone is a ship-builder. I think there are two main areas to really focus on regarding your shipbuilding. These two main areas are: building your partnerships and building your relationships. If you focus on improving and building these areas every day, then you will be purposeful, feel solid and steadfast, and you'll be unsinkable!

Wright

The elements of relationships and partnerships sound very similar, so what are the differences?

Moore

They are very similar, but yet have some unique differences. Let's look at them separately for a moment. With partnerships, the main area that comes to mind is the need *to really understand the other person*—what are his or her needs and circumstances? The most effective way to initiate a partnership is by asking great questions, listening carefully to the answers, and finding out what's important to the other person. This includes learning about and understanding what's going on in the other person's world—not just what's important to you. Then agree on what is important to each of you, establish your go-forward plan, what needs to be achieved, and how are you going to *work together* to accomplish it? *Then you can establish a working agreement with specific goals and objectives based on a clearly defined shared mission and vision.*

The second area of a successful partnership is *reciprocity*—finding out how you can work together and what the mutual exchange will be to meet the partnership objectives. I learned something a long time ago from my grandmother (who was probably the wisest woman in the world). She said, "Krista, there are givers and takers out there." And I'd go through life evaluating people: he's a giver, she's a taker. This might not have been the best way to view the world, but think about giving and taking for a moment. Just imagine building a ship or building a partnership where both people are takers. That's not going to be a solid and successful relationship. Reciprocity is a key concept in a partnership. Reciprocity means that your partner is holding up his or her end of the bargain and that there's always a give and take. When you are building your partnerships, be very clear and agree upon what the expectations are for each of you.

Another important aspect of a partnership is *execution*. Typically a partnership is an agreement where there is a task that needs to be executed or a plan implemented—you want to accomplish something together. You need to actually get some work done and you will want to focus on care, trust, and integrity to make it happen faster. Ideally this means getting things done through staying focused and both parties having a clear understanding of what they're supposed to be doing separately and together.

Sometimes people in partnerships get discouraged and think, "I've given it all I have—I can't give anymore." It is then when each member in the partnership needs to try and *exceed* what the other expects. If you don't continuously do that, people will get tired and complacent and feel taken for granted. We see this with internal business relationships, external partnerships and with customers.

I teach a lot of sales executives this: the number one reason customers leave is because they feel undervalued or ignored—it isn't because of price.

The customer, however, isn't going to say, "Well, you didn't pay attention to me," or "I really needed more from you," or "you're not doing anything above and beyond being the supplier or the business partner." The customer will just begin doing business with someone else. It is up to you to continuously look for ways you can exceed what the other person expects. If both partners do that, you have a solid partnership. Too often I see customers leave and salespeople be surprised because they thought they had such a great relationship with them.

Think about it: what have you done to exceed expectations and build customer loyalty *today*?

As for relationships, as you pointed out, there are elements similar to partnerships. What's the difference between partnerships and relationships? When I think about the differences, I believe there is more of an emotional component and a personal connection within relationships.

When you start to build a relationship it's very important to know your role and your purpose in that relationship. For example, are you the boss, are you the leader or the manager, are you the mom or the daughter or the father? What is your role and what is your purpose? If that's unclear, it's difficult for you to build upon that relationship and really understand what value you bring. Ask yourself, "What value do I bring to this relationship?" If I'm in a marriage and I don't bring any value for the other person or I'm not clear about what my purpose or my role is in that relationship, then it becomes very uncomfortable and can be very stressful.

I'm recently married for the second time, so now I'm a wife and I want to be the best wife in the world. I never really thought of myself as wifely, but understanding what's expected of me is extremely important—does he expect me to have dinner on the table every night and have the laundry done and be a working mom, and do all the work? I don't think so. But being clear about what value you bring and what's expected from the other person builds the foundation for the relationship, and establishes ongoing communication.

Another aspect of relationships that is different from partnerships is empathy—having an emotional connection and understanding. Empathy is not easy for a lot of people. In business, sometimes we feel that we can't show empathy, but it's extremely important. It involves trying to feel what the other person feels. When I'm working with business owners and leaders and they are trying to build relationships with their peers or their subordinates, we talk about finding a place for empathy and thinking with your head, your heart, and your gut.

Often, we're talking about the bottom line, goals, objectives, tactics, and not really relating to and understanding what the other person in the relationship might be thinking or feeling. But, once we recognize the impact we can have by coaching in these areas, we see amazing results.

For instance, in a relationship between a manager and a sales rep who does a good job, the manager might leave the sales rep alone, thinking that he doesn't need to attend to him or her because the rep is doing good work. Actually, the manager is neglecting that relationship—the sales rep may not be getting any support to continue to develop his or her skills, and eventually the rep isn't challenged or motivated and may grow complacent.

You constantly need to work on relationships. Sometimes, with our customers or our closest personal relationships, we might say they love us, everything is fine, and we may take that relationship for granted. What this really means is that we have stopped building our ships and have taken the attention way from what really matters and things start to deteriorate. Therefore we may not feel solid and purposeful in who we are and what we stand for.

Many of the focus areas for relationships and partnerships may sound alike, but the key elements they have in common include continuously showing you care, demonstrating trust, exceeding expectations, and ensuring reciprocity.

Wright

So how do you bridge the gap between executive coaching and shipbuilding?

Moore

For a coach to be effective, the coach needs to be great at building relationships with clients. You want to create an atmosphere that is open and honest and comfortable, confidential, with mutual trust and respect for each other so that you can begin working on those predetermined coaching objectives. So define clearly what your role and responsibilities are—what is the client's role and what are you going to do as the coach? And then define what success will look like, and if we reach certain objectives, what will that feel like? An effective coach will clearly define what the expectations are and will understand what value he or she brings.

A coach becomes a partner, helping clients reach their goals, instilling confidence in them, and having a genuine working relationship.

I think I've realized the importance of shipbuilding with my clients, and have intentionally worked on that and they have experienced great success with this focus. I would have clients for three or four years, and I'd think, "Wow, that can't be very effective coaching or we would be done, right?" But it's constant, it's ever-turning. The partnership is working. If I'm coaching one individual, there's another department, there's another area for coaching. It's constantly building great productive coaching relationships that evolve into other areas through departments and referrals.

Most importantly, the leader is the captain of the ship, and directions change. Great leaders are constantly building relationships themselves and developing followership internally within a company and externally in their personal lives. The leader is continuously looking for areas to grow, improve, and focus. Once the ship is built, it doesn't mean that it's complete. There will be new direction or changes that will take place or maybe the perfect storm comes. So you can build a good sturdy ship, but you can't then just rest on your laurels or sit on your ship with your feet up. You have to care for it and keep it seaworthy. It's constant work. So there is always a need for executive coaching focused on leadership and shipbuilding.

Wright

The thought of bringing such a personal aspect into business seems taboo. How well is it being received and what are some of the results?

Moore

I think many coaches realize that there's a personal aspect to coaching. It's essential, and building ships brings closeness. Sometimes "closeness" is a word that people want to stay away from in business. But again, that trust and a comfortable environment need to be created in order to really feel and see progress. That's not easy for many coaches and certainly not easy for a lot of executives, but it needs to be there to really make a difference.

Some examples of results would be, if you think of the leader at the top and you've heard it's lonely at the top; well, if that leader is feeling lonely, then he or she is not very good at shipbuilding because at the top he or she should feel anything but lonely if that leader has a solid ship. Sometimes a coach or mentor can fill that void—be a third-party sounding-board, so to speak, and just be someone there to listen. But the personal aspect is that nobody, whether a leader or not, or in business or not, wants to be alone. Some people hope that when they get old they are not alone. If that's the case, I'd suggest looking at your personal ship and figuring out where you can start working and building relationships and partnerships so that you're not alone.

As far as being taboo, I think years ago you could not bring that emotional connection into the office. Work-life balance is the ideal, and I certainly have experienced that in my life as an executive woman and single mom, raising two teenagers. I had to balance all of that along the way. But everyone needs to feel a sense of purpose, whether that's at home or at work, and it needs to be rewarding. Sometimes just hitting goals and focusing on the bottom line doesn't get you there. So I would say that there is a balance between the personal aspect and the business aspect.

Here's a good example: I have a client who is on the verge of resigning. He's a terrific individual, extremely talented, and critical to the future success of the organization. My client is going to resign primarily because of his relationship with the boss. My client feels undervalued and ignored and not appreciated. As I said, this is a person critical to the organization. So, do you throw all that away or do you build a ship here? Do you figure out how to focus on this relationship? Some people just walk away and avoid crucial conversations and confrontation.

So we decided we're going to give this ship a chance. We've outlined steps and rather than just avoiding confrontation or avoiding an emotional discussion, we're going to meet it head on. We prepared for the discussion by role-playing because my client believed the situation was worth working on. He believed it was critical to fix this relationship. He is a high-level executive who has a knot in his stomach every day he drives to work. Nobody wants to live that way. After a few months of working on the crucial relationship with his boss, he is still with the company, happy as ever, and taking on new rewarding opportunities.

From a pure business standpoint, a typical coaching engagement might have more consulting elements involved such as: defining vision and mission, creating clarity, putting strategies together, ensuring that everyone's aligned to the vision, and executing the plans. But we still have to think about shipbuilding tactics, first with our clients and then with their business relationships and customer relationships. What are they doing above and beyond to create loyalty with their customer base? When they determine the answer to that, then we put tactics in place toward achieving this. We might put together a formal business review process or a special promotion to really exceed whatever the client might be expecting. We've seen greatly improved retention rates because of a pure focus on the customer relationship. Instead of just taking the customer for granted or thinking that if you give good service, you're nice to them, and you follow up that they'll be there forever, but we know this is not the case.

There's also a shipbuilding tactic for leaders that is more focused on employees. We know how important employee retention is and so we've put together a simple recognition schedule. This is a great shipbuilding activity for managers and leaders. Employees want to feel empowered, right? They want to feel that they're a part of something bigger. In the old days they just came to work, earned a paycheck, they got a turkey at Thanksgiving, and a Christmas bonus. But today it's different—this new generation is looking for a whole lot more. So rather than sending an e-mail, pick up the phone or put a handwritten thank-you note together. A great exercise includes coming up with two or three key relationships in business and in your personal life, posting those, and intentionally scheduling attention and recognition activities. That's starting to build your ship. You might not see results within a couple of weeks, but you'll see people reacting differently over time. It's a terrific shipbuilding activity.

Wright

It sounds as though the key to leadership and success is creating sustainable, loyal ships with customers, business partners, and employees.

Moore

Yes, I think so. As we looked at successful leaders and analyzed them, we knew that they didn't get there alone—they understood the importance of hiring talented people, pulling those people along, and creating sustainable, loyal ships with customers' business partners and internally— with employees. So if one day a leader stops working on his or her relationships and partnerships, what do you think is going to happen? Many people might argue that reaching the highest level of happiness is success. The Roadmap might twist and turn a bit and the circumstances might change, but balance between work and family is important, as is continuously looking at all aspects—employees, business partners, and customers. I think that's what a good leader does well.

One of the best books I've read recently is Stephen M. R. Covey's book, *The Speed of Trust.* It is about the great things that can happen within organizations when trust is there and how fast progress can be made. If leaders are working on caring, on trusting, and treating these relationships with integrity in all aspects, great things are going to happen, and they'll happen a whole lot faster.

Wright

You are obviously very passionate about this subject. Is there a personal side to shipbuilding for you?

Moore

Once I connected with this, I became more aware of the shipbuilding within my own coaching practice. It became clear that almost every client I had was talking about personal development—interpersonal skills, communications, handling crucial and difficult conversations, and delegating and time management. It's centered on the people issue and creating better relationships. I have taken it to heart and am very passionate about being an effective coach who can develop great leaders so they can improve crucial relationships and partnerships and have sustainable positive changes. So I take my role very seriously and I constantly work on my own development.

The other personal side to shipbuilding for me is I began thinking about my own personal shipbuilding. I looked in the past at where I did well and where I failed in the different aspects of my life. I remember arriving the first day in a new leadership position and learning that the company had just lost seventeen million dollars in revenue the previous six months. They had "forgotten" to tell me that important fact during the interview. All of a sudden I'm thinking, "Oh no, what am I going to do?" Then I thought, "Okay, we have to take care of our people internally and take care of our service levels to our customers." So, we had a lot of hard work ahead of us, which included rebuilding relationships with customers so that they could trust us again, and internally building and inspiring and motivating the employees to get them refocused on what's important.

That was building a ship. The loyalty and trust component was rebuilt, both internally and externally. And guess what? The sales organization began thriving. I remember thinking, "Okay, now I'm on a yacht"—my ship had become a yacht. I was feeling good, my feet were up, I had a fishing pole out, and I was relaxed. I didn't pay much attention to those relationships and partnerships anymore. I thought I was done and I could rest on my laurels.

But then service levels started to deteriorate, customers weren't being taken care of, my family was suffering because I had been working more hours trying to fix the problems in the company. My kids didn't know they had a mom, my husband didn't know he had a wife. My relationship with my boss deteriorated; I lost trust and respect for him. Then came the perfect storm and I jumped. I was no longer in a yacht—I was in a canoe or a lifeboat paddling upstream! I literally found myself in the middle of the ocean and realized that I had to start all over again. My marriage ended, and my attention immediately went to my children as we worked through this emotional transition and rebuilding our relationships. I was also without a career and decided to build my own company. So I started to build my ships all over again, pulling from past business relationships, and counting on great friendships to begin the healing and rebuilding process.

When I think about this whole shipbuilding concept, I can certainly relate to it. I think about where I am today in building my business or building my personal relationships and it really does involve a bit of introspection. It requires a great deal of focus to get this message out there, to communicate it, and realize its importance. If I can continue to talk, write, and coach around shipbuilding, what a difference it's going to make in other peoples' lives as well as for me personally. It definitely makes me feel more purposeful and solid in who I am.

Wright

I love the concept; it seems to have many possibilities. What do you think those are?

Moore

I remember speaking at a conference on shipbuilding. I was speaking to a room full of high-level executive men. I began talking about the personal aspects, and when I started to bring the heart into it, the whole audience's demeanor and mood changed. They were connecting. I was getting them what I call, "below the neck"—they were no longer thinking just with their head, they were thinking with their heart and their gut and they were relating to it.

So I believe that the possibilities are tremendous when people connect to it. When I considered the aspect of "what does your ship look like?" I realized that many of my clients are tug boats. They're just pulling people along, they're not doing a good job delegating; they're getting where they need to go, but very slowly. I have plenty of clients I would call speed boats. They're just going through life at 50,000 miles an hour and they're not looking to the coast or right or left. They're just going full speed ahead, not concerned about anybody else around them, and not stopping to smell the roses. They're only interested in getting from point A to point B faster than the next guy. Then there are those who remind me of the Titanic. They built this glamorous ship and it was all about image and prestige; but they didn't have enough life support or life jackets for their employees and customers.

When I start relating to different types of ships it gets somewhat contagious. I discovered that there are over five hundred words that contain "ship." These include words like: citizenship, stewardship, and friendship.

In another shipbuilding presentation I was talking about these five hundred words and all the different kinds of ships. There was a lady in the front row getting excited—she was relating it to her personal life and what she could do different to make her life more meaningful. Later she told me, "I loved it. These ship words—they're all so positive."

Well most of them are, but what about the word *shipwreck*"? It's a scary thought. We work long and hard at building these ships and they can be destroyed in an instant if we don't pay attention to them. So it's just constant work. But imagine the possibilities. If everybody is building ships at the same time, intentionally working on this aspect of their life, how much reward and reciprocity will everyone have? It's a beautiful thought.

Wright

So I have to ask you, what does *your* ship look like?

Moore

Well, I think and dream about that often I'm out in the middle of the ocean and my ship is a wooden plank, it is just a small piece of flat wood and I'm surfing—I'm surfing the waves, the wind is fierce, the rain is beating down and stinging my face, and my hair is flying. But I'm balanced and smiling. Nothing is going to knock me off because I am solid and steadfast about who I am, what I'm doing, and my purpose. I'm working on my personal relationships as well as my business partnerships, and its smooth sailing.

Wright

So what is the one thing that you want people to take away from your shipbuilding message in this book?

Moore

I'd like them to think about one or two key relationships or partnerships that are important to them and what specifically they can do different to begin intentionally building them. They could use the elements described in this chapter, and begin scheduling time and attention for their shipbuilding.

A great example is the one relationship we all have—the one with our mothers. Well, I need to call my mother more and I know that. I'm busy, I'm traveling, and she's eight hours away and home alone; but I'm her daughter, we need each other and there's a responsibility I have to this relationship.. So, as silly as it may sound, I am going to schedule "attention time", I'm going to call her, at a minimum, on Wednesday evenings and Sunday afternoons, and hopefully this leads to our ship building.

The same time allocation and attention can be applied to many business relationships as well. For example, for many business leaders—they have a role and responsibility to their people and they need to recognize the importance and the impact of the personal connection and building their relationships. They need to make time to get to know their employees personally so they can inspire, motivate, and get better results, through making their relationships more meaningful.

If there are any takeaways in this chapter I hope readers remember to apply shipbuilding in all aspects of their lives. I hope they take some of the thoughts I have mentioned here on how to build your ship. Pick one or two relationships and try it and see what a difference it can make!

Wright

What a great conversation. I've learned a lot about shipbuilding here today and I know our readers will. I really appreciate the time you've taken to answer all these questions.

Moore

Thank you I enjoyed it. And smooth sailing to you!

Wright

Today we've been talking with Krista Moore. She is the President of K. Coaching LLC, an executive and team coaching practice. She combines twenty-five years of sales and business experience with her business coaching certifications to help others reach their highest level of achievement. In addition to her daily coaching clients, she is a highly sought-after international events speaker, presenting seminars and workshops on subjects such as: "Save Your Business with CPR," "Motivating Others with a Coach Approach," and her popular and inspirational, "Shipbuilding to Last a Lifetime." As we have found today, she is very passionate about that.

Krista, thank you so much for being with us today on *Roadmap to Success!*

Moore

Thank you.

About the Author

Krista Moore is known to many as a dynamic leader and mentor, with great passion and dedication to her cause. As President of *K.Coaching*, she is a results-oriented Executive Coach who is passionate about her clients having outstanding success in their lives and in their careers. Krista brings to her practice 25-plus years of corporate business experience, working as a sales leader for Boise Cascade and as a VP of Sales for Corporate Express.

Over the past five years she has built a successful coaching practice by combining her real life business experiences, certified business coaching and an energetic coaching style to help others reach their highest level of achievement. Krista addresses hundreds of businesses internationally, through her powerful seminars, coaching programs and learning resources.

To Contact Krista Moore...

K. Coaching, LLC

14460 New Falls of Neuse Rd

Suite 149-155

Raleigh, NC. 27614

Phone: 919-554-4505

E-mail: Krista@kcoaching.com

www.kcoaching.com

www.buildyourships.com

ROADMAP *to* SUCCESS 4

An interview with...

Buck Jacobs

David Wright (Wright)

Today we're talking with Buck Jacobs, the Founder and Chairman of The C12 Group, America's leaders since 1992 in equipping Christian Chief Executives to "Build Great Business for a Greater Purpose." Buck has authored several books and articles and has been a popular speaker. Previously, as a Senior Executive for S.H. Mack & Company of Chicago, Illinois, he oversaw a ten-year, ten-fold increase in sales and the global development of a Christ-centered business. The Mack Company was a founding member of the Fellowship of Companies for Christ (FCCI), for which Buck later served as Florida Director. His earlier roles include Managing Director of Sta-Power Italia, Rome, Italy, President of R.G. Haskins Corporation, and CEO of the Executive Development Institute. Buck is happily married to Bonnie, and has three daughters and five grandchildren.

Buck, welcome to *Roadmap to Success!*

Buck Jacobs (Jacobs)

Thank you David, it's my pleasure to be here.

Wright

So what is C12, why does it work, and what is its unique business proposition?

Jacobs

Actually David, C12 exists on two levels. First, there is the organizational level. The C12 Group, LLC is a franchise-granting business and has a national representation of over 600 members. The business began in 1992 and has been growing about 30 percent annually for the last four or five years. We recruit and train franchisees who build a local C12 practice by organizing Christian business owners and CEOs into groups of twelve to fifteen. The groups meet together for a full day each month to learn together, share "best practices" as a group of peer advisors, and to also hold one another accountable for implementation and application of what they study and share in these group meetings.

This basic format works in many arenas and is not really a unique formula or format to C12. There are similar groups, called "10 Groups" or "20 Groups," that builders, car dealers, and retailers have used historically. There are many non-Christ-centered roundtable organizations for CEOs and owners. The C12 concept is one that's been used for a long time very successfully. In fact, Peter Drucker said not too long before he passed away that "Peer coaching is a way of the future." *INC* magazine once recommended it as a piece of "Every thinking CEO's toolkit."

The concept works well because it's a microcosm of the design of the Christian Church or the Body of Christ. In the Church all the uniquely gifted and talented members are intended to work interdependently and to share one another's strengths and gifts for the common good. Whether the Church operates that way all the time or not, that is God's design, which is why this small interactive group of peers is so powerful.

C12's unique business proposition is that our foundation is firmly based on the Christian, biblical worldview. You know, there are many implications and cultural challenges a Christian faces in a leadership role that are unique based on his or her faith and desire to live a coherent life consistent with that faith.

Let me give you an example of what I mean. Some years ago I had the privilege of meeting a gentleman named Max DePree who was the Chairman and CEO of the Herman Miller Corporation of Zeeland, Michigan. Max was the second generation CEO of a company that had been founded by his father on a Christian foundation. Herman Miller is annually recognized as one of the "one hundred best places to work" and is a Fortune 500 company.

When I first met him he asked me what I did. I said, "I try to help Christian business owners integrate their faith into their business." Mr. DePree looked at me for a minute and he said, "Buck don't you have that just backward? Shouldn't we be bringing our business to our faith? Isn't our faith central to our life, and aren't all other aspects of life informed by our faith, rather than vice versa?" That was an epiphany for me. If faith and belief are real, then this is the center of our lives and should represent the context and lens through which we filter everything else.

We need to bring our business to our faith, not vice versa. In C12 we acknowledge that paradigm and focus on its real day-to-day application by building great businesses that allow for a balanced and consistent Christian lifestyle that is first modeled by the leader. That's what's uniquely different about C12 and how we are differentiated from many other similar organizations.

Wright

So what are the differences or similarities between the biblical leadership model and other models? In other words, how does C12's goals for productive companies and chief executives differ from those espoused by, say, the American Dream or our contemporary culture?

Jacobs

The American Dream says to get yours, achieve personal independence and "security," hopefully by selling to the highest bidder, and to seek a life of leisure and recreation while you're still young enough to enjoy it. We see life quite differently.

For CEOs operating under the Lordship of Christ, the perspective is very different. Our timeline and security include the eternal dimension. We view ourselves as desiring to finish strong while being forever dependent on a loving God. What we do with the proceeds from a business profit or sale is a matter of accountability before God and a clear personal testimony before those who are watching. For example, for Christian leaders, Jesus Christ is our model and He said, "I'm among you as one who serves," and, "he who would be greatest among you must be servant of all." So our fundamental model is servant leadership, which can be very different from some of our culture's accepted norms.

Jim Collins, in his wonderful book, *Good to Great*, identified one of the qualities that was common to leadership in businesses that significantly outperformed peer competitors. He identified a quality that he calls "Level 5 Leadership." Are you familiar with the book, David?

Wright

Yes.

Jacobs

You remember, then, that when Collins identified these "great" companies that had distinguished themselves by hugely outperforming their peer competitors for years, he was surprised to find that they were not led by the high-profile "superstar" leaders we constantly read about in business headlines and best-selling books. Their chief executives were men of unusual humility, diligence, and loyalty. They focused on the good of the organization and developing their people, rather than their personal recognition, money, or reputation. Level 5 leaders are those who lead with firm humility and selflessness, with the greater good of the organization in mind rather than personal gain.

Jesus was the greatest and most successful model of servant leadership ever. He took twelve ordinary men and mentored them for three years before sending them out to execute His strategic plan and purpose. His growing organization is still going strong 2,000 years later. So we attempt to follow the Lord's example, and we strive to build great businesses for a different and a higher purpose. Our vision is not only to build a great business according to all the normal business metrics. We believe that as we do this it's a witness to God's truth and way in life; such enterprises provide a God-given platform for authentic Christian ministry.

Another very significant difference is that in our paradigm we believe that we operate as stewards, not owners. We base our understanding on our common belief that God is Creator and Sovereign Father and He owns everything. The Bible says that, "The earth is the Lord's and all that it contains" (Psalm 24:1) and, as Christians, we accept that as just a simple truth. Roughly 80 percent of the American population would identify themselves as Christians, and about half that number would identify themselves as "born again" Christians. For us, this is simply reality—God is sovereign and He owns it all.

So we see a business as a vehicle that's given to us to manage for God as stewards, and not as a means to our greater personal benefit, merely so we can have access to a higher standard of living or more personal comfort than other people. It's a stewardship—something that we do as part of what we're called to do. As Christians we believe that each person is created by God with a definite purpose and role to play in His infinite plan. As such, we are to play it to His glory and according to His principles and ways. Our struggle is how to integrate all that into building a thriving business in today's culture.

There are some significant differences in leadership style and purpose as well. The contrasting paradigms of "I own it" and "God owns it" are fundamentally mutually exclusive. However, to me it's very interesting (and I've been at this for almost thirty-five years now) to discern what I understand to be long-term successful business principles, and to find that there is an obvious coherency between things that produce long-term success and biblical principles that undergird them.

Wright

So how do you define success?

Jacobs

Well, in these terms, looking at life as a Christian and a Christian leader, ultimately success will be found in hearing Jesus Christ say, "Well done, good and faithful servant!" and the criteria that will be used to judge success in Jesus' eyes won't necessarily be the same that our non-Christian contemporaries would acknowledge. But they will be consistent with the criteria He uses to judge all of His leaders, whether they're pastors, priests, CEOs, or whatever. Leadership is a gift and all leaders will be accountable for how well it is used. The Bible teaches that all authority is derived from God and those who exercise authority do so as accountable stewards. Their success will be judged based on His values.

Wright

Who do you think exemplifies such success?

Jacobs

I like to think about success on two levels. On one level there are examples such as Mother Teresa, George Müller, and Hudson Taylor. We all know Mother Teresa as a great saint of our contemporary times. She founded the Missionaries of Charity in Calcutta, India. Starting by herself, against the wishes of her superiors, with no resources except for her faith in a Sovereign God who could supply all she needed to do all He wanted, her order became a universally respected global organization. She was awarded the Nobel Peace Prize and was loved by millions.

George Müller founded a series of orphanages in England in the 1850s, and Hudson Taylor is the founder of the China Inland Mission, the first successful Christian outreach into China. The significance that they bring to this conversation is that when they first applied to be allowed to do what they felt God wanted them to do they were all turned down. They were told that they weren't gifted, talented, or physically strong enough to do the work they believed they were called to do. They had to persist, going back time and again to gain the opportunity to simply go and do what they felt called and equipped to do. As I've studied each of their lives, I see many commonalities.

They each had great faith in God's providential ability to provide what they needed to do the work that He had called them to do and a strong desire to obey Him. They each had a serious morning quiet time where they established intimacy with God. They adopted the native dress and style of the arena in which they were working and none of them (and this is interesting in today's culture) allowed fundraising on their behalf. They simply relied on prayer and God's providence to meet their needs and those of their organizations. George Müller specifically wrote in his diary that he chose to live by faith as he did to give an example of God's providential ability to "businessmen" who lacked the faith to trust Him in their work. All three of them built globally celebrated organizations, which have survived the transition to new leadership after their time on earth was finished.

In the context of contemporary business we have role models such as Charles Letourneau, Max DePree, Norman Miller of Interstate Batteries, Bill Pollard of ServiceMaster, Truett Cathy of Chick Fil-A, and David Dunkel of KForce Incorporated. Each of these men either led, or currently lead, billion-dollar businesses and strive to do so in ways that are consistent with their Christian faith and witness while keeping the eternal perspective of life.

So in C12's orientation we believe that there is a potential for greatness in an individual's obedience, and that success isn't only the result of their talents, gifts, opportunity, and resources. When the power of God can be engaged in the will of God, then even ordinary people can do extraordinary things. When God calls someone to start a company or to lead and grow a business, and that person is connected and operating in coherence with God's will, the business can become an extremely vibrant, vital, and strong business, able to grow to be as big as God wants it to be and to demonstrate His ways in the process.

Wright

So what does it mean to have an eternal perspective of life and how does this relate to living under the Lordship of Christ?

Jacobs

The eternal perspective is rooted in a biblical understanding of God's work, plan, purpose, and principles with our eternity in mind. This concept was expressed well by Tielhard DeChardin who said, "We are not physical beings who have occasional spiritual experiences, we are spirit beings who are having a temporary physical experience." We believe that we originate in the heart of our Eternal Father, are sent here for a season to do specific things as "ambassadors for Christ," and will return to our eternal home to experience rewards for our obedience in this role on Earth.

We see many parallels with national ambassadors. For example they: 1) are sent, 2) don't choose their place of service, 3) represent the interests of the sending nation to others, 4), are compensated by the sending nation (not the nation they're sent to), 5) model the ways and customs of their home country and, when their tour of duty is over, 6) are recalled and rewarded for loyal service.

In our culture, there is a pervasive influence to live for self and for the moment. This has spawned such a powerful attempt to privatize our faith today that living according to the eternal perspective, even within our Christian culture, isn't seen as the priority that it should be. From the eternal perspective, C12 is all about building great businesses, since that's what we were called to do. But, there is an additional dimension and purpose to our lives. This doesn't eliminate any of the pressures, qualifications, or requirements associated with doing business with excellence felt by others who don't have the eternal perspective. But there is an additional awareness of the fact that everything we do while we're here on earth has eternal significance. The reality of life after death is foundational to the Christian faith. I recognize that not everybody shares this perspective. But as a Christian, it informs my whole view of life and is a vital input that helps to shape our entire vision and purpose through business.

The eternal perspective of life simply says that there's much more to life than just the daily grind. When our life in the flesh is over there is eternal life to come. Importantly, though, what we do while we're here on earth, as called and chosen sons and daughters of God, has a great effect on what we experience in that life to come.

Wright

So how do the results of your members compare with those of other similar non-member businesses?

Jacobs

Great question! Living with eternity in mind is our priority. But, at the end of the day, we've got to be profitable to be sustainable and we've got to obey all the legal and societal requirements of every other business to stay in business. We certainly acknowledge that. It's not a matter of putting on long robes and sandals and lighting a bunch of candles and walking around like super-spiritual beings. We live in the real world and our members all live and operate in the real world.

When I started this business sixteen years ago I recognized that what we do is to ask the CEO or owner of a business to take a full day each month out of his or her busy schedule and to spend it with us and *pay* us to do so! My background is in business and organizational development, primarily as a president and CEO, so I knew full well that I would never pay to allocate a day a month unless there was a very significant payback attached to it. Over time, we have seen that there is great value being provided to our members.

In 2006 we did a study of long-term C12 group members—those who have been members for ten or more years. We compared their results with a group of leadership companies in a study sponsored by The Business Roundtable that were selected based on their reputation for being well-managed. The performance of this "blue chip" group of 350 businesses was evaluated during the years 1995 to 2005.

We asked our long-term members to give us their results in four basic areas over this same timeframe. The first three were metrics directly comparable to the other, largely non-Christian, companies. The fourth area of inquiry is more specific to C12. We asked them for their top line revenue numbers in the year that they joined C12 (i.e., 1992–1996) and again for 2005. We also asked them for the bottom line profit numbers and a computed real productivity measure over the same period. Finally, for our members, we also asked them to describe their ministry activities and results when they joined in comparison to 2005.

In terms of gross revenue, the compound annual growth rate (CAGR) of the Business Roundtable sample over the ten-year period was 4.3 percent. The composite top line revenue CAGR of all ten-year C12 Group members was 15.2 percent, more than three times what the BRT study group had achieved. The average profit CAGR among the Business Roundtable group was an impressive 8.5 percent, but the C12 sample enjoyed a profit CAGR of 22.1 percent. Further, real ten-year business sector productivity growth, as recorded by the U.S. Bureau of Labor Statistics, was 2.9 percent CAGR, while C12 member companies attained 5.1 percent.

While we don't claim this to be a totally definitive study, it's the best one we could do based on the numbers that were available to us. Going forward, we will be continually and objectively refining how we measure our impact, but these results seem to speak for themselves.

Regarding ministry results, we asked our long-term members to tell us their perceptions of the role of business as a ministry platform when they had joined C12 compared to what it had become ten years later. Their answers in this dimension were, from our perspective, even more exciting in that they had all begun to see their businesses as great opportunities to model and share God's love and truth with the stakeholder community that each one represents.

Every business has a natural circle of influence made up of customers, employees, suppliers, and other trade associates with whom they interact in the natural course of business. During a typical year there is a surprisingly large yet identifiable number of people who are touched by every business in various ways, ranging from brief and casual to very deep and intense. Our thinking is that, when a business and its leaders and employees are intentional about it, they can use those business touches to demonstrate the love and principles of Christ in tangible ways.

With our member companies we found that the increase in the awareness and effectiveness in this dimension was huge. In fact, two particular long-term C12 companies, each with only a hundred or so employees, had each seen over two hundred and fifty people come to faith in Christ through business relationships during that ten-year period. If they had been churches they would have ranked in the top 5 percent of all churches in America in evangelical effectiveness. So they not only experienced exemplary business success as a group, but also made outstanding strides in Christian ministry in the process.

We see this as the natural result of good people striving to do good things God's way over time.

Do you remember, for instance, the movie *Chariots of Fire?* There is a scene in that movie where Eric Liddle refused to run the Olympic race that was his specialty because it was to be run on Sunday. Instead, he committed to run in a different mid-week event that was totally out of his "sweet spot." Just prior to the race, an American runner named Jackson Schultz came up to Eric and put a note in his hand that read, "God honors those who honor Him," a quote from the Bible (1 Samuel 2:30). C12 believes that this is foundationally true—there is a spiritual dimension of life in which God is intimately engaged with us. He *does* honor those who honor Him!

Wright

What is the foundation for building eternally significant success such as great businesses for a greater purpose?

Jacobs

My first response is that Christ and God's Word provide the foundation along with God's providential gifting of abilities and opportunities. This is where we start. From there, I like to cite Dr. Covey's first three principles given in his wonderful book, *The 7 Habits of Highly Effective People,* as extremely helpful to establishing a solid personal foundation. They are:

1. "Be proactive"—Take responsibility for acting positively on the things I can control.
2. "Begin with the end in mind"—Establish a definition of success that can serve as "true north."
3. "Put first things first"—Focus my life and activities on the things that feed the end or vision that I have chosen.

Since we have defined success as hearing Jesus say, "Well done" at the end of our journey through life, this is the ultimate end we strive to keep in mind. We seek eternally significant success in all of our roles and we must have a strong foundation on which to build our business and life.

We have found that there are three common elements that we see consistently utilized to build the kind of foundation that leads to eternally significant success as it applies to organizations:

- *They are led*—it doesn't "just happen." The organizations that really perform and produce in these areas are led by proactive, intentional leaders with a vision firmly in view.

- The leader(s) have a *significant daily quiet time* that builds intimacy with God, both to better know Him and to learn to apply His ways in their lives and roles.

- They have *mission statements that are God honoring and that keep them focused on their first things.* For example, the mission statement for Bill Pollard and ServiceMaster has been; "To honor God in all we do, to help people develop, to pursue excellence, and to grow profitably." This is an articulation that helps us remember where to find true north and really is a tremendous tool and help. In Mr. Pollard's book, *Serving Two Masters,* he demonstrates how he used this mission statement to prepare for and guide ServiceMaster board meetings and how it guided their decision-making process.

We want to seek eternally significant success in all our roles. Beyond the role of CEO or owner we are spouses, parents, members of the community, and so forth. We certainly don't exclude any of them. We focus on the need to build a coherent and integrated life under the Lordship of Christ in all areas. Ultimately our lives and our legacy are going to be a reflection of thousands of choices, and our choices will be reflections of our beliefs. Our beliefs are nurtured by our quiet times with the Lord.

The typical picture of an American Christian leader today is one who is overly burdened, busy, and stressed. These leaders don't seem to have enough hours in each day and find themselves running from dawn to dusk. The product of such a life is not pretty. What tends to happen is they get so busy that they don't take time to work "on" their lives and companies, since they're so busy working "in" them. They don't do strategic and intentional planning for their lives. Most of them get up in the morning, fall out of bed, grab a cup of coffee, race off to the office, react to whatever first hits them in the face, and then keep reacting the whole day until they come home too late at night to have dinner with the family. They watch television for a few hours, fall asleep, get up the next day somewhat sleep-deprived, and do it all over again. Unfortunately, that is an all-too typical picture. It's not the picture of successful leaders in the terms that we discuss in C12, but it's typical of twenty-first century America.

This picture describes too many of today's Christian leaders. We're striving to help them change, gain control of their lives, and become outstanding leaders. Change isn't easy but it is certainly possible and available to anyone willing to engage. The best way I have found is to follow those first three habits or disciplines. We must determine to begin acting on the things that we *can* control. Directionally, we know where we want to go by beginning with the end in mind. Then we need to discern from among the many choices we might make. Leaders have many more choices than most people do because of our positions. We need to become adept at assessing the alternative paths to determine which options will best feed the end we truly seek.

So it's all about taking time to get away from the stress of life on a consistent basis to plan, prepare, and then to enter into each day with a clear sense of purpose, priority and focus. Now, no matter how well we do so, things still happen that knock us off stride because none of us can control everything. But if we have the discipline or healthy habits established in our life that are intentionally designed to keep us close to the path and bring us back into focus, we will make consistent progress. With such discipline, we may get knocked off form from time-to-time, but we won't stay off stride for long or perhaps so dramatically.

Wright

So how do I get a proactive handle on my time and priorities?

Jacobs

That's another great question. So many of our members cite getting control of their lives and schedules as their number one priority! We spend a lot of time here and can promise that, not only is it possible to make huge progress in gaining control, it doesn't require a complicated system.

There are two basics I advocate and that we teach in different ways through the materials we publish for use with our groups. They're so basic that often they're overlooked due to their simplicity. But for most of us, it's the simple things that work best. Beyond being simple to administer, these methods are equally available to anyone willing to make the effort.

The first tool is to establish the discipline on each Sunday night to sit down with a calendar or PDA—whatever vehicle you use to schedule and order your life—and book appointments for the most important things in your life, in priority order.

Let me expand on that. As Christians, the most important relationship we have is our relationship with God. And for any relationship to be healthy, there are two ingredients that cannot be shorted: time and honesty. We all recognize this fact in our marriage relationships. If we don't spend the time that's required to build a healthy marriage, our marriage is going to suffer and we'll struggle. Marriage also requires a level of honesty or transparency that leads to true intimacy. If we spend a lot of time together, but never get beyond the surface by being honest with one another, it doesn't work and our relationship is stunted. So time and honesty are non-negotiable and integral to any healthy relationship.

Developing the intimacy with God that leads to a healthy relationship is no different. God is a "person" in that sense, and our relationship with Him will be developed in much the same way that we would build a relationship with anyone who is important to us. An intimate relationship with God is the foundation that, if cultivated and strengthened, will allow Christians to hear from God the, "Well done, good and faithful servant" that we're seeking.

It will take considerable focused time to intentionally build intimacy with God, where we not only learn about God and speak to Him, but where we also hear from Him as well. So we advocate spending daily "quiet" time with God; we purposely book that time in our calendars each day. In order to get each day off to a good start and enable us to keep God's principles in view from the first, we recommend doing this daily. Allowing thirty to sixty minutes is a good place to start. As with an appointment with our banker or best customer, we require all the other less important priorities and pressures of life to adjust to these pre-committed appointments.

Next to our relationship with God, our marital relationship (assuming we're married) is most important. And there is no way to have a healthy marriage without investing time in that relationship. This time can take the form of date nights, couch time, or sharing activities together as life-mates to nurture and cultivate our marriage relationship. We book that time each week in advance, before we find ourselves carried along by the current of "what's happening now."

Those of us who have children have a God-given parenting responsibility that no one else in the world can fulfill for us. To be healthy, our kids require our time as well. So we book the appointments needed to go to their ball games, help them with homework, have a special date with our child, or do whatever it is that we conclude is necessary.

We also need to take care of our health. The Bible tells us that our bodies are the temple of the Holy Spirit (1 Corinthians 6:19). If our bodies break down we can't be as effective in any of the roles of our lives, so we book time for whatever kinds of healthy exercise are needed. Basic fitness requires spending time in regular physical exercise. So we book an adequate amount of time during the week, typically a minimum of three thirty- to forty-five-minute appointments. Each individual determines what that is for him or her and books it.

After we have made provision for all of the more important priorities, we use the remaining time available to work on building our business. So many of us have it backward. We make every provision for our business and then try to fit the *more* important things—the things we care about most— into whatever time is left. Unfortunately, that method doesn't work very well and leads to damaged or stunted relationships with the most important people in our lives. No one ever comes to the end of life saying, "I just wish I spent more time at the office."

I will give you an example of how this works out in real life. We have a C12 group member who is CEO of a publicly traded business that was doing just less than $100 million per year when he first joined C12. He asked me in one of our early meetings, "Buck, how big does God want me to grow my business?"

"That's the wrong question." I replied.

"Well, what's the right question?"

"The right question is: how many hours a week does God want me to work in building my business?" I then went through the discussion with him of how I discern God's priorities for our lives as I just described above. Together we looked at truly making our first priorities our relationship with God, spouse, parenting, and so forth. We actually sat down with his calendar and booked time for each. He had six teenagers at this time. It was a "blended" family, and every one of those kids had a real need for parenting time.

When we finished the exercise, he said, "Based on this I should really only be working at my business forty to forty-five hours a week."

I asked, "How many hours are you working now?"

"About eighty," he answered.

I said, "That's going to require some changes."

After a moment, he said, "That's right; in order to do this I'm going to have to do three things very differently. Number one, I'm going to have to hire better, because, second, I'll need to be able to delegate a whole lot more effectively than I have until now. Third, I've got to learn to leverage technology so that I can be productive when I'm not actually physically at work."

He began to work this system ten years ago. Today that company is a billion dollar company and he has maintained a 40-50 hour workweek for ten years. There have been, of course, seasons where the workload temporarily spikes; but the point is, because he's being proactive about his life, even when it goes up it doesn't stay up—the bad habit doesn't become a permanent lifestyle. He's consistently working toward the good habit of keeping first things first. And he accepts the first things that will build him a successful life are those that build his relationship with God, his wife and children, and his health. His business is going to be whatever it can be in those hours that are left.

Jack Welch used to brag that he ran GE on forty-five hours a week. The model of the ninety-hour-a-week, hyper-stressed CEO may be a cultural icon, but it's not a valid, biblical model that leads to our God's best and highest for our life and those we touch along the way!

So, our first step is to start to schedule our time based on biblical priorities. Next, we seek to begin each day with a consistent, focused, quiet time. This will be a time for Bible reading and study, prayer, and personal, professional, and spiritual development. As we do this, we recommend recording thoughts and life events through brief journaling. This practice, and what it enables one to "see," will be the foundation for building both eternal and temporal success.

Daily quiet time is a standard Christian discipline and has been advocated as a basic practice necessary to develop an effective Christian life for hundreds of years. The testimony of every great Christian hero—historically and in contemporary terms—unequivocally supports it. I credit this discipline to be the foundation for whatever success I have had as a Christian leader.

The uniqueness of what we're advocating here comes from not only reading the Bible but also from spending a portion of our quiet time reading and studying things that are helpful for our professional and our spiritual development. Since God has called us to the role of leader it is our responsibility to strive for excellence in it through committing to personal development and continuous improvement in all the facets required to be an excellent and productive example.

Years ago, before I even thought about becoming a Christian, I attended a seminar taught by Earl Nightingale. In that seminar he said that if average people would spend as little as five minutes a day studying something to improve their understanding of their business and the specific skills involved in operating the business, within five years they would become experts in their fields. I believed him, and I've been practicing and expanding on his theory for over fifty years.

A little bit of improvement and the incremental acquiring of knowledge day-by-day over a long period of time really does add up. In fact, it will set us apart from all those who stop learning when they leave school or who don't engage in this practice. It's key to being a lifetime learner, both on the spiritual and the practical level, and lifetime learning is an integral piece on the pathway to success.

In today's fast-moving world we cannot succeed over the long-term merely with today's knowledge. Peter Drucker said, "Most companies are being led today based on knowledge that is obsolete." We have to stay ahead of the curve and keep learning and growing to keep our minds young. We need to keep reaching to build sustained success that results in a spiritual legacy as well as observable performance. Knowing and applying biblical principles and commandments in all of life is a key to a coherent, integrated, and fruitful life for a Christian.

Wright

So how do you see the Bible—how does it relate to business and leadership?

Jacobs

The Bible is God's guidebook for life and it contains God's truth both for mankind and mankind's relationship with Him, as well as for relationships with each other. It's both vertical and horizontal.

When I started on this path that God has guided me on for thirty-five years, I was working in a small business with a friend in the Chicago area. There were no organizations like C12 to be found where we could go for advice. So we just met together for about thirty minutes before work each day. We would read a chapter from the Bible and then ask, "God, how do we apply what we've read to the situations we're facing in life and business?" It was incredible how quickly we saw ways that biblical principles, eternal wisdom, and truth would be brought to bear, relationally and in various dimensions relating to integrity and business ethics.

As I passed through this time of learning and revelation, it became clear to me that the reason for the Bible's amazing relevance is that it's all about relationships. First it's about God's relationship with mankind—His created beings—and secondly it's all about mankind's relationship with others under God's commands and principles. You know, a lot of people who might struggle with the first dimension—with God as a creator God—can still apply and benefit from the person-to-person principles in the Bible because they're universal. They apply whether you understand them and know them or not. When people apply the Golden Rule it works whether or not they are Christians. The Bible is God's written way of communicating His principles and commandments. Following God's ways will produce healthy relationships—and business is all about relationships.

A business that is a collection of unhealthy relationships is an unhealthy business. In a recent popular business book, *Firms of Endearment,* the authors studied a number of firms recognized as organizations that sincerely attempt to balance the legitimate needs of the four stakeholder groups in every business or organization: owners, employees, customers, and suppliers. Among other things, the research compared the results that these businesses achieved with those studied in *Good to Great.* The *Firms of Endearment* group significantly outperformed the comparable sample group from *Good to Great.* So these businesses that even in a secular sense strive to serve the legitimate interests of all stakeholder groups do exceptionally well. Some people term this, "doing good by doing good." The Bible, then, is a Christian's guide to a healthy relational life in every sphere of our existence, including business.

Wright

So how do I have a successful quiet time?

Jacobs

I've been at this for over thirty years and this section—how to be successful in starting each day with God our Father—has benefitted others more than anything I've ever shared. If I could only tell a young business leader (or any person) one thing that I feel is most important, this would be it: have a daily quiet time, begin *every day* with an hour of quiet reflection with God.

The first decision about daily quiet time is perhaps the most important of all. It's simple and, if applied, will eliminate hundreds and even thousands of other difficult decisions. This critical decision is that we must make this commitment *non-negotiable!* We all regulate our lives from the time we get up in the morning based on our commitments and the requirements of the day. I've always known since I started out in my work life that I had to be in my car at a certain time in order to arrive at work at the time I needed to be there. I backed up from that time to the time I needed to get out of bed in order to have breakfast, clean my face, get dressed, and so forth; so living a life based on that kind of regulation is not abnormal. The key is to make the first hour, or part of an hour, of your day non-negotiable and dedicate it to being with God. That's all there is to it—getting up one hour, or part of an hour, earlier.

Now the fear is that we think (or we're led to think) that if we get up an hour earlier we're going to be that much more tired at the end of the day. My question is this, "How do you measure how tired you are at the end of the day?" If you're a CEO or business owner, at the end of each day you're going to be tired. You'll be tired whether or not you sleep in that extra bit of time from 5:00 to 6:00 AM, or 6:30 to 7:00, or whatever increment you want to use. You're going to be wiped out at the end of the day, and there is no measurable difference! In terms of how tired we are at day's end, the time we get up (within reason) is really insignificant. Making it non-negotiable means, for instance, if on Saturday I don't have any work commitments and I'm able to sleep until 9:00 AM, then my quiet time is from 9:00 until 10:00. If I'm on vacation I may need to get out of the room, away from the family, and find a quiet place; but I can still have my quiet time with the Lord. If we're going to depart at 8:00 AM to go to Disney World I can get up at 6:30 and have my hour of quiet time before meeting the family for breakfast.

I understand that it may be too much for some of our readers to start with an hour. If so, begin with thirty minutes and test the process. Even ten minutes a day is infinitely better than none and I believe such trial steps will lead to increased focus and commitment over time. The value proposition is pretty incredible. What are a few minutes each day with the One who created heaven and earth worth?

The first key is to make it non-negotiable, and the second is to commit to keeping a daily journal. Journaling—systematically recording our thoughts, prayers, confessions, thanks, and questions—helps us remember our thoughts and God's responses. It also helps us to clarify our thoughts and move toward application. To start, I recommend using just a simple three-ring binder because they are so readily available. You can easily add pages as necessary. To aid in later historical reflection, I recommend you start your quiet time by recording the date, day, and time. In my case, I also record what I weigh, because I've been on a diet for thirty years!

On the top line, note the Scripture passages you will read that day. I recommend two chapters: one from the Gospels and one from another Old or New Testament book. Some people might read more, some might read less. It's most important to start with God's Word, whether it is a brief passage or multiple chapters. Record the portion of the Bible that you're to read that day. I choose to always read at least one Gospel chapter because Jesus is my model and I always want to be reminded of what He said personally. The method of selecting specific day-to-day chapters is secondary, since what we're discussing is a lifetime commitment and practice. Over time, your approach can and most certainly will vary. We can approach it one-way when we start and a year later be doing something else. For depth and freshness, I like to change my pattern over time. To get started, just select something from the Bible and record what you're going to read.

For me, the next most important feature to my quiet time is the practice of considering how the Lord has counseled, blessed, and provided for me over the previous day. Following a subtitle, "Blessing," I serially record that day (e.g., Day 1, Day 2, Day 1,789, and so on) and simply reflect for just a couple of minutes on how God has blessed my life in the previous twenty-four hours. It's amazing how quickly we forget if we don't take the time to think about the good things that have come to our lives from God's hand and due to our faith and obedience. It is so healthy and inspiring to cultivate an "attitude of gratitude." When we reflect for even a few moments we see His hand in our lives in so many ways. We have so much for which to be grateful and it helps us to adjust our thinking when we just write a few of them down each day.

In my personal journal (in which the consecutive entries have just passed Day 7,050), I start by writing "Thank you Father for—" and then reflect on the twenty-four hours just passed. These notes don't take more than a couple minutes, but I believe that this practice fosters a grateful heart and an understanding of God's grace and sovereignty that is so vitally important in a Christian leader's life. It reduces stress, provides a sense of peace, and helps us see God's providence flowing into and through our lives. And, as we realize how He has touched and helped us in the past, it helps us to trust Him for the upcoming challenges of each day.

Next I recommend reading the Bible passages you have planned. Ask the Lord to help you, in fellowship with His Spirit, to approach His Word with an open and teachable heart. Try to read it slowly, and *really* think about *what* the Lord is saying to you and *why*. Basically, ask yourself, "How does this apply to what I'm experiencing in my life today?" Don't hurry and don't be discouraged if you initially have trouble concentrating. When you find yourself distracted, just refocus and continue. Simply read and think through the Scripture. Note your thoughts if you feel you want to remember something particularly pertinent.

After you finish your Bible reading, select something to read that's of a professional or a spiritual or combined professional/spiritual development nature. I read business books, such as *Good to Great, Passion for Excellence,* and *The 7 Habits* in my morning quiet time, as well as inspiring works written by great Christian heroes such as A. W. Tozer, Watchman Nee, George Müller, Thomas á Kempis, and D. L. Moody. I've read literally hundreds of books and God has used them all to teach, equip, inspire, and shape me. It really doesn't matter so much who you prefer or where you start, as long as you select purposefully based on the potential to learn something to apply to your faith and calling. There are scores of ancient and contemporary writers to choose from and it is great to vary your choices. I have been blessed by and learned much from writers from every business field and Christian denomination, both Catholic and Protestant.

I truly believe that one hour is an ideal amount of time to truly benefit from the discipline of quiet time. It only takes fifteen to twenty minutes to read a chapter or two from the Bible and another fifteen minutes to read something for our daily personal development that will pay huge dividends over time. Cumulatively, this continuous learning discipline can create a tremendous competitive advantage.

Next, I write a brief letter to God in my journal. I write whatever is on my heart. Some days, when I've learned something noteworthy, I thank Him for that. Some days, when I've been convicted, I pause to talk to Him or maybe confess some things. I sometimes write questions and occasionally I even write down what I think His answers to the questions are. That doesn't happen every day, but this practice is intended to be a dialogue with God. It's designed to build both intimacy and awareness of our vital, life-giving relationship. This is what God wants with us—you and me—and with every one of His children. He wants a solid day-to-day relationship. All healthy relationships are two-way affairs. We're not talking about an organizational thing or an inanimate experience—it's a personal relationship. And we cultivate and nurture that relationship by writing our thoughts to God as our loving and active Father. I write, "Dear Father," on the first line and then just pour my heart out to Him. I urge and encourage everyone who reads this to accept this as a challenge or opportunity and, as Nike says, "Just Do It!"

The last thing I do during my quiet time is to have a time of prayer where I just talk to God and "listen" for His leading and conviction. I talk to Him primarily about what He has for me to do—His plan for my life—and I focus on praying for other people and their needs. I've found that keeping a prayer list in my journal is very helpful. Since I'm not a great prayer warrior, my prayer time isn't all I would like it to be. But over time, if you discipline yourself to do it every day, you can cover an awful lot of people. In sustaining this process over time, you'll see tons of prayers answered. This practice really builds faith since recording and writing things down helps to remember them!

Another habit I've developed that I think is key is taking a little extra time each Saturday morning, when I have a little more flexibility, to review my journal for the week. It's amazing how we forget so quickly the good things that come to our lives. When I review my journal and the blessings of the week, I'm often struck by the fact that I've already forgotten so many good things that have happened in my life. This helps me to be thankful and to recognize God's kindness to me. It feeds my understanding of the whole concept of God's grace, honor, and favor. I'm able to develop an acute awareness that I really deserve nothing on my own merits and to realize and appreciate what I have been given. It's such a great way to look at life.

So that's the process of quiet time and, at the risk of being accused of being dogmatic, I'll say that I believe no man or woman will ever be all that they were designed to be in God's kingdom apart from having a serious daily quiet time.

I've studied the lives of numerous great Christian leaders, three of whom I mentioned—Mother Teresa, George Müller, and Hudson Taylor—and each of them practiced this daily quiet time discipline. Martin Luther said, "I require an hour with God every day, but if I have a busy day I do two hours." It's an overlooked and under-utilized discipline in our current post-Christian culture, but one essential for those who are going to accept the challenge and excel in the practice of Christian leadership in the twenty-first century. The benefits are immeasurable, both now and in eternity. For a Christian leader it's an indispensable step on the Roadmap to Success.

Wright

Well, what a great conversation. I really do appreciate this. This is, I think, the discipline that you have to have in your industry and should also be great fodder for some of our readers, especially those who are in leadership roles.

Jacobs

Thanks David, I'm really just trying to share what I've learned along the way with others. Thirty-five years ago I stepped onto the narrow way and have stumbled and fallen off many times. I'm just a learner trying to help others learn as well. I believe that great leaders are really great mentors and it's a mentoring relationship that we have with each other in C12 groups. I've heard that teachers impart knowledge, but mentors impart life, and that's what gives C12 groups the vibrancy they have—life-on-life sharpening and accountability.

Wright

Today we've been talking with Buck Jacobs, Founder and Chairman of The C12 Group, America's leaders since 1992 in equipping Christian chief executives to *Build Great Business for a Greater Purpose.* He has authored several books and articles and is also a very popular speaker.

Buck, thank you so much for being with us today on *Roadmap to Success.*

Jacobs

It's been my pleasure, David. Thank you.

About the Author

BUCK JACOBS is Founder and Chairman of The C12 Group, America's leaders since 1992 in equipping Christian Chief Executives to "Build Great Business for a Greater Purpose." Buck has authored several books and articles and is a popular seminar and conference speaker. Previously, as a Senior Executive for S.H. Mack & Company of Chicago, Illinois, he oversaw a ten-year, ten-fold increase in sales and the global development of a Christ-centered business. The Mack Company was a founding member of the Fellowship of Companies for Christ (FCCI), for which Buck later served as Florida Director. His earlier roles include Managing Director of Sta-Power Italia, Rome, Italy, President of R.G. Haskins Corporation, and CEO of the Executive Development Institute. Buck is happily married to Bonnie, and has three daughters and five grandchildren.

To Contact Buck Jacobs...
141 Sunset Oaks
Cornelia, GA 30531
706.717.0234
buck.jacobs@c12group.com
www.c12group.com

ROADMAP to SUCCESS 5

An interview with...

Dina Emser

David Wright (Wright)

Today we're talking with Dina Emser. Dina brings her training and experience as an educator, director of a not-for-profit corporation, and a certified professional development coach to business professionals, educators, and parents. Dina has spoken nationally and internationally to such groups as Women in Leadership, National Association for the Education of Young Children, North American Society of Adlerian Psychology, and the Association of Professional Fundraisers. She is a member of the International Coach Federation, Positive Discipline Association, and the International Speakers Network.

Dina, welcome to *Roadmap to Success!*

Dina Emser (Emser)

Thank you, David.

Wright

So tell me, what is a professional development coach?

Emser

Well, as a professional development coach I work with business professionals to identify their career goals and I help them chunk down those goals into doable steps. Having a coach provides accountability. I help clients recognize their progress and sometimes we revise their steps a bit. I often give them feedback about their leadership style and where it might be getting in the way of their progress and I provide a sounding board for them. It doesn't seem to matter whether they're small business owners with five to ten employees or members of a corporate team for a Fortune 100 company, people need someone they trust to offer them an alternative point of view. And, maybe most importantly, I acknowledge their strengths and help them recognize when they're using them.

Wright

So you're in for the long haul; you actually do some tracking.

Emser

Yes, absolutely. I work with clients for a minimum of three months. I've worked with some clients for several years. After we've established some structures to support them, they often continue with one call a month as a check-in. A structure might be a way to prioritize daily tasks or a way to delegate things to staff members or a way to notice other perspectives when a client is stuck.

Wright

So how do you connect professionalism to parenting?

Emser

I really encourage parents to consider themselves as leaders. Leadership has similarities both at work and at home. My former life as an educator puts me in front of audiences of teachers and parents across the country. I often speak about teacher and parent leadership styles and how each style invites a certain response from children. I started noticing that understanding leadership styles was coming up with both parents and my business clients as well. Sometimes the problems arising at home are a reflection of the parent's leadership style. For instance, a stern parent leadership style may invite a strong child to rebel and a less confident child to become overly compliant. A permissive parent leadership style may invite the child to become manipulative and overly attached to getting his or her own way. It just got me wondering—what if parents were more intentional, as professionals are, about coming up with plans to improve their leadership at home? What if they did exactly what the pros do? I started making some connections between what I see with my professional clients, and I came up with a list of ten things that parents can do to *"Parent Like a Pro."*

Wright

So what are some of the things parents can learn from these pros?

Emser

The first one on the list is to cultivate the desire to be the best they can be. Professionals take themselves pretty seriously and are always interested in being their best. Have you ever known of an Olympic athlete who wanted to come in second? They practice and practice in order to be sure they will give their top performance. They hire the best coaches and they dedicate time, energy, and resources to achieve their goals. I think we'd all agree that being a parent is a pretty important job. If parents got more intentional about doing their best as parents, they would want to have plans for increasing their own effectiveness.

Pros always have long-range plans for success and they know how to capitalize on their natural talents. You don't often see someone make it at a professional level doing something that is not natural to him or her. However, parents are inclined to pay attention to the things that they don't do very well, rather than to their natural strengths. I like to help them identify what they already do well and utilize these qualities more fully. These qualities might include having a sense of humor, having empathy, being good problem-solvers, promoting teamwork, and getting children involved so that they want to cooperate.

Wright

I heard you mention a long-range plan. How does this relate to a professional's Roadmap to success?

Emser

Pros have visions of where they want to go and they know how they're going to get there. I think parents should create their own Roadmaps to success. If they could imagine their children all grown up and create a list of skills and qualities that they want their grown children to have, they could concentrate on helping children develop those skills. A long-range plan or a vision of how they want their children to be can help parents focus on what they want with intention, very similar to what professionals do. Their vision of their children as young adults is like the destination on the map. The tools they use and the experiences they provide for their children in order to develop and grow these important skills are like the roads and the landmarks on the Roadmap. Think how much easier a trip is when you know where you're going and you have the route mapped out!

Wright

You seem to be emphasizing strengths on your top ten list. Why is it so important for parents to pay attention to a child's strengths?

Emser

Strengths are a part of all of us, and often in our society we're more experienced in dealing with our weaknesses. We hear about them from our parents, our teachers, and from other well-meaning adults. Just imagine for a moment what a child's life would be like if his or her parents spent time developing natural talents instead of focusing so much time on weaknesses.

And parents would have a lot more fun with their families if they focused on their parenting strengths rather than on their weaknesses. We often don't give ourselves any credit for the things that come to us naturally, and these qualities can make parenting a whole lot more fun and can make us more effective doing it. I've seen parents who were just naturals at inviting cooperation with kids. They use their natural team-building skills to give kids jobs based on their interests and abilities. Getting kids involved is a great way to increase their feelings of connectedness and importance, and of giving them a sense of competence. I've seen other parents who accomplish consensus in their families effortlessly by using their natural skills in negotiation and problem solving.

I also really believe that what we focus on expands, so if we're constantly focused on our child's faults or inadequacies, that's what we're going to see. If we focus on our own shortcomings, those will show up for us time and again. Doing this breeds a feeling of discontent and fear that we're never good enough. But our increased happiness might just be a simple shift away.

If we trained ourselves to notice our children's natural talents and interests and gave them time and attention to develop those, they could turn into something quite extraordinary. For example, let's say a parent became aware that his daughter is always drawing. Anything he can say in words, she can represent with pictures. She even seems to pick up subtle nuances in the illustrations of her picture books. She sees things that he hasn't even noticed. The first thing he may want to do is to acknowledge her abilities with a sense of true admiration. Then, he may want to be sure she has the tools to develop her abilities. He doesn't have to go over the top and begin planning her career as an artist and sign her up at the best art school for preschoolers. What our kids do need is our genuine attention and our heartfelt acknowledgment of their gifts.

Wright

What other kinds of plans do you think parents need to put in place in order to be the best parents they can be?

Emser

Besides a long-range plan for success, I also think parents should have plans for what they will do and say when they are in the spotlight. Pros know what to say when they're in the spotlight! In an interview or public appearance, they often write their own questions or scripts and they practice! Parents have lots of opportunities to be in the spotlight when they are in public with their children or without them. How will they talk about their children to family members, to care providers and teachers, to adult friends? What will they say if they are asked a hard question by their children in front of their friends or other adults? We all know these things are going to happen. I propose that it is a very good idea to make a plan ahead of time, even if the plan is simply, "This isn't the time to discuss this. We'll talk about it when we get home."

Parents need plans for how they want their children to behave when they're outside the home. Kids have lots of opportunities to embarrass parents in public. When parents work with their children to come up with a plan and role-play it, this is a great way to communicate expectations and to do some training. When we involve children in the planning, it also increases their desire to cooperate. An important part of the plan should be what will happen if things don't go smoothly. That might include "We're all going to get back in the car and go home and we'll have another chance to practice next time." It's not about blaming and shaming our kids. An effective, respectful parent is pro-active about coming up with a plan ahead of time and respectfully communicating it so that he or she will know how to handle situations that arise on the job, and children will know what to expect.

One of the most important plans I think parents need is a plan to take care of themselves. Parents need time away from their kids to nurture their relationships as married couples and if they're single parents, they need time away from their kids to develop their own interests and to cultivate other relationships. It is nearly impossible to consistently care for others when our own needs for self-care are not met. This is not selfish! It is wise.

Wright

So actually, you're just talking about planning and emphasizing things at the parent level. I'm so interested in your top ten things, would you mind running through the list?

Emser

I would be delighted to do that. Here are ten things I think parents can learn from the pros:

- Pros are interested in being the best they can be.
- Pros have long-range plans for success.
- Pros know and utilize their strengths.
- Pros demonstrate a professional code of conduct.
- Pros know their audience and their needs.
- Pros partner with others to get what they need and to create a win-win.
- Pros get ongoing training and they practice a lot.
- Pros have and use the best tools of their trade.
- Pros know how to handle being in the spotlight.
- Pros take care of themselves because they know they are their own best assets.

Wright

Those are great. When you think of the professionals whom you coach, what issues do they have in common with parents?

Emser

My business clients often have communication concerns such as how to tell an employee a hard truth or how to motivate and encourage employees without enabling them, how to say what they really mean as leaders without seeming bossy, and what to do when they feel like they're involved in a power struggle. All of these issues are really similar to things that happen to us as parents, and for me, it comes back to something I learned as a school principal. Psychologist Alfred Adler believed that all people have a basic human need to be included. We all need to feel that we belong in whatever group we're with, and we learn about this first with our families. We also need to believe that we contribute in meaningful ways and that we are important to the group. When you can figure out how to help people feel a sense of belonging and significance—whether they're children or adults—they're going to be much more likely to cooperate and to be more fully engaged. They will give to their team, whether it is their company team or their family.

Business clients and parents want and need tools for more effective and respectful communication and ways to encourage others.

Wright

It sure seems that there are more and more examples of pros in the spotlight who don't set a very good example, so what do you think we can learn from them?

Emser

That's a good question, David. I think that one actually comes to the mind of a lot of people when they think about pros. Just because people are in the spotlight—and it doesn't matter whether they're professional athletes or entertainers or politicians—it certainly doesn't mean they are good role models for young people. If we have conversations and dialogue with our children, I believe they can learn a lot from people who don't model integrity, honesty, and respect. We can ask children what they would do differently. We can discuss our points of view about their behaviors, and help our young people learn about empathy. How would it really feel to have so many people watching you? What would your life be like, considering other aspects than just the huge income we associate with professionals? What is the responsibility of someone who has so much power over the public?

Then when we do see a role model who seems to be able to balance his or her professional responsibilities and a personal life, we really sit up and take notice because we have seen so many people who don't do that very well. It's almost as though the people who don't do it give increased value to those who do. It's a tricky balance, but I think it really does boil down to being intentional and having a plan for how you're going to navigate that increased notoriety and increased success.

Wright

So I know you do a lot of public speaking. What's the message you really want people to hear from you?

Emser

For me, it really comes back to reminding people that even if they can't change their immediate circumstances, they can always change their minds. We tell ourselves very powerful stories and we believe these stories to be true. We create stories about ourselves, about others, and about the way the world works. I want people to become more aware of their stories and always to see that they have a choice—that if they don't like what they have, they can change their story about it. Sometimes changing your story makes all the difference.

I believe that we are very connected and have more things alike about us than we have different. I like to encourage people to be more intentional about what they want in their lives and to find ways to create more of that! Find ways to more fully use their natural talents and gifts to make a difference in the world. We all have it in us!

Wright

As a parent of a forty-six-year-old daughter, a forty-four-year-old son, and a nineteen-year-old daughter, I've had all kinds of opportunities to do some of the things that you have said here; but I learned these things so late in life, it didn't really help with the first two. I wonder what we could do as a nation to train parents, to give them some tools? I had no training and one day I was a parent. Do you have any suggestions? Do we do that through the school systems?

Emser

It's a really good question, David. I feel strongly that it's each parent's responsibility to get training. One of my "Ten Things the Pros Know" (number seven) is, "Get ongoing training and practice a lot." Professionals are constantly adding to their skills. The business world is always changing, so ongoing education and training are critical to professional success. Parents need to be willing to admit that they don't know everything there is to know about parenting—nobody can.

Many schools do offer programs for parents, and I know from experience that they are often poorly attended. There are always places that we can go, either to seminars or to hear people speak, and there are a myriad of wonderful books out there for parents. But, parents must take the first step to get the help they need. And, parent educators have to continue to find helpful and inviting ways to offer tools and information to parents—not from a place of judgment, but from a place of encouragement and sharing.

Wright

It does seem a little strange that we would give billions and billions to scholarships for high school students going into college and, as far as I know, nothing to teaching parents. I would think it would be much more important to be an effective parent that it would be to be a college graduate.

Emser

You know it's a tricky thing because we have so much impact on the lives of our own young children—the ones that come through our households—and it's a very challenging job that changes with each stage of our child's development. Parents often don't want to parent the way they were parented, but they don't really have a very good place to look for an alternative. They need information, they need tools, and they need encouragement. Even as I hear the different ages of your children, I'm reminded that it's a job that never ends. It just keeps changing and our responsibilities and relationships with our adult children clearly change too.

My children are also adults. One is twenty and one is twenty-four. I think that having them be the ages that they are really adds to my increased understanding and desire to help parents when their kids are young because that's the time. It's never too late, but certainly it's a lot easier when they're younger—when we can see a vision of what we want for them as young adults. What would it really look like for my children to be successful and what would they need? Want if I could help them develop those skills and qualities right now, growing them day by day?

Wright

Well, what an interesting conversation. You certainly have an interesting job.

Emser

I love my job. I am constantly learning from the people I work with, which keeps it challenging and fun.

Wright

I really appreciate all the time you've spent with me this afternoon answering all these questions. I've learned a lot.

Emser

Thanks, David. It's been a pleasure.

Wright

Today we've been talking with Dina Emser. She coaches professionals, educators, and parents, and as we can see from her answers to these questions today, I think she knows what she's talking about. I've really enjoyed listening to her, and I hope that you will learn from reading this unusual chapter.

Dina, thank you so much for being with us today on *Roadmap to Success*.

Emser

Thank you, David.

About the Author

DINA EMSER is a Certified Professional Development Coach who coaches business leaders, educators, and parents to better utilize their natural strengths to improve effectiveness and satisfaction. Dina is the author of *The Fortune Within* and is a sought-after public speaker. She is also a veteran facilitator providing training to organizations across the United States and abroad. She is an adjunct faculty member at the Adler School of Professional Psychology, Chicago, IL and is a member of the International Coach Federation, Positive Discipline Association, International Speakers Network and Women in Leadership.

Dina has been happily married for 30 years and is the mother of two young adults.

To Contact Dina Emser...
Professional Development Coach
207 E. Campus Street, Suite B
Eureka, IL 61530
309.467.4429
dina@dinaemser.com
www.dinaemser.com

ROADMAP *to* SUCCESS 6

An interview with...

D. Trinidad Hunt

David E. Wright (Wright)

Today we're talking with D. Trinidad Hunt. Trin is President and co-founder of two training and consulting firms, Élan Enterprises LLC and Élan Asia-Pacific. Trin is an International author, consultant, trainer, and keynote speaker with over thirty years of experience in the area of program development and training. As cofounder of Élan Enterprises LLC, Trinidad has developed programs for business leaders nationally and internationally for such companies as Pepsi Cola, Frito Lay, Sprint, and The Royal Bank of Canada. As a result of her expertise in business and leadership, Trinidad has been invited to speak in Australia, China, India, Canada, and the Philippines.

Trinidad has hosted her own radio talk show on the East Coast in the United States and has spoken to leaders across the United States and Canada on her newest model of IQ, EQ, SQ, and how it affects leadership in the twenty-first century.

Wright

You run a successful international consulting and training firm as well as a non-profit for children. Tell us how you got started.

Trinidad Hunt (Trin)

You know, David, I started out like most young people, fresh out of college with no money to my name. To the outsider, the success in my life today may appear to be luck or even destiny. However, in hindsight, I realize that it really wasn't either of these. From my perspective, the Roadmap to success is not a linear path. On close inspection it looks more like a relief map, multi-dimensional in nature with elevations and depressions representing the hills, valleys, and summits of challenges and achievements along the way. Ultimately, it is a combination of intention, attitude and actions applied along the way.

For myself, success started with a positive desire and a passion for what was possible. I spent my first few years out of college thinking about what I *didn't* want. I was teaching at the time and I didn't want to do what I was doing. I loved the kids, but I didn't want to be in a classroom all day long. I knew I wanted do something more, but I didn't know what that something was.

I must have complained about my lot in life because one day a friend of mine said something that changed my perspective forever: "I have heard what you don't want in your life," he said. "But you've never told me what you *do* want."

That evening I went home and thought about what my friend had said. "What do I want?" I wondered. So I made a list of what I *did* want. It was a very short list, but it was the best I could do at the time. It was the first time I had clearly stated a positive desire on paper. Looking back, I realize now that it was the beginning of my transformation. I wrote:

1. I want to do more and give more than I am now.
2. I want to be the best that I can possibly be.
3. I want to use my gifts and talents in whatever I do.

4.   I want to make a positive contribution to the lives of others.

I wasn't even really clear about what my gifts and talents were then. But I sensed from my work with young people that all human beings come in with certain propensities, certain talents, or things they are naturally good at. I also intuitively felt that the fulfillment of a life was involved in using these natural talents in service to the larger body of humanity. So even though the edges of my picture were not clearly defined in the beginning, I had enough information to begin formulating an image. It was the beginning of my visioning process and the clarification of my purpose, although I didn't know it at the time.

At the same time, I began to develop a fascination with the idea of genius and "geniuses"—those men and women who had made a remarkable or extraordinary contribution to humankind. I spent hours at night pouring over biographies and autobiographies of these men and women. What became evident was that in each and every case, these were individuals who were using their gifts and talents to achieve some incredible task that they had set before themselves.

I began to identify with these people as I read about them. Like me, these men and women were challenged. Life did not make it easy for them by opening a perfect path to their objective; rather, it was just the opposite. After these individuals made a decision to achieve some goal, blocks, barriers, and obstacles appeared at every turn in the road. In every case these men and women learned to turn adversity into an ally. Adversity seemed to strengthen them by forcing them to stretch the muscle of their mind and heart in order to find deeper resources within themselves. In no case were these individuals ever willing to give up. Even though they sometimes hit a wall and sank to the ground in despair, they would soon find the power within to get up and get going once again.

I was teaching at the time. So as I read and reflected on these ideas at night, my mind went through a radical transformation. I began to develop a passion for what might be possible in my life. I began to realize that my life circumstances were exactly what I needed to master at this time. I needed to turn this challenge—this seeming adversity—into an opportunity and use it as a stepping-stone rather than a barrier. As I continued to immerse myself in this study by night, I vowed to put what I was learning into practice in my own life circumstances during the day.

I tried in every way to follow the path of those men and women who had come before me. Much like Hansel and Gretel, who had left the telltale signs of their trail, these men and women had left a trail of insights and discoveries. I knew that for those who could read the signs and the secrets, the path would become visible. While it might have appeared to others that I was a fifth grade teacher, I knew that I was a fifth grade teacher with a purpose. I was in the process of discovering and harnessing the genius within so that I might direct it in service to mankind.

I made a promise then to always give my very best. I call it my "best always principle." This meant that I had to be willing to do what others were not willing to do. It became evident that this was a core practice of every great contributor. It was this practice that carried great leaders beyond the mediocre. I discovered that there was only one small inch of difference between mediocrity and brilliance; but that small inch could be compared to the difference between a marathon and a triathlon. It would require every ounce of courage and strength within me. It would also require the willingness to turn daily practice into a consistent habit.

I was working with fifth graders at the time and it was because of this principle that I began exploring the borders and pushing the conventional boundaries of education. I decided to give my students everything I had, so I started teaching them the principles and practices that I was learning. I showed up earlier than any other teacher and I left later. I found that over-preparation was one of the keys to excellence. So I prepared my lesson plans with a passion.

Further, I decided to do the unthinkable at the time—I taught my students goal setting, visioning, and time management. I created personal files that they could access at their discretion. I set aside time for monthly goal setting at the beginning of each month. Then, at the end of every month, I gave the students time to assess their development and score themselves on what percent of their goal they felt they had achieved.

My class rose to such heights that year that the principal began to notice the change. My students' grades showed steady upward progress and they exhibited greater self-control than their peers on the playground. One of the parents called a television station in our area and they came and did a five-minute news story on our class.

As the year came to a close, the principal called me to her office. She asked if I would be willing to leave the classroom the following year in order to share my knowledge with other teachers. So during the next year I had an office and began training other teachers to do what I had done with my students.

The next step was obvious. At the end of that year, I left the school to join a small training and consulting firm. A year and a half later, I purchased the company and became my own employer. I eventually sold that company to my business partner and co-founded two other companies as well as a non-profit that serves students and teachers in the school system.

Let me sum up the lessons of those early years—lessons that I use in my consulting business to this day. First, I discovered that *the only way out is through*. In other words, the stepping-stone to the next level of expansion in your life is through doing what is right in front of you exceptionally well. Excellence is a principle and a practice. It is a habit and we must start developing the habit in the here and now.

The other lesson is something I call P to the seventh power or P^7. P^7 is made up of a constellation of seven interrelated, mutually reinforcing elements: *Purpose and Passion, Principles and Practices, People and Partnership,* and *Perseverance.*

Wright

I notice that you've linked some of the words together such as purpose and passion, principles and practice. Is this intentional?

Trin

It is, David. The various aspects of P^7 are interdependent. Let me explain. P^7 begins with Purpose and Passion. People often think that they have to be crystal clear about their purpose. However, you don't really need to know every single thing you want in order to set a personal change in motion. I always ask those I coach to define what they *are* clear about. If you remember, I was only clear about four things when I started. Yet having this amount of clarity regarding my purpose provided a skeletal framework to begin the process of change or growth. So it is with those I coach. I ask those I coach to start with what they do know and commit these goals to paper. Writing it down always helps people clarify their purpose or objective.

Then, when we couple *purpose* with *passion*, which includes enthusiasm, zest, and a desire to achieve, we create a powerful thrust to move us forward. Passion is an *e-motion—energy-in-motion*. In the case of P^7 it is the energy of purpose put into motion. So passion is what moves us to action. Without passion, purpose can become a laborious task. Purpose determines the direction while passion ignites the spark that sets the process in motion. Purpose together with passion turns every labor into a labor of love.

Again, P^7 consists of seven mutually reinforcing related elements. This means that we can't have any one of the seven without the other. All of the elements are related and reinforce or support one another. You can, therefore, begin by determining your purpose or you could begin by clarifying your principles.

So now let's look at the next two words: Principles and Practices. *While purpose determines our direction, and passion energizes us, principles guide our actions.* Principles are our deeply held values—the fundamental beliefs that guide us. Our principles are our ethics, our compass, and our true north on that compass. As business leaders, our principles may include such things as ethics and personal integrity, quality, excellence, service-oriented, and so on.

Further, Principles and Practices are irrevocably intertwined. Our practices—the actions we take and the things that we do—must be aligned with our principles. To be successful in business, we must be both trustable and trustworthy. And we only become trustworthy when our behaviors are congruent with our principles, beliefs, or values. We must say what we will do and do what we say. The question is not whether or not we influence people—the real question is what kind of influence will we have on people? When our principles and our practices are aligned, our positive influence exceeds the ordinary. Gandhi put it very succinctly when he said, *"You must be the change you wish to see in the world."* Simply put, we must walk the talk. We must be what we are asking others to be and do what we are asking others to do.

Now let's look at People and Partnership. While purpose determines our direction and principles guide our actions, it is people who will help us achieve our goals. Our people are our partners in the game. As for myself, I believe in this principle so much that I have taken on partnerships in all of my major endeavors. Then in the process of building the company, we hire for both attitude and skill.

I learned in my early years that a person with a negative attitude or a lack of skills in an area that is critical to job success can demoralize an entire team. Therefore, hiring, placement, and training are extremely important when fitting a team for success. It takes time to hire effectively.

Today, we recommend a three-step hiring process. The first screening begins with the resume and dialogue with previous employers. The second step is a battery of inventories that gives an added understanding of the person from various perspectives. And the final step is an interview with the team of people who will be working with the person.

Another important aspect of people and partnership are our vendors and our customers. All are seen as partners in the game. This means that a great part of our success will be dependent on our ability to create and sustain positive supportive relationships.

Finally, in our P^7 model is perseverance. Perseverance includes the determination and stamina to stick with your purpose. It includes endurance and commitment as well as our intention to stay the course. Life will always throw blocks and barriers along the path in our quest for success. As we accept the challenges, we become stronger. Challenges test and strengthen our will and our resiliency.

If I could summarize P⁷ for people, David, I'd probably say, "Do the best you can at getting in touch with what you want. You may not know your full purpose, but you do know something. Write down what you do know. Next, to the best of your ability, define the boundaries of your principles. I wanted to make a positive contribution to the lives of others and use my gifts and talents in the process. To this day, this intention guides my actions.

Then surround yourself with good people—people who are willing to support the purpose and vision you hold. Passion will help you persevere, and as you persevere with the support of your partners, your vision will get clearer and your intention stronger. In time, your goals will begin to crystallize and the results will begin to reveal themselves. Persist and be patient. Don't expect instantaneous success. Remember, you are strengthening a muscle—the muscle of your will and mind and heart. As you continue to persevere, you will notice an upward spiral of positive change.

Wright

So are you saying that the concept or theory of P⁷ will work for everyone?

Trin

Absolutely, David, I have seen the results of the P⁷ concepts with everyone we coach. The P⁷process will work for those who want to grow into a leadership position as well as for those who are already in a leadership position. It works for people who want to sharpen their skills and increase their effectiveness.

Wright

So is this what distinguishes your work with business managers and leaders or is there more?

Trin

Actually, David, P⁷ is only part of the picture. It falls within the framework of a new style of high performance leadership. We call it

"Facilitative Leadership." As you know, the word "facilitate" comes from the Latin derivative *facilis,* which means, "to make easy." A facilitative leader, therefore, makes things easier or smoothes the way, and enables, assists, helps, or aids his or her team. These leaders speed up, accelerate, advance, or promote people and business. They also encourage and are catalysts for positive change.

For the facilitative leader, success in business—organizational success—depends on P^7 as well as a combination of other elements. Further, success depends on arranging those elements relative to one another in order to produce a positive outcome.

Another way of looking at this is that anyone who plays any sport or game of any kind has to bring a lot of elements to bear in order to be successful at his or her game. It is just the same in the game of business. In order to play the game in a masterful way, facilitative leaders must align and balance many elements both within themselves as well as within the team.

Wright

You call business a "game'?

Trin

I do, David. Business has all the elements of a game. You have to go out there to the field every day and play as if your life depends on it. At the same time, you have to remember not to get caught in your own self-importance. You have to be aware of the score. Yet you have to take your eyes off the scoreboard and focus on the play, giving it everything you've got.

In a game you also have to develop the skills and skill sets that define greatness in your chosen sport. Then you have to practice every single day to improve in each of those skills so that you can play a competitive or exceptional game. It is no different in business. You have to develop the skills of a great leader. Then you must hone these skills so that, like a finely tuned instrument, you play your part perfectly.

Again, in a game you have a competitor. And in business it is just the same. You have a competitor or competitors in the marketplace—

companies that present a formidable challenge and that push you to find and play at your personal best. And when you've made a mistake or fallen down, there's no time to hesitate, you have to get up and dust yourself off and get back into the game.

At the end of the day, after your play on the field, you have to assess your game. You must review your wins and reflect on your mistakes. Then you have to release them, let them go, and envision how you will improve the next day.

Then on the following day you have to get up, go back to the field, and give it everything you've got one more time. This practice repeats itself day after day ad infinitum. In other words, you must aspire to excellence, and then execute your play each day with all the purpose and passion in you. And finally you must make *Kaizen* a regular part of your daily process and practice.

Wright

What is *Kaizen?*

Trin

Kaizen is a Japanese word. *Kai* means "change" and *Zen* means "for the better." In Chinese it is pronounced *Gai San, Gai* meaning "the action to correct" and *san* meaning an action that benefits all people rather than one individual. In English, the connotative meaning of *Kaizen* has come to be known as "gradual, orderly, and continuous improvement."

In working with people in leadership positions or with those who want to move into a leadership position, we ask them to make *kaizen* a part of their daily practice. They soon develop the habit of using the *kaizen* methods to improve their systems and processes as well as their own personal leadership practices on a daily basis.

Wright

So business is a game and part of the game includes making *kaizen* part of our daily process and practice?

Trin

Absolutely! You see, the primary element in any game begins with us. It starts with me and you or the "self." We have to bring ourselves to the game and to the team. As leaders, we influence others. As leaders we are the "set point" for the team. The leader determines the tone the team develops and the zone the team plays in. It is leaders' actions, behaviors, and words that set the tone in their departments and organizations. We do this by who we are and how we "be." It is our "being-ness" that sets the tone or feeling in the organization. Self-development, therefore, is not an option when it comes to business leadership. Instead, self-development is a responsibility of leadership.

In this regard, when I start the coaching process with any of my people, I ask the question, "Who do you want to be?" Not "What do you want to do?" What a person does will flow from who they are. Or, *what we "do" will naturally flow out of who we choose to "be."*

We commence with each executive's "Philosophy of Leadership." We ask each executive to reflect deeply on what they feel good leadership looks and feels like. We ask executives to reflect back to what inspired them as followers. We ask them to think about the managers and leaders who influenced them. Then we ask them to consider their own values and beliefs. We ask them to ask themselves, "Who am I in relationship to the people I work with and lead?"

It takes quite a bit of time for a leader to clarify his or her philosophy. The wheels of business don't come to a halt or even slow down so that a leader can get clear. So this process becomes a backdrop to a leader's ongoing work. We ask leaders to hold four questions before them as they go about their day:

- What is a leader? And what is the role and responsibility of a leader?
- As a leader, what do I believe in with all my heart and mind?
- What do leaders "do"? What actions do they take?

- Why lead? What's the point of being a leader?

Then we ask leaders to take five minutes at the end of each day to reflect on what they have learned that day in relationship to these four questions. We ask them to reflect on their words and behavior in relationship to what they believe. We ask them to imagine sitting in front of a mirror at the end of each day. There, in front of the mirror in their mind, we ask them to review their words and actions in the light of their dawning philosophy.

As they review their day and reflect back over their thoughts and actions in the light of the four questions, we ask them to add their insights and ideas to their philosophy. In the beginning, their philosophy will appear hazy. Yet over time, through the process of self-reflection, their thinking will begin to clarify.

It is much like looking into a pool after a rainstorm has stirred the sediment in the water. In the beginning, the pool will appear murky. Yet over time, the sediment will settle and the water will become clear. It is the same with one's philosophy. Most of us are not used to self-reflection, so the beginning stages seem murky. Over time, however, one's thoughts and feelings become clear.

Wright

Once this process is underway, what's next?

Trin

Once this process is underway, it becomes the backdrop for the next phase of the process. Here we coach the leader in developing the skills, skill sets, and competencies of those truly great leaders who have made a positive impact on their organizations and in their communities. In this phase we look at the anatomy of a true leader—the mind, the heart, and the hand of the great leader.

The mind represents the intellect—the reasoning power of the leader. The heart is the emotional component or the passion and intensity of the leader. The hand represents the leader's connection with other people—his or her relationships. To simplify the metaphor so that it is easily comprehensible, we use something called the IQ, EQ, SQ Model™. This model provides greater clarity to the people we are working with.

The IQ, EQ, SQ Model™

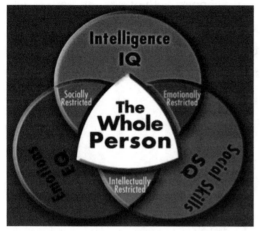

I developed the IQ EQ SQ Model™ in answer to a clear need to help business leaders easily understand and integrate what might otherwise appear to be a complex set of skills and competencies. Essentially, the model makes the process less complicated and more manageable.

Let me start with a brief overview of the model, and then we'll delve into the deeper levels and the implication of each of these areas.

In the IQ EQ SQ Model™ (also referred to as the "Whole Person Model"), IQ stands for the *quality* of our intellect rather than the numeric measure of our intellect. It is *how we use our minds and how we think.* Here IQ includes, but is not limited to, some of the following characteristics: curiosity, forethought, visioning, creative thinking, focus, reasoning, self-reflection, decision-making, and problem-solving skills. It includes the capacity to see a situation from a holistic viewpoint, understanding both the broad perspective as well as the cause-and-effect relationship in a situation.

EQ is the capacity to accurately identify our emotions, understand them, and manage them. It also includes the ability to use our emotions to facilitate and support our goals and objectives. Again, it includes, but is not limited to, such qualities as self-control, trust, integrity patience, courage, resourcefulness, resilient optimism, perseverance, psychological hardiness, and self-discipline.

The quality of our social relationships (SQ) is an often overlooked, yet pivotal factor in achieving success and happiness in life. With SQ, we enlarge our understanding of what it means to be a human being. As the saying goes, "no man is an island." We don't live in a vacuum nor do we lead in a vacuum. Here we expand our psychology to include two or more people.

SQ is about what happens when we connect with others and learn to act with wisdom in our relationships. It is through collaborative effort that almost everything we do comes into fruition. SQ includes, but is not limited to, such things as helpfulness, respect, dignity and consideration, collaboration, empathy, teamwork, and compassion.

Wright

How did you develop the IQ, EQ, SQ Model?

Trin

I developed this model over a period of about twenty-five years. I had been working with a series of different corporations in various industries during those years. Over time I began to notice a pattern or trend throughout. Most of the high level managers and executives seemed to be very good at thinking skills. Most of them had been hired for their intellectual capacities. They were usually very good at the core mental skills such as problem solving, reasoning, and decision-making. However, some of them did not have the capacity to develop loyalty in their team members. Others were moody and often acted irrationally under pressure. These fluctuations in mood and temperament proved to be confusing to members of the team, causing uncertainty, insecurity, and even high levels of stress. Further, some of the teams had become fractured and dysfunctional. Others had developed a "watch-your-back" attitude when it came to management and even to other members within the team.

Although members of the team expressed their distress, they were not able to initiate a complete change in their departments. They were able to do self-work and initiate self-change, but they weren't capable of bringing about a complete change within the department organization. This was because the atmosphere in each of these departments was a direct function of the leadership in those departments. It was more than a trickle-down effect—it was more like an aura of energy that surrounded the leader and permeated the department. Change the leadership, and the atmosphere changed.

Every once in awhile we would come across a highly effective, productive department. Usually team members in these departments were happy and people got along well with each other. What was the distinction? The difference was the leadership in that department. Team members saw them as fair-minded and equitable, slow to get upset, and emotionally even-tempered. They also often viewed them as open and responsive. They were even described as warm and friendly.

We began to study these distinctions between happy, healthy teams and somewhat dysfunctional teams at close range. And, as we did, we were able to isolate some of the core qualities that were vital to the success of the leader.

The next question we asked ourselves was, "Are these skills and skill sets learnable?" It wasn't the old nurture or nature question. It wasn't that black and white. But it was a question of whether or not people in leadership positions could really change behavior. Our answer to that question today is an unequivocal, yes—*if they want to*. As usual, desire and intention along with patience, practice, and *kaizen* were the critical factors in any successful effort.

Today, we start by first assessing the qualities and competencies that must be mastered for success in each of the three domains. Then we focus on developing one or two competencies at a time. Over time, as the executive's skill improves, and the person begins to feel that he or she is improving and gaining proficiency in any given area, the individual takes on more and greater challenges.

Wright

So tell me more about this IQ, EQ, SQ Model.

109

Trin

In order to understand how we isolated the core qualities, let's take each of the domains and look at them in greater depth. First let's look at the mental skills—the area of IQ—as it pertains to leadership.

There are a certain number of qualities or skills within this domain that are fundamental to leadership success. When we say "fundamental," we mean that if a person does not develop a capacity in this skill, success cannot be fully realized. Let's look at two of these in each of the three domains.

Within the area of IQ, the first of these qualities is self-awareness. Naturally, self-awareness has always included being aware of your strengths and weaknesses. However, our working definition for this competency is "awareness of yourself in action." This includes being aware of yourself as you move through your department or organization. It also means being aware that you are making an impact on your environment and the people in your environment.

The way one develops self-awareness is to study how people in the environment respond to them. At its entry level, one has to begin to observe every single person he or she interacts with while interacting with them. This means studying the changes in facial expression, body language, or vocal pacing of the other person. At the advanced level, one has to develop a capacity for dual observation. This means calibrating the change in front of you and noticing what you might have done or said to cause that change.

This is not as easy as it appears to be at first glance. We are asking people to develop new habits, and changing habits takes practice and it takes time. In the case of self-awareness we are asking people to change something as fundamental as where they put their attention. What we pay attention to is usually habitual. Asking people to expand their awareness to include the response they are getting from the people in front of them takes a tremendous amount of practice.

The second competency within the IQ domain is self-reflection. Our working definition for self-reflection is, "reflecting back on past words or actions and/or reflecting forward to improve on words, actions, and/or behaviors."

Self-reflection is such a critical factor that we ask the people we coach to take five minutes at the end of each day to "wind down." During the wind down process we ask them to reflect on three questions:

1. What did work during the course of the day?
2. What could have worked better today?
3. Where do I want to improve tomorrow?

This kind of rigorous self-observation will heighten sensitivity and lead to consistent course correction. And course correction is how we ultimately improve our game.

While Tiger Woods might observe and improve his swing through the use of video, we teach people that they can improve their game through consistent self-awareness and self-reflection. In either case, if one is committed, one will improve over time.

There are, of course, other competencies that are vital to leadership success within the IQ domain. Mental acuity or sharpness, forethought and planning, focus, and decision-making skills are all part of the tool chest of leadership. The reason we highlight self-reflection and self-awareness is because both practices help leaders improve their results in all areas. Both practices help the leader develop the "eagle's view"—the ability to view one's self as well as the surrounding landscape. This perspective helps people see what was always visible, but not seen. Once something is seen or brought into conscious awareness, a natural process of improvement begins to occur.

Wright

How about the area of EQ?

Trin

Okay, let's look at the domain of EQ—the quality of our emotional reactions and responses. Although this was an area made famous by Daniel Goleman in his book, *Emotional Intelligence,* my discovery of EQ peaked during an eighteen-month stretch of teaching in a boys' home in Honolulu.

Let me digress for a moment. The year was 1990. I was completely engaged in my consulting work. So I was quite surprised when my office received a call from someone in management at the home. They had heard of our work and wondered if I would come in to work with the boys. They were facing a formidable challenge. They had seventeen boys, all of whom had a high recidivism rate. All of them were between sixteen and seventeen years of age, and the next time they were incarcerated they would go into the adult penitentiary.

John Shinkawa, the head at that time, explained to me that a young person who goes to prison will most likely be lost for life. "Research has shown," he said, "that by the time they reach twenty-one or twenty-two years of age they will probably be hardened criminals." He paused, "Your job would be to turn them around so that they can make a healthy long-term re-entry into society."

Needless to say, I accepted the challenge, as long as I could take a male member of my team with me. Lovell Harris agreed to go and was excited about the assignment. He is an African American with a prison record, a man who had mentored under me and transformed his life. He saw this as an opportunity to reach young people before they made the same mistake he had made years ago.

To make a long story short, we worked with these young people over an eighteen-month period of time. Here I discovered that "hurt people, *hurt people.*" These kids had been hurt and as a result, they hurt others. And if they didn't hurt others they often turned their hurt inward and hurt themselves.

It was here also that the pieces of the puzzle regarding the IQ, EQ, and SQ qualities began coming together for me. My awakening occurred as a result of being bounced back and forth between two worlds. By day I was training associate staff and consulting with the managers and executives in corporations, while twice a week at night I was with Lovell training these institutionalized boys.

I discovered that these young men were smart. They did not in any way lack in the IQ or intelligence area. It was *how* they were using their intelligence that got them in trouble. What they lacked was forethought—the ability to connect consequences to the actions they engaged in. The other thing that was missing in these young men was what most middle class students pick up by osmosis in home and school—*management of their emotions and appropriate social skills.*

Here my understanding of emotional and social qualities began to crystallize. Although the issues were in no way the same as those in corporate America, there were similarities. I started to see each of the emotional and social skills as operating along a continuum. It was soon after this time that I began developing the IQ, EQ, SQ Model™ that we use to this day.

Now let's take a look at the domain of EQ, representative of the heart or courage and passion. These include such things as self-control, self-discipline, perseverance, resourcefulness, enthusiasm, integrity, the ability to delay gratification for a long-term goal, resiliency, and optimism. Although all of these are vital to the success of a leader, I'd like to focus on two of the other items that we haven't listed in the foregoing group.

The first quality I'd like to highlight is self-motivation. This is the ability to initiate action and move forward based on one's own inner determinism. Most self-motivated people are also driven by purpose. Purpose lights their inner fire, giving them strength in the face of challenges, endurance in the face of resignation, and hope in the face of despair. For the true leader, purpose converts all barriers that come up along the way and turns them into opportunities.

Psychological hardiness is the second quality I'd like to highlight in the EQ area. We describe this as an inner emotional resiliency. We can sum it up in an old well-worn phrase, *"when the going gets tough, the tough get going."* It is the ability to quickly pick yourself up and dust yourself off after a failure and get back in the game.

Psychological hardiness is the quality that gives highly developed athletes the endurance they have. It is a mental and emotional toughness of spirit, and might just as easily have fallen into the IQ area, but for the emotional fortitude and vigor that must accompany the mental strength.

Truly great leaders exhibit an added ability that is inherent in psychological hardiness—the ability to learn from their failures. Again, using self-reflection great leaders study the results of a failed project or event so as not to repeat the process in the future.

Wright

This is really interesting. Everything you talk about seems to be circular and relate to everything else. So how about the SQ area or "domain" as you call it?

Trin

You're right, David. Everything is interrelated and interdependent. So let's complete the picture with the SQ domain.

SQ is the quality of our social relationships and it is absolutely critical to leadership as it is the area that connects the leader to his or her people. As Theodore Roosevelt put it years before our time, *"The most important single ingredient to the formula of success is knowing how to get along with people."* You see, as leaders we either *affect* or *infect* our people and our team!

To highlight a couple of items in the SQ domain takes a supreme effort on my part, because many of the items in this area are so very intertwined. You usually can't have one without the other. It starts with respect—having a high regard for people. When you respect people, you care about them and want to support them in achieving success. It also includes teamwork, cooperation, and collaboration. Further, it includes communication and dialogue with team members about growing the business in order to build an information rich culture.

However, I'd like to highlight both a quality and a competency that underpin all of these in the SQ area. Again, both are pivotal to the success of the leader.

The first of these is the quality of empathy. In the past there was a lot of confusion around this word. Most people thought that it didn't belong in the business arena. Empathetic people were thought to be weak or even "wimpy," wishy-washy, and vulnerable.

Empathy is the ability to notice and understand other people. An empathetic person can feel what the other person is feeling. Because of this, the empathetic person will usually respond in an appropriate manner. Feelings and emotions play out on a scale, much like a musical scale. In other words, there's a "tone" to emotions. When we can tune into this "tone," the other person feels understood.

Empathy is probably one of the most critical factors in building a loyal team. One can inspire people to high levels of excellence, pushing them to achieve their personal best, if one is "in tune" with them. This means being responsive, yet not permissive, sensitive and tolerant, yet not indulgent.

When you combine empathy with some of the primary attributes necessary for success in the IQ and EQ domains, one becomes sensitive yet mentally sharp and psychologically strong. This is not a leader who is a pushover. Far from it, this is a leader who understands himself (or herself) through expanded self-awareness and self-reflection. From that vantage point, the person's understanding of human beings begins to deepen. Great leaders understand the heights and depths of the human condition. They recognize the human foibles within themselves. Therefore, they push themselves and their team members to achieve at their personal best.

The second item within the SQ domain is more an art form than a competency. It is the art of listening. Listening is very close to my heart because I used to be a terrible listener. I would find my mind wandering and as it did, I would lose the essence of what the other person was saying or I would do just the opposite—I'd find myself finishing people's sentences for them. In either case, the message the other person received was that I didn't care or, in the case of finishing their sentence, I was impatient and unwilling to hear them out.

Finally, realizing that neither behavior served me, I brought the subject up with Joann, a friend of mine. I told her that I was concerned that it might be damaging my relationships, and she agreed because she had experienced my mental wandering too.

Living in Hawaii, you can imagine that my friends are of every nationality. Joann was of Chinese ancestry. We were sitting in her kitchen having coffee and she pulled a piece of paper out of the kitchen drawer. "Let me show you the Chinese character for listen," she said, reaching for a pencil. "It is made up of a combination of characters," she continued, "and it is almost a training session unto itself."

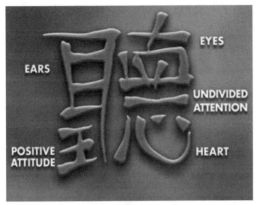

As she drew the character and wrote the meaning next to each portion of it, I started to understand what she had said. It was indeed a teaching.

"I usually focus with eyes ears and heart on the speaker," I said. "And my attitude is usually positive. But it's the undivided attention that I lack."

"Listening is a process, not a product," Joann said with a subtle knowing smile. She wasn't critical. It was the character itself that spoke to me.

From that day on, I began observing my listening. With the tenacity of a scientist on a quest, I coached myself using the three questions we discussed earlier.

As I began improving in my listening skills, I started to share what I was learning. As it turned out, I discovered that I was not alone. There were many who shared a similar experience. People told me that they were not exempt from the "wandering mind syndrome" or the "finishing others' sentences" situation.

Naturally, this became part of the leadership training. Today we help leaders become proficient in the skills and skill sets that make up the totality of listening.

In a sense it is somewhat like tennis or any of the sports. You don't learn tennis in one fell swoop. Instead, the tennis coach takes the game apart. One has to learn the serve, backhand, and volley, etc. Finally, the coach helps you bring all of the pieces together in order to produce fluid movement. You become a powerful player by learning the fundamentals well and then blending and improving on them. Listening is just the same. We start with the fundamentals and build from there. In fact, with all of the items in the IQ, EQ, SQ Model, we help people master the fundamentals and then build capacity from there.

Wright

People need to know where they are before they decide where they want to go. How do you determine where they are when they start the process with you, Trin?

Trin

We start by giving the leaders a self-scoring inventory. Then we often follow up by having some of the people on their team score them. Again, just like coaching in a sport, we begin coaching, training, and practice in the area of the gaps. The gaps are the difference between how leaders view themselves and how their team members view them.

Just for fun I've added a couple of sample questions from our inventory as an addendum to our discussion. I thought the reader might like to see something tangible so I chose two items in the SQ area—empathy and listening. Our full inventory includes many items within each of the three domains, but I thought readers might enjoy a taste of what we do. We also provided a sample of our rating scale in case readers want to have some fun by scoring themselves on the questions.

Wright

That's great, Trin, but if I'm hearing you, it seems that you're saying there is no quick attainment or quick fix in this thing called "business success, right?

Trin

Sorry about that, David, the path to success in business and in leadership is similar to the path of the pro. It is everything we've shared in our discussion, from P[7] to *kaizen,* and the IQ, EQ, SQ Model, and it is one thing more.

It seems to me that the defining moment between mediocrity and brilliance is the moment when each player isn't in the mood to do the work. The defining moment is what each player does on the day when he or she doesn't feel like going to practice. On that day, the mediocre player gets up, isn't in the mood, and doesn't go to practice. The true Olympiad, on the other hand, isn't in the mood but gets up and goes to practice anyway.

It takes that same kind of commitment to become a true professional in business and leadership. For those who are willing to do what others who are less successful are not willing to do, for those who are willing to put in the extra effort that others aren't willing to put in, the supreme achievement will be theirs.

Wright

And what would you tell young people just starting out in life, Trin? Would you have a word of advice for them?

Trin

I haven't really spoken of it, David, but I do a lot of work with young people through my non-profit organization. I view it as my contribution to the community. It is a way for me to give back for all I have received. We do written and experiential activities from the P[7] model. Naturally, these are scaled down to match the age level of the young people we're working with, but the work centers on the same fundamental teachings. However, if I had only a minute with a young person and I had to cut to the chase, I'd say this:

There are many paths to the top of the mountain. The journey begins wherever you are and will lead wherever you choose to go. Study and learn from the trail that others have left, and then make your own path, for you are special and unique. No one on Earth can do your life the way you can. Embrace your life, for it is your one great work of art!

Then, no matter what field you choose, give it everything you have. Play ball with all the passion and gusto you can muster. Play an exceptional game and you'll get an exceptional result.

Wright

This has been a terrific, thought-provoking conversation. We've been talking with D. Trinidad Hunt, President of Élan Enterprises LLC, and Élan Asia-Pacific, training and consulting companies that operate in the United States and throughout the Australia and Asian Pacific market.

As we also learned, Trin is founder of the World Youth Network International, a non-profit organization dedicated to serving students and teachers by teaching principles of self-esteem, character, education, and achievement. Trin's knowledge and expertise is definitely far-reaching.

Thank you so much, Trin, for sharing your wisdom today regarding the *Roadmap to Success.*

Trin

Thank you, David, I've thoroughly enjoyed our conversation, and I'm honored to be a part of the project. It is my hope that everyone who reads this book grows from the insights offered in it.

Addendum

Almost Never	Rarely	Occasionally	Sometimes	Frequently	Usually	Almost Always
1	2	3	4	5	6	7

Empathy

	I am very aware of the feelings of others when I am speaking with them.
	I watch people carefully when working with them because I know that people's feelings often show and communicate more than their words can say.
	I am sensitive to the feelings and needs of those on my team.
	I consciously modulate my energy for I am highly aware of the impact of my moods and feelings on those around me.
	I listen to the speaker from the speaker's perspective, putting myself in his or her shoes.
	I listen to hear the true meaning between the lines so that I can really understand what is being said.
	I am sensitive to the moods of other people.
	I think before I present an idea to someone so that I can frame the subject in a way that the person will open up to it and understand it.
	I am careful not to make sarcastic or caustic remarks when engaged in a conversation with someone.
	I like people and I let my warmth and friendliness show when working with people.
Total Score	

Listening

	I listen with my eyes and ears focused on the speaker.
	I stay focused and keep my mind from wandering during a conversation.
	When interrupted by a member of my team who needs to speak with me, I stop what I am doing and give up my personal agenda for the moment.
	When someone is speaking to me, I give up what I want to say and listen with full attention.
	I let people finish their thoughts and do not finish their sentences for them.
	I listen to hear between the lines.
	Even though I've heard what is being said before, I listen intently to hear what I might not have heard before.
	I align my heart with the heart of the speaker to get a "feel" for what he or she might really be trying to say.
	Instead of jumping to conclusions or making snap judgments, I keep a positive attitude and an open mind when listening.
	If working at my desk or on the computer, I stop what I am doing and turn to face those who come to speak with me, giving them my full attention.
Total Score	

For those readers who want to score themselves on empathy and listening, here is a short version of the meaning of their scores:

Total score between 65–70

You show great consistency! You walk the talk and those around you experience certainty and stability in your presence. It may be tempting to rest on your laurels! Instead, pick an item that you feel you could improve on from the inventory and set a self-improvement goal. Continue to use daily self-reflection in order to enhance self-awareness. This will help you improve in the subtleties of exceptional leadership. Look for ways to expand and stretch. Challenge yourself to take on new opportunities for professional growth both within the organization and in the community.

Total score between 59–64

Your self-work shows! To develop greater consistency, continue your self-development work and self-assessment on a daily basis! Pick one item from either the empathy or listening questions. Examine your attitudes and motivations around this item and set goals for improvement, then use self-observation as you go through your day. Establish a daily practice of three to five focus minutes in the morning and three to five assessment minutes in the evening. For greatest advancement, focus on no more than two or three self-improvement goals at a time until you experience a positive shift. Then move on.

Total score between 53–58

You show frequent bursts of clarity and reliability. Now is the time to focus on accomplishing consistency in word and deed. Pick one item from either the empathy or listening questions. Examine your thoughts and attitudes around this item and set goals for improvement. Study the lives and thinking of great leaders. List your top seven behavioral change goals. Prioritize the list and focus on no more than one or two things at a time, then establish a daily practice of three to five focus minutes in the morning and three to five assessment minutes in the evening. Move to another item only after you feel a positive shift in behavior. This will help you catch your unconscious behavioral patterns so that you can begin to self-correct a little more quickly and easily.

Total score between 40–52

Now is the time to commit to personal and professional self-improvement. This inventory serves as a reminder that leadership is not passive. Instead, it takes a progressive and proactive attitude to harness the varied energies and forces within each of us. It is important to remember that this is not about you personally; rather, it is about the path and progress of becoming an effective leader.

Pick one item from either the empathy or listening questions. Examine your thoughts and attitudes around this item and set one self-improvement goal. Commit to a daily practice of three to five focus minutes in the morning and three to five assessment minutes in the evening. By focusing on a single behavioral change item at a time, you will strengthen your resolve. Through this method of self-reflection and goal setting, you will begin to experience small progressive changes. You will then begin to shed some of the old outmoded behavioral patterns that are no longer aligned with your goals at this time.

About the Author

D. TRINIDAD HUNT, an International author, consultant/trainer, and keynote speaker has over thirty years of experience in program development and training. As cofounder of Élan Enterprises LLC and Élan Asia Pacific, Trin has delivered organizational training programs for business leaders nationally and internationally for such companies as Pepsi Cola, Frito Lay, and Sprint. As cofounder of World Youth Network International (WYN) in the United States, Australia, Malaysia, Philippines, and Canada, she designed, developed, and delivered curricula for students, parents, and teachers. The resultant effect has been education for the entire community.

Trinidad's *Learning to Learn: Maximizing Your Performance Potential,* a national best seller, has been used by accelerated learning courses in universities and colleges. Her novel, *The Operator's Manual for Planet Earth an Adventure for the Soul,* was published by Hyperion Press, a division of Disney. *Wisdom's Way, the Art of a True Leader* was released in August 2008.

Over the last ten years Trin has turned her attention to youth, believing that children hold the hope of the generations to come. Her programs are now in over 250 schools both nationally and internationally.

As a former member of the National Speakers Association for twenty years Trin has received many awards for her work in Leadership. She has been recognized in Who's Who American Women in Business.

To Contact D. Trinidad Hunt...
Élan Enterprises LLC
Office Manager, Lisa K. Kupau
E-mail: lisa@trainingbyelan.com, elantrin@aol.com
Toll free: United States & Canada 800.707.3526
Phone: 808.239.4431
Fax: 808.239.2482
www.elan-learning-institute.com
www.quest4values.com.au
www.endbullying.com

An interview with...

Kenneth Blanchard

David E. Wright (Wright)

Few people have created a positive impact on the day-to-day management of people and companies more than Dr. Kenneth Blanchard. He is known around the world simply as Ken, a prominent, gregarious, sought-after author, speaker, and business consultant. Ken is universally characterized by friends, colleagues, and clients as one of the most insightful, powerful, and compassionate men in business today. Ken's impact as a writer is far-reaching. His phenomenal best-selling book, *The One Minute Manager*®, coauthored with Spencer Johnson, has sold more than thirteen million copies worldwide and has been translated into more than twenty-five languages. Ken is Chairman and "Chief Spiritual Officer" of the Ken Blanchard Companies. The organization's focus is to energize organizations around the world with customized training in bottom-line business strategies based on the simple, yet powerful principles inspired by Ken's best-selling books.

Dr. Blanchard, welcome to *Roadmap to Success.*

Dr. Ken Blanchard (Blanchard)

Well, it's nice to talk with you, David. It's good to be here.

Wright

I must tell you that preparing for your interview took quite a bit more time than usual. The scope of your life's work and your business, the Ken Blanchard Companies, would make for a dozen fascinating interviews.

Before we dive into the specifics of some of your projects and strategies, will you give our readers a brief synopsis of your life—how you came to be the Ken Blanchard we all know and respect?

Blanchard

Well, I'll tell you, David, I think life is what you do when you are planning on doing something else. I think that was John Lennon's line. I never intended to do what I have been doing. In fact, all my professors in college told me that I couldn't write. I wanted to do college work, which I did, and they said, "You had better be an administrator." So I decided I was going to be a Dean of Students. I got provisionally accepted into my master's degree program and then provisionally accepted at Cornell because I never could take any of those standardized tests.

I took the college boards four times and finally got 502 in English. I don't have a test-taking mind. I ended up in a university in Athens, Ohio, in 1966 as an Administrative Assistant to the Dean of the Business School. When I got there he said, "Ken, I want you to teach a course. I want all my deans to teach." I had never thought about teaching because they said I couldn't write, and teachers had to publish. He put me in the manager's department.

I've taken enough bad courses in my day and I wasn't going to teach one. I really prepared and had a wonderful time with the students. I was chosen as one of the top ten teachers on the campus coming out of the chute!

I just had a marvelous time. A colleague by the name of Paul Hersey was chairman of the Management Department. He wasn't very friendly to me initially because the Dean had led me to his department, but I heard he was a great teacher. He taught Organizational Behavior and Leadership. So I said, "Can I sit in on your course next semester?"

"Nobody audits my courses," he said. "If you want to take it for credit, you're welcome."

I couldn't believe it. I had a doctoral degree and he wanted me to take his course for credit—so I signed up.

The registrar didn't know what to do with me because I already had a doctorate, but I wrote the papers and took the course, and it was great.

In June 1967, Hersey came into my office and said, "Ken, I've been teaching in this field for ten years. I think I'm better than anybody, but I can't write. I'm a nervous wreck, and I'd love to write a textbook with somebody. Would you write one with me?"

I said, "We ought to be a great team. You can't write and I'm not supposed to be able to, so let's do it!"

Thus began this great career of writing and teaching. We wrote a textbook called Management of Organizational Behavior: Utilizing Human Resources. It came out in its eighth edition October 3, 2000, and the ninth edition was published September 3, 2007. It has sold more than any other textbook in that area over the years. It's been over forty years since that book first came out.

I quit my administrative job, became a professor, and ended up working my way up the ranks. I got a sabbatical leave and went to California for one year twenty-five years ago. I ended up meeting Spencer Johnson at a cocktail party. He wrote children's books—a wonderful series called Value Tales® for Kids. He also wrote The Value of Courage: The Story of Jackie Robinson and The Value of Believing In Yourself: The Story of Louis Pasteur.

My wife, Margie, met him first and said, "You guys ought to write a children's book for managers because they won't read anything else." That was my introduction to Spencer. So, The One Minute Manager was really a kid's book for big people. That is a long way from saying that my career was well planned.

Wright

Ken, what and/or who were your early influences in the areas of business, leadership, and success? In other words, who shaped you in your early years?

Blanchard

My father had a great impact on me. He was retired as an admiral in the Navy and had a wonderful philosophy. I remember when I was elected as president of the seventh grade, and I came home all pumped up. My father said, "Son, it's great that you're the president of the seventh grade, but now that you have that leadership position, don't ever use it." He said, "Great leaders are followed because people respect them and like them, not because they have power." That was a wonderful lesson for me early on. He was just a great model for me. I got a lot from him.

Then I had this wonderful opportunity in the mid-1980s to write a book with Norman Vincent Peale. He wrote The Power of Positive Thinking. I met him when he was eighty-six years old; we were asked to write a book on ethics together, The Power of Ethical Management: Integrity Pays, You Don't Have to Cheat to Win. It didn't matter what we were writing together; I learned so much from him. He just built from the positive things I learned from my mother.

My mother said that when I was born I laughed before I cried, I danced before I walked, and I smiled before I frowned. So that, as well as Norman Vincent Peale, really impacted me as I focused on what I could do to train leaders. How do you make them positive? How do you make them realize that it's not about them, it's about who they are serving? It's not about their position—it's about what they can do to help other people win.

So, I'd say my mother and father, then Norman Vincent Peale. All had a tremendous impact on me.

Wright

I can imagine. I read a summary of your undergraduate and graduate degrees. I assumed you studied Business Administration, marketing management, and related courses. Instead, at Cornell you studied Government and Philosophy. You received your master's from Colgate in Sociology and Counseling and your PhD from Cornell in Educational Administration and Leadership. Why did you choose this course of study? How has it affected your writing and consulting?

Blanchard

Well, again, it wasn't really well planned out. I originally went to Colgate to get a master's degree in Education because I was going to be a

Dean of Students over men. I had been a Government major, and I was a Government major because it was the best department at Cornell in the Liberal Arts School. It was exciting. We would study what the people were doing at the league of governments. And then, the Philosophy Department was great. I just loved the philosophical arguments. I wasn't a great student in terms of getting grades, but I'm a total learner. I would sit there and listen, and I would really soak it in.

When I went over to Colgate and got into the education courses, they were awful. They were boring. The second week, I was sitting at the bar at the Colgate Inn saying, "I can't believe I've been here two years for this." This is just the way the Lord works: Sitting next to me in the bar was a young sociology professor who had just gotten his PhD at Illinois. He was staying at the Inn. I was moaning and groaning about what I was doing, and he said, "Why don't you come and major with me in sociology? It's really exciting."

"I can do that?" I asked.

He said, "Yes."

I knew they would probably let me do whatever I wanted the first week. Suddenly, I switched out of Education and went with Warren Ramshaw. He had a tremendous impact on me. He retired some years ago as the leading professor at Colgate in the Arts and Sciences, and got me interested in leadership and organizations. That's why I got a master's in Sociology.

The reason I went into educational administration and leadership? It was a doctoral program I could get into because I knew the guy heading up the program. He said, "The greatest thing about Cornell is that you will be in the School of Education. It's not very big, so you don't have to take many education courses, and you can take stuff all over the place."

There was a marvelous man by the name of Don McCarty who eventually became the Dean of the School of Education, Wisconsin. He had an impact on my life; but I was always just searching around.

My mission statement is: to be a loving teacher and example of simple truths that help myself and others to awaken the presence of God in our lives. The reason I mention "God" is that I believe the biggest addiction in the world is the human ego; but I'm really into simple truth. I used to tell people I was trying to get the B.S. out of the behavioral sciences.

Wright

I can't help but think, when you mentioned your father, that he just bottom-lined it for you about leadership.

Blanchard

Yes.

Wright

A man named Paul Myers, in Texas, years and years ago when I went to a conference down there, said, "David, if you think you're a leader and you look around, and no one is following you, you're just out for a walk."

Blanchard

Well, you'd get a kick out of this—I'm just reaching over to pick up a picture of Paul Myers on my desk. He's a good friend, and he's a part of our Center for FaithWalk Leadership where we're trying to challenge and equip people to lead like Jesus. It's non-profit. I tell people I'm not an evangelist because we've got enough trouble with the Christians we have. We don't need any more new ones. But, this is a picture of Paul on top of a mountain. Then there's another picture below that of him under the sea with stingrays. It says, "Attitude is everything. Whether you're on the top of the mountain or the bottom of the sea, true happiness is achieved by accepting God's promises, and by having a biblically positive frame of mind. Your attitude is everything." Isn't that something?

Wright

He's a fine, fine man. He helped me tremendously. In keeping with the theme of our book, Roadmap for Success, I wanted to get a sense from you about your own success journey. Many people know you best from The One Minute Manager books you coauthored with Spencer Johnson. Would you consider these books as a high water mark for you or have you defined success for yourself in different terms?

Blanchard

Well, you know, *The One Minute Manager* was an absurdly successful book so quickly that I found I couldn't take credit for it. That was when I really got on my own spiritual journey and started to try to find out what the real meaning of life and success was.

That's been a wonderful journey for me because I think, David, the problem with most people is they think their self-worth is a function of their performance plus the opinion of others. The minute you think that is what your self-worth is, every day your self-worth is up for grabs because your performance is going to fluctuate on a day-to-day basis. People are fickle. Their opinions are going to go up and down. You need to ground your self-worth in the unconditional love that God has ready for us, and that really grew out of the unbelievable success of The One Minute Manager.

When I started to realize where all that came from, that's how I got involved in this ministry that I mentioned. Paul Myers is a part of it. As I started to read the Bible, I realized that everything I've ever written about, or taught, Jesus did. You know, He did it with the twelve incompetent guys He "hired." The only guy with much education was Judas, and he was His only turnover problem.

Wright

Right.

Blanchard

This is a really interesting thing. What I see in people is not only do they think their self-worth is a function of their performance plus the opinion of others, but they measure their success on the amount of accumulation of wealth, on recognition, power, and status. I think those are nice success items. There's nothing wrong with those, as long as you don't define your life by that.

What I think you need to focus on rather than success is what Bob Buford, in his book Halftime, calls "significance"—moving from success to significance. I think the opposite of accumulation of wealth is generosity.

I wrote a book called The Generosity Factor with Truett Cathy, who is the founder of Chick-fil-A. He is one of the most generous men I've ever met in my life. I thought we needed to have a model of generosity. It's not only your treasure, but it's your time and talent. Truett and I added touch as a fourth one.

The opposite of recognition is service. I think you become an adult when you realize you're here to serve rather than to be served.

Finally, the opposite of power and status is loving relationships. Take Mother Teresa as an example—she couldn't have cared less about recognition, power, and status because she was focused on generosity, service, and loving relationships; but she got all of that earthly stuff. If you focus on the earthly, such as money, recognition, and power, you're never going to get to significance. But if you focus on significance, you'll be amazed at how much success can come your way.

Wright

I spoke with Truett Cathy recently and was impressed by what a down-to-earth, good man he seems to be. When you start talking about him closing his restaurants on Sunday, all of my friends—when they found out I had talked to him—said, "Boy, he must be a great Christian man, but he's rich." I told them, "Well, to put his faith into perspective, by closing on Sunday it costs him $500 million a year."

He lives his faith, doesn't he?

Blanchard

Absolutely, but he still outsells everybody else.

Wright

That's right.

Blanchard

According to their January 25, 2007, press release, Chick-fil-A was the nation's second-largest quick-service chicken restaurant chain in sales at that time. Its business performance marks the thirty-ninth consecutive year the chain has enjoyed a system-wide sales gain—a streak the company has sustained since opening its first chain restaurant in 1967.

Wright

The simplest market scheme, I told him, tripped me up. I walked by his first Chick-fil-A I had ever seen, and some girl came out with chicken stuck on toothpicks and handed me one; I just grabbed it and ate it; it's history from there on.

Blanchard

Yes, I think so. It's really special. It is so important that people understand generosity, service, and loving relationships because too many people are running around like a bunch of peacocks. You even see pastors who measure their success by how many are in their congregation; authors by how many books they have sold; businesspeople by what their profit margin is—how good sales are. The reality is, that's all well and good, but I think what you need to focus on is the other. I think if business did that more and we got Wall Street off our backs with all the short-term evaluation, we'd be a lot better off.

Wright

Absolutely. There seems to be a clear theme that winds through many of your books that has to do with success in business and organizations—how people are treated by management and how they feel about their value to a company. Is this an accurate observation? If so, can you elaborate on it?

Blanchard

Yes, it's a very accurate observation. See, I think the profit is the applause you get for taking care of your customers and creating a motivating environment for your people. Very often people think that business is only about the bottom line. But no, that happens to be the result of creating raving fan customers, which I've described with Sheldon Bowles in our book, Raving Fans. Customers want to brag about you, if you create an environment where people can be gung-ho and committed. You've got to take care of your customers and your people, and then your cash register is going to go ka-ching, and you can make some big bucks.

Wright

I noticed that your professional title with the Ken Blanchard Companies is somewhat unique—"Chairman and Chief Spiritual Officer." What does your title mean to you personally and to your company? How does it affect the books you choose to write?

Blanchard

I remember having lunch with Max DuPree one time. The legendary Chairman of Herman Miller, Max wrote a wonderful book called Leadership Is an Art.

"What's your job?" I asked him.

He said, "I basically work in the vision area."

"Well, what do you do?" I asked.

"I'm like a third-grade teacher," he replied. "I say our vision and values over, and over, and over again until people get it right, right, right."

I decided from that, I was going to become the Chief Spiritual Officer, which means I would be working in the vision, values, and energy part of our business. I ended up leaving a morning message every day for everybody in our company. We have twenty-eight international offices around the world.

I leave a voice mail every morning, and I do three things on that as Chief Spiritual Officer: One, people tell me who we need to pray for. Two, people tell me who we need to praise—our unsung heroes and people like that. And then three, I leave an inspirational morning message. I really am the cheerleader—the Energizer Bunny—in our company. I'm the reminder of why we're here and what we're trying to do.

We think that our business in the Ken Blanchard Companies is to help people lead at a higher level, and to help individuals and organizations. Our mission statement is to unleash the power and potential of people and organizations for the common good. So if we are going to do that, we've really got to believe in that.

I'm working on getting more Chief Spiritual Officers around the country. I think it's a great title and we should get more of them.

Wright

So those people for whom you pray, where do you get the names?

Blanchard

The people in the company tell me who needs help, whether it's a spouse who is sick or kids who are sick or if they are worried about something. We've got over five years of data about the power of prayer, which is pretty important.

One morning, my inspirational message was about my wife and five members of our company who walked sixty miles one weekend—twenty miles a day for three days—to raise money for breast cancer research.

It was amazing. I went down and waved them all in as they came. They had a ceremony; they had raised $7.6 million. There were over three thousand people walking. A lot of the walkers were dressed in pink—they were cancer victors—people who had overcome it. There were even men walking with pictures of their wives who had died from breast cancer. I thought it was incredible.

There wasn't one mention about it in the major San Diego papers. I said, "Isn't that just something." We have to be an island of positive influence because all you see in the paper today is about celebrities and their bad behavior. Here you have all these thousands of people out there walking and trying to make a difference, and nobody thinks it's news.

So every morning I pump people up about what life's about, about what's going on. That's what my Chief Spiritual Officer job is about.

Wright

I had the pleasure of reading one of your releases, *The Leadership Pill.*

Blanchard

Yes.

Wright

I must admit that my first thought was how short the book was. I wondered if I was going to get my money's worth, which by the way, I most certainly did. Many of your books are brief and based on a fictitious story. Most business books in the market today are hundreds of pages in length and are read almost like a textbook.

Will you talk a little bit about why you write these short books, and about the premise of The *Leadership Pill?*

Blanchard

I really developed my relationship with Spencer Johnson when we wrote The One Minute Manager. As you know, he wrote, Who Moved My Cheese, which was a phenomenal success. He wrote children's books and is quite a storyteller.

Jesus taught by parables, which were short stories.

My favorite books are Jonathan Livingston Seagull and The Little Prince. Og Mandino, author of seventeen books, was the greatest of them all.

I started writing parables because people can get into the story and learn the contents of the story, and they don't bring their judgmental hats into reading. You write a regular book and they'll say, "Well, where did you get the research?" They get into that judgmental side. Our books get them emotionally involved and they learn.

The Leadership Pill is a fun story about a pharmaceutical company that thinks they have discovered the secret to leadership, and they can put the ingredients in a pill. When they announce it, the country goes crazy because everybody knows we need more effective leaders. When they release it, it outsells Viagra.

The founders of the company start selling off stock and they call them Pillionaires. But along comes this guy who calls himself "the effective manager," and he challenges them to a no-pill challenge. If they identify two non-performing groups, he'll take on one and let somebody on the pill take another one, and he guarantees he will outperform that person by the end of the year. They agree, but of course they give him a drug test every week to make sure he's not sneaking pills on the side.

I wrote the book with Marc Muchnick, who is a young guy in his early thirties. We did a major study of what this interesting "Y" generation—the young people of today—want from leaders, and this is a secret blend that this effective manager uses. When you think about it, David, it is really powerful in terms of what people want from a leader.

Number one, they want integrity. A lot of people have talked about that in the past, but these young people will walk if they see people say one thing and do another. A lot of us walk to the bathroom and out into the halls to talk about it. But these people will quit. They don't want somebody to say something and not do it.

The second thing they want is a partnership relationship. They hate superior/subordinate. I mean, what awful terms those are. You know, the "head" of the department and the hired "hands"—you don't even give them a head. "What do I do? I'm in supervision. I see things a lot clearer than these stupid idiots." They want to be treated as partners; if they can get a financial partnership, great. If they can't, they really want a minimum of a psychological partnership where they can bring their brains to work and make decisions.

Then finally, they want affirmation. They not only want to be caught doing things right, but they want to be affirmed for who they are. They want to be known as individual people, not as numbers.

So those are the three ingredients that this effective manager uses. They are wonderful values when you think about them.

Rank-order values for any organization is number one, integrity. In our company we call it ethics. It is our number one value. The number two value is partnership. In our company we call it relationships. Number three is affirmation—being affirmed as a human being. I think that ties into relationships, too. They are wonderful values that can drive behavior in a great way.

Wright

I believe most people in today's business culture would agree that success in business has everything to do with successful leadership. In The Leadership Pill, you present a simple but profound premise; that leadership is not something you do to people; it's something you do with them. At face value, that seems incredibly obvious. But you must have found in your research and observations that leaders in today's culture do not get this. Would you speak to that issue?

Blanchard

Yes. I think what often happens in this is the human ego. There are too many leaders out there who are self-serving. They're not leaders who have service in mind. They think the sheep are there for the benefit of the shepherd. All the power, money, fame, and recognition move up the hierarchy. They forget that the real action in business is not up the hierarchy—it's in the one-to-one, moment-to-moment interactions that your frontline people have with your customers. It's how the phone is answered. It's how problems are dealt with and those kinds of things. If you don't think that you're doing leadership with them—rather, you're doing it to them—after a while they won't take care of your customers.

I was at a store once (not Nordstrom's, where I normally would go) and I thought of something I had to share with my wife, Margie. I asked the guy behind the counter in Men's Wear, "May I use your phone?"

He said, "No!"

"You're kidding me," I said. "I can always use the phone at Nordstrom's."

"Look, buddy," he said, "they won't let me use the phone here. Why should I let you use the phone?"

That is an example of leadership that's done to employees, not with them. People want a partnership. People want to be involved in a way that really makes a difference.

Wright

Dr. Blanchard, the time has flown by and there are so many more questions I'd like to ask you. In closing, would you mind sharing with our readers some thoughts on success? If you were mentoring a small group of men and women, and one of their central goals was to become successful, what kind of advice would you give them?

Blanchard

Well, I would first of all say, "What are you focused on?" If you are focused on success as being, as I said earlier, accumulation of money, recognition, power, or status, I think you've got the wrong target. What you need to really be focused on is how you can be generous in the use of your time and your talent and your treasure and touch. How can you serve people rather than be served? How can you develop caring, loving relationships with people? My sense is if you will focus on those things, success in the traditional sense will come to you. But if you go out and say, "Man, I'm going to make a fortune, and I'm going to do this," and have that kind of attitude, you might get some of those numbers. I think you become an adult, however, when you realize you are here to give rather than to get. You're here to serve, not to be served. I would just say to people, "Life is such a very special occasion. Don't miss it by aiming at a target that bypasses other people, because we're really here to serve each other."

Wright

Well, what an enlightening conversation, Dr. Blanchard. I really want you to know how much I appreciate all the time you've taken with me for this interview. I know that our readers will learn from this, and I really appreciate your being with us today.

Blanchard

Well, thank you so much, David. I really enjoyed my time with you. You've asked some great questions that made me think, and I hope my answers are helpful to other people because as I say, life is a special occasion.

Wright

Today we have been talking with Dr. Ken Blanchard. He is coauthor of the phenomenal best-selling book, *The One Minute Manager*. The fact that he's the Chief Spiritual Officer of his company should make us all think about how we are leading our companies and leading our families and leading anything, whether it is in church or civic organizations. I know I will.

Thank you so much, Dr. Blanchard, for being with us today.

Blanchard

Good to be with you, David.

About the Author

Few people have created more of a positive impact on the day-to-day management of people and companies than Dr. Kenneth Blanchard, who is known around the world simply as "Ken."

When Ken speaks, he speaks from the heart with warmth and humor. His unique gift is to speak to an audience and communicate with each individual as if they were alone and talking one-on-one. He is a polished storyteller with a knack for making the seemingly complex easy to understand.

Ken has been a guest on a number of national television programs, including Good Morning America and The Today Show. He has been featured in Time, People, U.S. News & World Report, and a host of other popular publications.

He earned his bachelor's degree in Government and Philosophy from Cornell University, his master's degree in Sociology and Counseling from Colgate University, and his PhD in Educational Administration and Leadership from Cornell University.

To Contact Dr. Ken Blanchard...

The Ken Blanchard Companies
125 State Place
Escondido, California 92029
800.728.6000
Fax: 760.489.8407
www.kenblanchard.com

ROADMAP *to* SUCCESS 8

An interview with...

Liz Christoffersen

David Wright (Wright)

Today we're talking with Liz Christoffersen. She is President of Empower Consulting Group, a company dedicated to helping others succeed. With over two decades of successful management sales and operations experience, and a proven track record for creating top producing sales teams and leaders, she has built a reputation in business as a contemporary authority on creating inspired teams who produce exceptional results. She has traveled the globe designing and delivering coaching, training, and consulting services for businesses and individuals who are serious about tackling challenges. Her extensive training in communication, relationships, and goal-setting enable her to share with leaders and professionals who wish to engage their true purpose, tap into their personal brilliance, be the example of excellence in action, and live a truly inspired and inspiring life.

Liz, welcome to *Roadmap to Success!*

Liz Christoffersen (Christoffersen)

Thank you, I'm glad to be here.

Wright

How do you define success?

Christoffersen

Success, like wealth, has many definitions. It is often associated with the accumulation of material wealth, position, or accomplishment. The true meaning of success to me is about the satisfaction and fulfillment of a job well done while serving the greater good. It is living life large, as it was meant to be experienced, and sharing life's lessons along the way. It is touching the hearts and souls of those on my journey and knowing that in some small way I've made a difference to them. Being able to share life's lessons with people drives a greater understanding of facing challenges and creating successful outcomes.

Everything we go through in life serves a purpose. Helping executives or business teams see challenges as learning and growth opportunities is critical. When we're challenged, there is an opportunity to reach beyond our perceived limitations. Success to me is seeing the greatness in others and helping them to tap into their source of power to achieve their destiny. When the people I work with tap into the core of their being and live with authenticity, miracles happen.

Wright

So how do you know when you've achieved it?

Christoffersen

There is a sense of satisfaction and fulfillment—a feeling of peace or bliss. It comes when people I've been working with share in conversation about an experience and how they've stepped outside their comfort zone to handle it. If my work has helped them to be clear about who they are, their potential, and the action they must take, then I've succeeded. It really is about helping them to be their most authentic self and in so doing, attracting success.

Wright

How do you measure it?

Christoffersen

The best way to measure success is really on a personal level. When you get up in the morning, are you happy and passionate about the work that you're doing? Do you feel contentment and bliss? Do you feel that what you're doing is contributing to the greater good? Measuring success is not necessarily about the material aspects of life. It's not about how much money you have in the bank or the car you drive or the house you live in. It is really about knowing what your gifts are and whether or not you are using those gifts to serve in the world.

Wright

When do you know it's enough?

Christoffersen

There's a sense of contentment, peace, and bliss that you feel when you've done a great job or you've done good work and it comes back to you. Someone calls to say thank you or sends you a note to express appreciation. When you work with an executive to create a philanthropy piece for the corporation to give back to the community, all of a sudden you realize the work that you've done has multiplied a hundred fold.

Wright

Knowing that you're successful, how did you create it?

Christoffersen

Sometimes life takes you down roads you never imagined. When I was in the corporate world, I thought I had a perfect life—a great career, a wonderful husband—all the trappings of material success. I thought I'd made it and was in complete control of my life.

As I was climbing the corporate ladder in Reno, my family in the Bay Area started falling apart. One day my father was out making deliveries for the business he and my mother owned and in a split second of time he was incapacitated by a seizure. While most families gathered over the Thanksgiving holiday to celebrate, we found ourselves staring at him through windows in the ICU/CCU, not understanding how such a strong, vibrant man could wind up like this.

Months of medical testing and physical deterioration tried our patience and our faith. In an attempt to ease the sorrow and pain, my husband and I opened our home to my parents as their caregivers. This fateful decision set us on a course of events that would change my life—all our lives— dramatically. We received the news just before the weekend of a planned spring getaway: "Inoperable brain tumor—three months at best." Those words bring tremors and tears, even to this day.

It was the following months of focused quality time creating memories and experiences I'll never forget. Dad's health and care consumed our world. Eventually he was transferred to a skilled nursing facility to live out his final days. Mother was quite brave and, unbeknownst to us, fighting her own health battles.

The day my father left this world I felt a part of me go too. Mother followed him shortly after and the grief was too much to bear. During this whole period of time I continued to work incessantly. I was rewarded with more responsibility and more money. The more I threw myself into my work to soften the challenges in my personal life, the more I realized I wasn't happy and hadn't been for some time. I had this deep feeling of emptiness and began to wonder if the work was really worth the effort when there was so little satisfaction. There was a deep sense that maybe I was really here for a greater purpose. Truthfully, I had that yearning long before Mother and Dad rejoined my life; I just didn't act on it.

Somewhere along the journey I came to realize that no matter what life handed me I had the power within to triumph. I started to visualize what a great life looked like for me and to take action with the belief that I had the power within to make it a reality. After gaining clarity, the first risk I took was to leave my comfy corporate COO role and venture off to pursue my passion through coaching, training, and strategy consulting. It felt incredibly awkward and frightening at first. Now I travel the globe sharing the strategies and actions that have helped many achieve success.

Wright

What has been the greatest factor contributing to your success?

Christoffersen

The greatest factor really has been my ability to tune in to my inner voice—to really understand what my intuition is telling me that I need to do, to focus on, and to take action.

Most people and businesses struggle because they're afraid to take a risk, to take an action step in the right direction. It doesn't have to be a big step; sometimes it's a little step. We allow our fears, our doubts, or the influences of other people to prevent us from actually doing the things we know deep down inside we need to do to create success for ourselves.

Hearing the internal message coupled with the strength of my faith and unshakeable belief has contributed to my success.

Wright

So what lessons have you learned along the way?

Christoffersen

We know intuitively in our hearts and in our souls exactly what we need to be doing at any given moment. We have the greatest struggles when we don't listen to that intuition. We just need to get clear, get focused, and take action.

All the experiences we have serve a purpose. They are lessons for us to learn. These lessons build the foundation to help us get to the next place, wherever that's going to be. It's when we're very, very challenged, during the dark moments in our life that we struggle instead of experiencing each moment with awe and appreciation for the value it brings.

We really do have the answers within ourselves. We just have to let go of limiting beliefs and of the influence of other people about how we need to live our lives. We allow these things to hold us back from our greatness when we really just need to be true to ourselves.

Life is meant to be enjoyed and our work is meant to be an expression of that joy.

Wright

So how did you get started in the business?

Christoffersen

Throughout my professional and personal life, I've always been in roles that involved some form of coaching, training, or mentoring. I've always enjoyed helping other people to grow personally and professionally. So when my parents passed away, I had this idea of creating a business that was fully focused on inspiring people to become world-class leaders. The idea of breathing spirit into corporate America to influence a better world fueled my passion and fit my purpose.

I attended Corporate Coach U to be certified to do coaching and have since participated in many other forms of professional development certification and training

Wright

Who influenced your process, or what influenced your process?

Christoffersen

My experience with my parents served as some of the best lessons for me during my childhood. Although I don't think I really realized that until years later when I was their caregiver in their final years. My mother certainly taught me the power of a strong woman and about unconditional love. My father taught me to believe in my own ability to accomplish anything I set out to do. He taught me at a young age to dream big dreams, to believe in them, and to take action to make them real.

I certainly spend a lot of time studying and reading the work of many of today's personal and professional development masters. I enjoy the work of Stephen Covey, Ken Blanchard, Cheryl Richardson, Jack Canfield, Louise Hay, and Laurie Beth Jones, plus many others.

Wright

Were they great leaders?

Christoffersen

Yes, absolutely. Truly great leadership is about seeing the greatness in other people and helping them bring that greatness to the surface. My parents challenged me to push beyond my perceived limits; the experience as their caregiver forced me to be very clear about the right actions to take.

Wright

So what do you think drives you, and how do you stay motivated?

Christoffersen

This quote from James Michener best describes what drives me: "The master in the art of living makes little distinction between his work and his play, his labor and his leisure, his mind and his body, his information and his recreation, his love and his religion. He hardly knows which is which. He simply pursues his vision of excellence at whatever he does, leaving others to decide whether he is working or playing. To him he is always doing both."

The love and the passion that I feel for the work I do drive my desire to be the best. I enjoy the interactions I have with the people I work with. As a wife and a mother, I want to create a nurturing environment to support my family in realizing their dreams. Seeing my clients blossom and their businesses flourish fills me with an overwhelming sense of gratitude for being a part of the experience.

Wright

So what is the message that you want to share with our readers and with our listeners?

Christoffersen

The secret to creating the kind of success we dream about is to take the time to get crystal clear about what our definition of success is. It is having the deep desire within to make it work and having strong faith and belief that it can work. Hold that clear, definite vision in your consciousness and see it working out step by step, without one thought of doubt or disbelief. Take action, do the things to make it come to fruition. Surround yourself with people who are like-minded, who support you, love you, and want to help you realize your dreams.

We live in an incredibly abundant world. Whatever we dream really can be ours for the taking.

Wright

So much has been written about "the secret" and the law of attraction recently; how does it really work?

Christoffersen

It's really a simple process: Be clear about what you want in life. Believe with unshakeable belief that it's on the way to you. Take the action to make it happen. Acknowledge with gratitude when it does come to you. Show that you appreciate the good things that are happening in your life. Don't forget to also acknowledge the challenges. We get caught up in the struggles of our daily life or our business and we fail to see that there is actually good there. Usually when we're struggling there is some type of a growth opportunity for us and we don't always see it when we're right in the thick of things. Later we can look back and say, Oh, yes, I went through this situation and here's what I learned about myself or my business or the people around me.

Wright

If it really is so simple, why do you think more don't embrace it?

Christoffersen

Most people allow their fears to hold them back. I've heard it called the "Terror Barrier." Change is one of the things we all fear. We fear what change means for us and those around us. Most people don't like to step outside their comfort zones. Many of the clients I work with will say, "If I change who I am in order to be the leader I need to be, how are the people around me going to react or respond? Is it going to be a good thing for them and a good thing for me?" Or, "What if they don't love me so much after I make these changes?" Or, "If Suzy changes and evolves, she may outgrow my relationship with her. What happens to me as a result?"

The nature of life is to evolve, so change is a constant. Yet, it is that which we fear the most.

Wright

Do you think success has changed you?

Christoffersen

Absolutely, I have become a much better person. I am a work in progress, continuing to evolve and grow, personally and professionally. Who I was a few years ago is a very different person than who I am now. I like the me that I've evolved to be so much better. I'm much more focused on the people around me, serving their needs and being more focused on giving to others. It is a great feeling.

Wright

So how about the maintenance—how do you maintain you success?

Christoffersen

Doing work with different coaches and trainers provides the forum to stay focused. When I'm getting off track I tend to have stress and to feel as though I'm struggling. My life becomes a little chaotic. I have learned to be aware of those moments. Taking a few minutes to think about where I am, what I'm facing, and what the best next action is helps me to get back on track.

Tuning out the noise of the world around me, taking a long walk, spending time in silence or meditation helps me to return to Source for direction. I live in the high desert at the base of snowcapped mountains and in the morning it's wonderful to get up as the sun is rising, take a long walk, think about what's really happening in my life and in my work, and what are the best things that I need to do to move forward today.

Wright

Do you attribute your success to timing, luck, know-how, opportunity, good fortune or to all of the above?

Christoffersen

It's a combination of all of those things. What I know now is that all of the experiences that I've had in my life have led me to this moment in time. Had I not gone through all of those experiences I would be a very different person. I've grown to love who I am—all the great things and all the flaws. I know that when I go to work with my clients, the person they're getting is the most authentic version of me and that feels really great.

Wright

What a great conversation. I've really learned a lot here, especially about success and achievement. I really appreciate all the time you've taken to talk with me today answering all these questions.

Christoffersen

Thank you.

Wright

Today we've been talking with Liz Christoffersen, President of Empower Consulting Group, a company whose mission is to lift the human spirit, accelerate business results, and develop world-class leadership. As a premier strategy and results company, ECG provides services designed to help individuals, groups, businesses, and organizations create their own amazing success stories. ECG is dedicated to making life and business simple, easy, and fun. Liz, thank you so much for being with us today on *Roadmap to Success!*

Christoffersen

Thank you. It's been a pleasure.

About the Author

LIZ CHRISTOFFERSEN has garnered a reputation as a remarkable individual and highly successful businessperson. She is an experienced speaker who has addressed audiences of all kinds. She has successfully coached hundreds of clients, including executives, public officials, entrepreneurs, and business owners around the world. She makes life happier and easier by helping people connect with their inner power. Her work focuses on personal well being, spiritual growth, and business success. Liz lives in the high desert at the base of the Sierra Nevada Mountains with her biggest passions in life—her husband and family. She spends her free time living life large, pursuing adventures in the great outdoors, reading, studying interior design, feng shui, enjoying all kinds of music, and most of all, laughter.

To Contact Liz Christoffersen...
Empower Consulting Group, LLC
3140 Cobble Ridge Ct.
Reno, NV 89511
775.853.2530
actnow@go2ecg.com
www.go2ecg.com

ROADMAP to SUCCESS

An interview with...

David Scheiderer

David Wright (Wright)

Today we're talking with David J. Scheiderer, MD, MBA, President of Tiberius Enterprises, Inc. in Roanoke, Virginia. An accomplished medical educator, Dr. Scheiderer is one of the most highly sought-after speakers in the nation on the topics of health and aging. He has served on numerous executive boards and currently provides professional and technical expertise to several international corporations. In addition to his busy lecture schedule, he maintains a private practice of age management medicine and psychiatry in Roanoke. Of his many roles, his favorite is that of father to his children, Jake and Cecily.

Dr. Scheiderer welcome to *Roadmap to Success!*

David Scheiderer (Scheiderer)

Thank you very much. I'm thrilled to be here. In fact, I jumped at the chance to co-author along side Ken and Stephen and the other impressive contributors to this very timely book.

Wright

A question I often ask individuals as accomplished and experienced as you are is what and who were your early and sustaining influences?

Scheiderer

I really appreciate that question because it gives me a chance to do something I rarely do—thank the people who, for better or worse, have made me the person I am. The list includes the usual cast of players: my parents, my sister, teachers, clergy, and colleagues. I suspect, however, that I owe the greatest debt of gratitude to these patients and clients who, over the years, have allowed me to accompany them on crucial legs of their life journeys. Seldom do I thank them, so I thank you, David, for the chance to do so now.

Wright

Over the past twenty years as a psychiatrist, and more recently as a practitioner of Age Management Medicine, you have helped thousands of individuals navigate their life road maps. Would you share with our readers what your experience has taught you about success?

Scheiderer

That could be a book unto itself. Let me answer that question with three general observations that apply not only to the vast majority of my patients and clients, but also to me:

At some point in our lives, we realize that we are following a road map drawn up by various and well-meaning others toward a learned or inherited version of success that may or may not align with our own desired destinations. How we respond to this realization fundamentally affects our future success.

Once we take responsibility for drawing our own life road map, we move from what I like to call *Measurable Units of Learned Acquisition (MULA) to deliberate adherence to a process*; in other words, a way of living. Ultimately, our road maps to success segue from an external journey to an internal one.

Wright

Would you mind elaborating on these observations?

Scheiderer

I'd be glad to. Let's take them one at a time starting with the idea that at some point in our lives it dawns on us that we may be using the wrong road map as we travel.

An enduring example of this comes from business motivational literature. In his book, *How to Enjoy Your Life and Your Job,* noted author, lecturer, and motivator, Dale Carnegie, tells the story of a woman oppressed by years of self-denial, false pretense, and fear-based living who was suddenly liberated by a chance remark. Her mother in-law was talking one day about how she had taught her children that no matter what happened, they be themselves. In a flash, the oppressed woman realized that she had caused much of her own misery by trying to force herself to become someone she was not. In essence, she had been following the wrong road map. Carnegie emphasizes that the only way to effectively pursue happiness and realize personal and professional success is to find out who you really are and be that person.

Wright

Why is this phenomenon so common?

Scheiderer

Well, you know, David, common wisdom holds that each of us has our own unique definition of success. Personally, I have found quite the opposite is true. Most of us never consciously and deliberately define success for ourselves at all. Rather, we follow a vague, predetermined road map that has been drawn for us by others. We remain largely ignorant of our own methods of seeking and earning success, because our means of defining and pursuing success results from early life conditioning. And as children, we did not realize or understand that this conditioning was taking place.

Eventually, whether by a sign from without or as a small voice from within, we are roused from our automated journeys and realize we may be traveling down the wrong path. I am reminded of this almost daily.

Just a couple of weeks ago, I was in Pittsburgh to give a lecture to a group of primary care physicians. I had arrived in town several hours early, so I checked into my hotel room to answer some e-mail and maybe take a nap. Alas, the heat in the room wasn't working so I asked the front desk to send somebody from maintenance. In no time Frank, the maintenance man, came up to my room, diagnosed the problem, and began working to fix it.

Frank, a first generation Italian-American, and I got to talking while he worked. It turns out that our fathers were roughly the same age and that his had just died. I asked Frank to tell me a little bit about his dad. Putting his tools down for a minute, Frank smiled and then relayed, replete with Italian accent and gestures, a conversation he had with his dad just before he had died.

"So Pop, what's the meaning of life—what's it all about?"

"Well, first you take care of your mom and pop and brothers and sisters."

"Yeah, Pop, and then what?"

"Well, then you take care of your wife and kids."

"Okay Pop, then what?"

"Then you take care of your grandkids."

"Yeah, yeah, yeah, then what, Pop?"

"Then you die, stupid."

We both laughed and then I asked the obvious question, "So Frank, what do you think life is all about?" Frank thought a few seconds and then replied, "Well, until I heard him say it, I never realized that he might as well have been speaking for me. It got me thinking—those things are very important, but I heard this voice inside telling me, there's more to life than that."

Frank chose to listen to that inside voice and act on it to remap his future. By enlarging his life view, he realized that there was more to life than taking care of other people and dying. Much of the work I've done with people over the years has been to help them turn down the amplitude of the noise and confusion of the fast-paced American life we all lead to allow them to hear that internal voice.

Such an admission—that we're following someone else's road map—brings us to a crucial crossroad in our life journeys. We can continue down the comfortable well-lit pathways forged by tradition, custom, and unexamined expectation or we can blaze our own trails and create our own road maps. If we refuse that call and play our life parts according to scripts written for us by others, anxieties mount. We fill our lives with busy work, extreme acts, or material acquisitions. Corralled by boredom, hard work, and culture, we lose the power of significant affirming action and we assume the role of victim. Even though we may have built wealth, status, and reknown, our lives lack meaning, our energies wane, our identities disintegrate, and our self-esteem plummets. Enter burnout.

If, on the other hand, we heed the call—if the road map we follow becomes one of our own crafting—then the journey toward success becomes our own true adventure. But it is not easy. This is why so many of us refuse the call of our inner voices. When the knights of the Arthurian round table were about to embark on their search for the Holy Grail, Sir Gawain challenged Sir Galahad saying that it would be a disgrace to go forth in a group. So each knight entered the forest at a place he alone had chosen where it was darkest and where there was no way or path. This is to say that each of us must find his or her own path. If we take a path already forged we follow someone else's destiny. The good news is that when we heed the call—when we decide to draft our own road maps—the path we follow is our true adventure. Doors will open and help will materialize along our way.

Think for a moment about the popular film series *Pirates of the Caribbean.* The male protagonist of the movies, Captain Jack Sparrow, has a compass that does not point north but rather only points to that which Jack's heart most desires. For many of my patients and clients over the years, it has been my job to help them read/discern their inner compasses. That is also the value of a book such as this.

Once we have taken responsibility for setting our own direction (which takes us to my second observation), we move from defining our success by Measureable Units of Learned Acquisition (MULA) – goals and benchmarks of others - to defining success by how true we are to our own path and way of living.

Wright

MULA—that's a new one; would you elaborate?

Scheiderer

Gladly. Although it might seem as though each of us defines success differently, in truth, most of us define it in measurable terms, such as the number of academic degrees or credentials one has amassed, the size of one's house, the prestige of one's neighborhood, the desirability of one's spouse, the intelligence of one's children, the importance of one's job position, the amount of power one wields, and so on and so forth. As we discussed a few minutes ago, most of these measurable units are learned from an early age and are never really examined or challenged, hence my cheesy, but memorable acronym MULA.

Wright

But aren't such things—these MULA—important to most of us?

Scheiderer

Of course they are. No one would deny that. Over the long haul, however, MULA alone, while important, won't satisfy the soul. Rather, I've come to believe what Henry David Thoreau wrote so eloquently: "to fundamentally affect the quality of each day, that is the highest of the arts."

I recently asked a very prominent, and by all external measures successful, client of mine to define success. Keep in mind, he's a former U.S. Navy fighter pilot, turned vascular surgeon, turned entrepreneur, turned author and pundit. He told me that he defines success by the quality of his day. He likes to wake up in the morning feeling refreshed after a solid night's sleep. His wife and he take turns being the first out of bed to make the coffee and start breakfast. They eat together, then take a ten- to fifteen-minute hiatus to plan that day's activities. After a spirited walk, they ready themselves to attack the imperatives of the day - work, chores, childcare and making sure the domestic trains run on time.

He likes to spend no more than 50 percent of his waking hours on daily labors, thereby ensuring he has plenty of time and mental energy to read and write and listen to music each day. Between two and two-thirty PM, two to three times a week, he takes a nap, for fifteen to twenty minutes. He eats three meals a day, with a snack in between and a snack before bed. At fifty-eight years old, he has sex two to three times a week. A good day for him is one wherein he has plenty of time and energy at the end of the day to be fully present with his loved ones at home in the evening.

I really like his version of success. He defines it by the moments of joy he experiences along the journey, not necessarily the destinations on his road map. So his working definition of success has evolved subtly over the years into a way of living.

Wright

Two of three observations down. Take us through your third insight into success.

Scheiderer

Once we draft our own life road map—once we move from MULA to a way of living—our maps segue from external journeys to internal ones. We become the road map we're traveling. Hopefully, before the death or illness of a loved one or before our own bodies begin to betray us, we stop taking our health for granted and start wondering how we can maximize our energy, vigor, and vitality. For no matter how comprehensive, detailed, and up-to-date our road map toward success is, if our vessel is not seaworthy we will not travel as far as we desire. At this point, when we give the same consideration to the vessel—ourselves—as we do to the map, we realize that the journey is less about the territory and more about us.

Think back on Stephen Covey's habit number seven from his epic work, *The 7 Habits of Highly Effective People: Sharpen the Saw.* Stephen, ever prescient, boldly asserted that preserving and enhancing the greatest asset you have—you—is the habit that makes all others possible. So important is this habit that Stephen, in his schematic diagram, encompasses all other habits with this one. When we understand the symbolism of saw sharpening, we begin to focus less on external measures of success in favor of the internal journey.

Wright

Well, thank you for sharing your observations about success, David, let's change directions just a bit. You practice Age Management Medicine and still maintain a small private psychiatric office in Roanoke. You're also known nationally for your efforts in teaching physicians, nurses, and other health care professionals. This seems like a departure for you, so what do you hope to accomplish in this interview, and what are your goals for contributing a chapter to this book?

Scheiderer

I've given that question much thought. My primary mission is to offer an overall attitude and approach to improving health and well being—a way, in fact, of living—founded in a commitment to a life-long journey of discovery in an era of exponentially expanding knowledge.

In addition, in the spirit of sharpening the saw, I would like to whet our readers' appetites with some very specific steps they can take immediately to move forward on their road map toward a successful and healthy future.

More specifically, I want to inspire readers, not only to contemplate, but to take the small incremental steps that will culminate in healthier lives.

Finally, I would like to begin to make existing medical knowledge more understandable and to show how simple changes in the way each of us lives can make us one to ten or more years younger.

Wright

Can you do all of that in this interview?

Scheiderer

Probably not, but at least I can get us started by introducing the discipline of Age Management Medicine (AMM). We've all attended workshops or read books or listened to books on tape (or CD) about building wealth, but where does one go to learn a comprehensive approach to building health? So think of this chapter on AMM as Health-building 101, and remember, regardless of our definitions of success, it stands to reason that the better our health, the better our chances of reaching our destination.

Many people try to make sense of the ocean of health related information out there and quickly become overwhelmed and discouraged. For that reason, in addition to a detailed map, we need a good guide; otherwise we will go down the wrong path or give up completely—pass the bon-bons. It reminds me of the wisdom of business guru, Peter Drucker, who wrote extensively about the new information revolution. It was not about a revolution in technology or machinery techniques or software speed; but rather, a revolution of concepts. According to Drucker, the prime mandate of contemporary society is to go beyond merely collecting, collating, and coordinating bits of "unformation" and thereby transforming them into information. Rather, the challenge is to assign meaning and purpose to the ever-growing din of random information. Nowhere does this challenge apply more than to the burgeoning of information in the health and wellness sector.

Not a day goes by that I don't read or hear on the news about the newest power food or the latest antioxidant or the best supplements and vitamins to take or the pros and cons of hormone supplementation. Health knowledge is growing at an accelerating pace and what few people know is that we now have an unprecedented ability to comprehend our biology at the level of the tiniest molecule. We also have the opportunity to vastly extend our longevity, improve our well being, and expand our ability to experience the world around us.

But who can help make intelligent sense of the plethora of information constantly flooding us? That is where Age Management Medicine comes into play. In a way, as a practitioner of AMM, I'm part cartographer, part signpost, part guide, part flashlight, part GPS, and part fellow traveler.

Wright

Would you tell us more about AMM and what you do as an AMM physician?

Scheiderer

In brief, Age Management Medicine (AMM) is state-of-the-art, evidenced-based, preventative medicine that focuses on optimum health and vigor. While we may not yet be able to increase longevity (though that day is just around the corner), we are able to delay and, in many cases, prevent premature disability and death, while enhancing quality of life. As such, Age Management Medicine is best seen as a pro-active, preventative approach to health, focusing on preservation of optimum functioning and quality of life for as long as possible making every effort to modulate the process of aging prior to the onset of disease and degenerative illness.

The basic precepts of AMM will be familiar to all: comprehensive patient evaluation, thorough medical history, lifestyle assessment, physical examination, and laboratory evaluation to establish personalized pro-active treatment plans consisting of proper diet, exercise, stress management, and appropriate medical interventions.

Another way of thinking about AMM (once again to borrow from Stephen Covey), is as advanced saw sharpening, which is preserving and enhancing your greatest asset—you. That's what I meant earlier when I said eventually your road map to success becomes an internal process.

Wright

So how does this differ from traditional medical care?

Scheiderer

Conventional medical care focuses on long-term degenerative processes only after they have erupted into advanced, and often life-threatening clinical illness. Keep in mind that the leading causes of death, which have not changed since the 1950s, are heart disease, cancer, stroke, respiratory illness, kidney disease, liver disease, and diabetes. These diseases do not develop out of a blue sky. Instead, they are the result of slow and relentless degenerative processes that are decades in the making.

Conversely, people can decide to consult with an Age Management physician in order to reduce body fat, increase lean muscle mass, improve cognition—clarity of thought, concentration, attention, and focus—lower cholesterol and overall heart disease risk, stabilize mood, improve ability to handle day-to-day stress and strain, bolster the immune system, and enhance sexual responsiveness. The emphasis is on education, skill building, risk reduction, and health enhancement, not solely on the relief of existing symptoms.

Specific goals will obviously vary among individuals. In general, what we try to accomplish in an AMM program can be broken down into three overlapping categories:

- Significant gains in how one feels on a day-to-day, moment-to-moment basis, including the alleviation of myriad discomforts, such as dyspepsia or fatigue, restless or inadequate sleep, low libido, depressed or erratic moods, irritability and difficulty maintaining weight

- Improved subjective sense of well-being, enhanced mental clarity, and better physical and mental energy

- The knowledge that today's steps for your health are propelling you toward long-term health, while significantly reducing your chance of chronic diseases that could cut your life and your health span short

Wright

You mentioned longevity and lifespan. Are you suggesting that we possess the knowledge and tools to live forever?

Scheiderer

In truth, if we froze all the scientific and technology available to us today, the answer to that question would have to be a resounding no. On the other hand, we do have the means to dramatically slow disease and the aging process far more than most people realize. Moreover, far from being stagnant, the pace of scientific and technologic discovery is accelerating exponentially.

For example, according to models created by Ray Kurzweil, one of the world's leading inventors and futurists, the paradigm shift rate (the rate at which technology is progressing) is doubling every decade and capability (which includes price performance, capacity, and speed of specific information technologies) is doubling every *year*. So to fully answer the question, yes, the knowledge exists (if applied aggressively and systematically) for us to slow aging and disease processes to a degree that we can be in good health and good spirits when more radical life-extending and life-enhancing technologies become available over the next few decades. The key is: will we be healthy enough when that quantum leap to life-prolonging technology comes along? The corollary question is, "what must we do today to make sure we are alive and well when said technology comes down the pike?"

Wright

You know, I've been on the planet for quite some time now. As a matter of fact, if I were middle age now I'd have to live to be 136, so why have I not heard more about Age Management Medicine?

Scheiderer

First of all, you're certainly not too old to benefit from AMM—no one is. That said, part of the reason most of us have not heard about this is pretty simple. For most of our lives, we take our health for granted. Sure, health issues command our attention the moment disease strikes. But most of us fail to focus on prevention and health enhancement in a timely manner before the onset of overt symptoms. When confronted with the reality of self-care—cutting back on processed foods, paying more for organic products, drinking that gallon of water a day, exercising more, rushing less, changing a generally unhealthful lifestyle—most of us cave and say, "Just give me the pill!" We have grown accustomed to taking the easy way out and look to merely ease our symptoms rather than address the real problems: inflammation, degeneration, early dysfunction, and death.

Compounding this phenomenon is that the health care system and medical profession, largely based on financial incentives, is oriented toward detecting and treating conditions only after the point of crisis has been reached. That is to say, our current health care system is great at treating acute illness or injury but poor at preventing disease and extending health/lifespan.

Furthermore, we operate under several myths that perpetuate our health lethargy:

Myth Number 1—"I have good insurance. The health care system will thereby take good care of me when I get sick." Such an attitude reminds me of a quotation from the Yellow Emperor's classic text of internal medicine, "To fight a disease after it occurs is like trying to dig a well when one is thirsty or forging a weapon once a war has begun." Unfortunately, that is precisely how our traditional, symptom-based medical system currently works. The financial incentives—the way doctors, hospitals, therapists, clinics get paid—are based on illness, not health building or wellness training. Self-neglect and fancy diagnosis and treatment of illness is big business in the United States. Of the excess of one trillion dollars we spend every year in America on healthcare, less than 5 percent is devoted to modifying high-risk health behaviors. We are simply a nation whose citizens passively sit back neglecting and even abusing ourselves, waiting for illness to strike. More than half of us who have heart disease learn that we have it only after we've had our first heart attack and 40 percent of us die from this first heart attack. The knowledge to delay or avoid the degenerative diseases that cause more than 90 percent of all deaths and disability is available, but the responsibility to apply this knowledge is ours, not the system's. David, I love what you wrote in your message from the publisher for your *Speaking of Success series:* others can shine a light on the path, but we ourselves must do the walking. Nowhere is that more true than when it comes to taking care of ourselves.

Myth Number 2: "There's no such thing as the fountain of youth." *Technically* this is true. But there is such a thing as the fountain of health along the road map toward youthful aging. Although we lack as of yet the tools we need to stop and reverse all aging processes, we do possess right now the means to significantly expand our health spans, stay in good health and good spirits until the revolution in bio and nano technology (hovering just around the corner) enables radical life extension.

Myth Number 3: "Why even try? My genes have already pre-determined my health and lifespan." As one of my favorite sports commentators would say, "Not so fast, my friend." Only 50 percent of our health span and lifespan are determined by genetics, the other 50 percent is determined by our health related habits.

Wright

Can you be more specific? How exactly do you accomplish all these lofty goals of creating longer lives and better lives?

Scheiderer

That again is a whole curriculum unto itself, but let me hit some of the highlights. My AMM program emphasizes twelve core domains:

- Body basics—breathing, posture, stretching, and balance
- Sleep
- Hydration
- Nutrition
- Supplements
- Hormonal Balance
- Sex
- Positive Psychology
- Pace
- Socialization
- Death
- Habit Management

Wright

Are there any components that are more important than the others?

Scheiderer

The AMM program is designed to be comprehensive and the components work indeed synergistically to provide optimum benefit. That said, some components probably provide more robust effects than others. There's a whole book dedicated to some of these things, written by a Harvard psychiatrist, George Vallaint, who summarized the finding of three large prospective studies designed to determine that very question: what variables correlate most strongly with health and longevity? The seven factors that he found were:

- Not being a smoker, or stopping young,
- The use of adaptive coping mechanisms for dealing with stress,
- Moderate use of alcohol and avoidance of alcohol abuse,
- Healthy weight,
- Stable marriage,
- Some exercise, and
- Years of education.

If you really pin me down, based on my reading of the literature, my years as a clinician, and examination of my own life, I'd say, sleep, nutrition, and activity (including sex and positive psychology) would form the base of my own pyramid of health.

Wright

I'd like to come back to a few of these core components, but you mentioned the importance of positive psychology. I suspect that involves more than just being merely upbeat, so what does all that entail?

Scheiderer

It turns out that very good data strongly suggest that a handful of attitudes correlates with longevity and happiness, and if practiced on a regular basis, can improve your health and possibly prolong your life. I actually prescribe exercises to help people cultivate the following six attitudes and inculcate them as daily habits:

- Gratitude
- Enthusiasm
- Interpretive Style (merit-finder versus fault-finder)
- Curiosity
- Optimism
- Forgiveness

People who practice these attitudes can lower their blood pressure, reduce visits to doctors, miss fewer days from work or school, and actually alter the structure of their brains.

Wright

So how do you use these precepts of positive psychology with your age management clients?

Scheiderer

Opportunities abound. I start by reminding clients of what Viktor Frankl teaches in his book, *Man's Search for Meaning*. Frankl, who lost his mother and father and wife in the Nazi concentration camps, wrote about how he himself survived the holocaust.

One of his most profound conclusions was that the last of all human freedoms is the freedom to choose the attitude with which we face our fates. Proper management of our attitudes provides a good source of fuel to propel us along our road maps toward success. Cultivation of these core attitudes also leads directly to increases in happiness and longevity.

To help people inculcate these attitudes as habit, I have them keep a gratitude journal wherein, for five minutes every night, they write down the five things they are most grateful for. The key is to not rush through writing down any old thing just for the sake of completing the assignment. Rather, I encourage people to quietly visualize and savor those things for which they are truly thankful.

Consistent use of such a gratitude journal has been shown to lower blood pressure, improve sleep, enhance mood and general outlook, reduce absenteeism and visits to the doctor's office, and improve circulation and oxygen utilization in specific parts of the brain. Pretty cool stuff.

Once people realize that consciously focusing on their attitudes can dramatically improve their quality of life, they readily embrace the rest of the AMM program.

Wright

Can people really change their attitudes?

Scheiderer

Yes, but it's not easy. Most of us resist mightily at first. Let's say a man has a heart attack or has a cardiac stent placed to reopen a closed blood vessel. Now, let's also say that he has received all the information he needs to modify his behavior and thereby reduce the chances of another heart attack or re-closure of his coronary artery. What are the odds that he will significantly change his health related behaviors even knowing the dire consequences of not doing so? The answer: 9:1 against changing. In other words, at any one time, only about 10 percent of Americans are, for whatever reason, ready to modify their behaviors. A certain few will be able to navigate for themselves the ocean of health information currently available. But most of us need structured programs to travel along our road maps.

Wright

You also mention sleep as part of the base of your personal health pyramid. Why is that?

Scheiderer

We average actually two hours less as Americans than we used to even fifty to one hundred years ago. And although most people know that chronic sleep deprivation will severely curtail our quality of life, most people don't know that daytime sleepiness accounts for more automobile and industrial accidents than alcohol and drugs. And even fewer people know that chronic sleep deprivation makes us more likely to die of heart disease, cancer, lung disease, and other medical conditions. Also, did you know that chronic sleep deprivation leads directly to obesity? As such, restoration of sleep makes up a critical aspect of my weight management strategies as well as my overall AMM program.

Wright

You mentioned hormones and supplements as part of your AMM core of components. Aren't those areas rather controversial at the present time?

Scheiderer

It is, and probably with good reason. I don't mind seeing the controversy because that means people are thinking about it. Unfortunately, because of the plethora of misinformation surrounding the ethical and legal use of hormones, many who need hormones are too frightened to be evaluated. I spend much of my time with clients, patients, and audience members educating them about the proper and improper use of hormone therapy.

These days I check hormone levels on nearly all my clients. They and I are often surprised to learn that they suffer from, and probably have for some time, a hormonal imbalance that is negatively impacting their health. For many men and women, "sharpening the saw" includes use of hormones

For example, a study published recently in the *Archives of Internal Medicine,* a well respected, peer-reviewed journal, looked at men over the age of sixty-five with respect to three hormones: DHEA, testosterone, and growth hormone. They found that subjects who had the lowest levels (in the normal range) for these three hormones, relative to those in the highest range (of normal values), were two and one-half times more likely to be dead of any cause in only six years. That association between low hormones and death is greater than the association between many of the parameters we in medicine routinely monitor including blood pressure, blood sugar, and cholesterol. And yet, how many people know what their DHEA, growth hormone, and testosterone levels are?

Wright

So I'm to become my own personal nutrition expert, spend more time with my friends and family, get more exercise, sleep more, relax regularly, and keep a gratitude journal. When, exactly, am I going to find the time to do anything else, such as keep a job and earn a living?

Scheiderer

That's a fair question and it turns out to be the number one objection I hear: when am I going to find the time to take better care of myself? Part of me wants to ask those same people, well, what are you doing that is so important now or that is more important than taking care of yourself? But I tend not to ask those as often as I'd probably like to. I do remind them of what William James, the father of modern American psychology, said well over a hundred years ago. Basically, it's neither the nature nor the amount of our work that leads to our nervous breakdowns, but the inane notion that we haven't enough time.

I have come to equate time with money. You can spend your money frivolously, you can keep your money in a safe or under your mattress, or you can invest your money so that it reaps dividends for years to come. Time is much the same. Where does your time go? If we think about our day-to-day actions, most of us waste, squander, and otherwise fritter away enormous amounts of time and personal energy in ways that are unproductive and probably don't contribute to a sense of well-being. Probably the best most of us ever do is learn to save some time through careful time management and improvements in efficiency and personal productivity. This is usually done by adopting habits that eliminate rework and redundancy, but it is not until we habitually take time to stop and sharpen our saws that we will actually create, down the road, more time and energy to reach the very destinations we have circled on our life's road maps.

Wright

You know, we are very near the end of our time together; do you have any parting shots or concluding remarks that you want to make?

Scheiderer

First, I'd like to thank you for your time and attention, and the good sparkling conversation. You're obviously very good at what you do.

Then, to summarize, a structured program in Age Management Medicine, like the one I outlined earlier, can without a doubt catapult you toward personal goals and infuse vim and vigor into your life. There is really no alternative. Although this is the end of this chapter, I hope it marks the beginning of a new chapter in your life, a new path on your life journey.

If you only take one message from this time together, I want it to be that we all have unprecedented opportunities to greatly improve our health and to sharpen not only our saws, but every tool in our chest.

Health comprises more than mere absence of disease; it incorporates the effectiveness and success of every level of our existence, and the effort we put into this endeavor will reap multi-fold gains and will fuel our journey toward whatever our life's goals may be.

In closing, there is no quick or easy path to health and happiness, only a slow and arduous one toward it. No finish line—only a starting point—there is neither a best time or place to start, so start here with this book, with this chapter, but soon. Start now.

Let me finally close with a quotation from Marcel Proust that the journey of self-discovery consists not in seeking new landscapes, but in having new eyes. I hope that as we all sojourn along our road map to success, it is with new eyes toward ourselves and our future.

Wright

What a great conversation. I really do appreciate all the time you've spent answering these questions. I have learned a tremendous amount here that I did not know and I am positive that our readers will also.

Scheiderer

Thank you, that is very kind. I hope you're right.

Wright

Today we've been talking with David J. Scheiderer, MD, MBA. He is an accomplished medical educator and highly sought-after speaker on the topics of health and aging in the country. As we have found out here today, this man really knows what he's talking about.

Dr. Scheiderer, thank you so much for being with us today on *Roadmap to Success*.

Scheiderer

Thank you.

About the Author

DAVID J. SCHEIDERER, MD, MBA, is the President of Tiberius Enterprises, Inc. in Roanoke, Virginia. An accomplished medical educator, Dr. Scheiderer is one of the most highly sought-after speakers in the nation on the topics of health and aging. In addition, he has served on numerous executive boards and currently provides professional and technical expertise to several international corporations. In addition to his busy lecture schedule, he maintains a private practice of age management medicine and psychiatry in Roanoke. Of his many roles, his favorite is that of father to his children, Jake and Cecily.

To Contact David J. Scheiderer, MD, MBA...
Tiberius Enterprises, Inc.
1328 Second St. SW
Roanoke, VA 24016
540.342.2844
E-mail: cc@tiberiusenterprises.com

ROADMAP to SUCCESS

10

An interview with...

Ellyn Traub

David Wright (Wright)

Today we're talking with Ellyn S. Traub, Founder and Executive Coach of High Performance Leadership, Inc. She rescues attorneys, executives, and professionals from frustration and from being overwhelmed and helps them gain control of their professional and personal lives. Ellyn shares her wealth of expertise through speaking engagements. As an executive coach and workshop facilitator, she delivers knowledge that results in measurable real-time and real-world application. Clients working with High Performance Leadership improve their internal and external relationships, utilize and leverage their time more effectively, find better ways to reduce stress, and gain a competitive edge. Company profits increase and clients learn how to make a life instead of just making a living. Work is no longer a bad four-letter word.

Ellyn, welcome to *Roadmap to Success.*

Ellyn S. Traub (Traub)

Thank you, David.

Wright

We know that communication is essential to success in the workplace and in our lives, but why is it so difficult?

Traub

Communication is something that we normally do not think about—we just open our mouths and talk. In reality, communication is a very complex process involving a sender and receiver, with many sources for potential errors. A simple message is not that simple! It's more than just words. It includes other information such as the sender's tone of voice, the timing of the message, and the way the sender expresses himself or herself. Does the message have an emotional undertone or is it matter-of-fact? All these factors enter into the equation. Once the receiver hears the message, he or she goes through the process of decoding it. The meaning of the message is then filtered through his or her values, past experiences, cultural and language differences, and biases. So the receiver's filters can alter the meaning of the message.

Our environment also affects our communication. We live in a fast-paced world that is also global and virtual. Everyone wants something from us and they want it now! We feel rushed and pressured to respond quickly, and we don't want to make the time to stop what we are doing to make our message clear. We send a quick e-mail with a sound byte of information and pass it off as communication. Without non-verbal cues, we just assume that what the person said is what was really meant. Given all these factors, you can see why so many organizational problems stem from ineffective communication.

Wright

Let's focus on non-verbal communication. How does it enter into the process?

Traub

Non-verbal communication such as facial expressions, posture, eye movement, and gestures, can either add to or detract from verbal communication. They can add to verbal communication by reinforcing the message and by emphasizing certain phrases or words. They can detract from verbal communication by not being consistent with the verbal message or by distracting the listener's attention from the message.

For example, we might say one thing with words, but our eyes and our bodies are telling the listener something very different. This could be intentional—to hide something from or to deceive—or it could just be a habit we've picked up that has nothing to do with the message. The listener is then forced to choose between the two scenarios. We assume that our message has been received and interpreted the way we intended it to be, while that may not be the case at all.

I'm sure you've been in situations where you are talking to someone who is pre-occupied with something else. He or she is not looking at you or even acknowledging that you are being heard. What are you supposed to think? You can interpret a vast number of possibilities, but you don't know for sure.

How we occupy space is another form of non-verbal communication. In certain cultures, standing very close and frequently touching another person, such as patting him or her on the shoulder, is commonplace. But in the United States, that type of behavior would most likely make us uncomfortable. We might even be offended by it. We may back away from the person and stop listening to what he or she is saying while we focus on wishing the person would just go away because we are feeling uncomfortable. The physical size of the speaker and tone (resonance) of voice in relation to the listener's size and voice plays a role as well.

Many factors go into communication—factors that we have to process quickly and act upon.

Wright

Are there specific strategies for interpreting non-verbal communication?

Traub

First of all, pay attention to the clues and pay attention to what you are doing. How is the receiver responding? Is the person not making eye contact because he or she is distracted or is the person afraid to make eye contact? Is the person fidgeting? That might mean you are rambling and the person is bored or it could mean nervousness. If you keep moving closer, but the receiver keeps backing away, that's a clue that you are making him or her uncomfortable. People who are backing away are shutting you off. They're "saying" I don't want to talk to you; you are in my space.

Your voice, tone, volume, pitch, and resonance can add or detract from your verbal message. Paying attention to the other person's facial reactions, physical size in relation to your size, and voice in relation to your voice will help you to adapt to a style that is comfortable for him or her.

Wright

From what you are telling me, effective communication is complex, but isn't it even less effective to analyze every conversation in detail?

Traub

On the surface that's true, David. But the bottom line is that in order to be more effective communicators, we need to understand more than the basics. Once we go beyond the basics, integrate them into our own behavior and apply what we have learned, our responses will become automatic and we won't have to mentally go through the process step-by-step. Bringing some of the complexities to the forefront will help us to understand the communication process, our behavior, and what we can do to maximize our interactions with others.

Wright

You've touched on several barriers to communication, Ellyn. How can we use this information to improve communication with others regardless of the venue?

Traub

Effective communication is showing courtesy and respect toward others and understanding our own behavior.

Once we learn to take a good look at ourselves—the good, the bad, and the ugly—understand and listen to ourselves, think about how others may perceive us, and change our behavior, we can then learn to appreciate the differences in others. This understanding and application leads to appropriate word choice, tone, cadence, and other non-verbal cues that will be appealing to the receiver of the message. This naturally results in more effective communication. All it takes to eliminate many communication errors is simply listening openly, actively, and with empathy to the other person.

In virtual interactions, many non-verbal cues are missing. Add to this global and cultural influences, different interpretations, slang, and words specific to particular regions (including regional-specific language within North America), and open, active, and empathic listening and communication becomes more critical. When relying on virtual forms of communication such as e-mail and voice mail messages, we need to take special care that our communication is clear.

We use the opinions of others and our own past experiences to anticipate the outcome of future interactions. We assume that our interaction is going to be the same as someone else's or the same as it was for us in the past. That isn't necessarily true

For example, based on past experience, we may perceive that our co-workers are trying to be difficult and are not cooperating with us. It might help to sit down with them and say, "We're not getting along" or "We are not working well together" or "There is something missing here. Let's figure out what the barriers are and what we can do to eliminate them." In all likelihood, they were just trying to get their own work done and weren't intentionally disrupting your day. Try it. This is not a new trick or magic; it's simply showing courtesy and respect toward the other person. It's showing a sincere desire to work together.

Wright

I'm sure you'd agree that giving information is only part of the process. What about the other side of the coin? What about listening?

Traub

Listening is critical. Listening goes both ways—we need to not only listen to others, but to ourselves. How many times have you not heard a message correctly or you only heard part of it because you were thinking about the other tasks you had to complete? Perhaps you were distracted by the "you've got mail" tone? Think about the last conversation you had with your boss, parents, siblings, or friends—were you really paying attention or were you formulating your response as the other person was talking?

We tend to listen to argue or listen to respond instead of listening to understand. In our desire to have a ready response, we begin thinking about what we will say even before the other person has finished talking. Sometimes we might be focusing on the messenger and not the message. For example, the messenger may be someone we respect or someone we don't want to talk to. When we are not focused, we cannot actively listen and we might respond inappropriately.

All the components of communication that we have reviewed in this chapter add to communication; there isn't room to get distracted by components that add little or nothing to the conversation.

Wright

Can we all learn to be effective listeners?

Traub

Absolutely! The key is to get involved. Listening is not hearing—listening is active. Active listening is being open and empathetic with the other person and being in an active body state. Listening is not just something you "do."

Fight the distractions, especially when you are on the phone. It's so easy to drop out of the conversation while you read an e-mail if you are in front of the computer. That's a distraction. Yes, it is hard not to multi-task and it is a difficult habit to break. Turn the screen away and turn off the speakers. You don't really need to know when an e-mail arrives. Keep your space free of distractions. Whether you're talking with someone on the phone or face-to-face, stop what you're doing and focus on the conversation. If you are interrupted when you are in the middle of work that requires your attention, you have to choose between the two. You won't be able to do both completely, and if you try, you are setting yourself up for making errors. Stop talking. Let the other person have his or her say. Ask the other person to clarify something on the spot if you don't understand. Paraphrasing what the other person has said helps your understanding as well. Communicate your feelings, don't act them out.

Wright

What special challenges are there to effective communication between different levels of employees within an organization? How can a manager benefit from improved communication with an employee?

Traub

Communication between managers and employees needs to be clear, open, and timely. There are several ways managers can communicate: they can dictate, they can parent, or they can coach their employees. Managing by team collaboration involves developing the strengths of others, asking good questions, and guiding others to solve and prevent problems.

As a manager, you need your people more than they need you. Management is the art of getting things done through others. Managers need to be savvy enough to use the right communication style at the right time with each employee. By understanding each employee's communication style, the manager can use the words and non-verbal actions that the employee will respond to in a positive manner in order to achieve results.

Communicate your expectations with your employees and ask them their expectations of you. Provide a supportive work environment where employees can practice new skills and aren't afraid to ask questions. Engage employees in their work, don't just give them work to do that has no meaning to them. Any type of work, even the most routine, has meaning and importance to the operation of the company. Sit down and talk with your employees and help them make this connection.

Create an environment where people can grow and take risks. Acknowledge work well done and use mistakes as learning opportunities. Not all employees are superstars; many want and enjoy playing supporting roles. Acknowledge the contributions of the supportive players; they are the keys to a manager's overall success. Walk your talk—actions speak louder than words. Employees watch what happens. As a manager, your role is to coach and guide employees, not to manage them.

Wright

For both managers and the employees, effective communication with customers is perhaps the most difficult and yet potentially the most rewarding for the health of the organization. How is communication with customers different—or is it?

Traub

Customers are people too! Communication with customers is not much different than communication with employees; only the context has changed.

Customer service is not a seminar; it is the life-blood of a business. Furthermore, customer service is part of every employee's job description. Consistency and frequency in communication is essential. All employees need to understand and believe in the philosophy and mission of the company. The message, actions, and words need to be in sync at all times.

Processes need to be in place to gather information about your customers—what they want and expect. You need to be able to anticipate new wants and expectations and be flexible enough to respond to them quickly. Processes need to be in place for changes and to handle problems. These processes can be enhanced by engaging employees in the process. In many cases, employees may have more direct information about an issue than the business owner or manager has.

In most cases, if you give average service, you will not hear from the customer. That service is expected. You may receive a call if you provide exceptional service. What you are striving for is customers who are advocates for your company—customers who tell their friends about the exceptional service they received. You want them to call you about the exceptional service and specific employees who made the experience extraordinary and detail what they did right so you can repeat the experience for future customers.

You may or may not hear when something goes wrong or is not up to expectations. Unfortunately, many times the unhappy customer has told the "horror story" to dozens of friends and/or business colleagues, long before you—the business owner—hear of it. When customers complain, they're in a highly emotional state. It's your job to actively listen and understand, not to argue. Own the customer's question or complaint; uphold and improve the reputation and standards of your organization. Show respect and compassion. Take personal responsibility for the problem or issue. If you don't have the answers, give the customer your name, take the person's name and number, and call back with the information he or she needs. Find out exactly what the problem is. Let the customer fully tell his or her story without interruption. In a neutral voice, paraphrase what you heard so you completely understand the problem. Ask the customer how you can solve the problem. Most of the time the customer just wants to let you know, for your own information, about encounters that didn't go well. You want customers to tell you when things are not going well, when things are just okay, and when things are great. That will give you the measure of what you need to do, things you need to do more often, and things you need to do less often.

Make it a non-threatening experience for the customer to give feedback, both positive and negative. Listening to the voice of the customer can guide you to where necessary improvements are needed. Don't overlook the details.

Look at both the process and your personnel. If the process is the problem, work to improve it. If it is a personnel issue, then work with the employee. He or she may need more training, more information, and better guidelines and boundaries of their authority. The issue may be both a process and personnel problem.

The goal for effective communication, whether it is with your customers or with your employees, is to always raise the bar, never to lower it.

Wright

Another difficult situation managers encounter is providing feedback to employees. How can they make it a more productive and positive experience?

Traub

Managers must keep their communication clear, open, and timely. We have discussed several ways managers can improve their communication. Now is the time for them to implement what they've learned. Here's what I would advise:

Engage your employees. By that I mean, make sure that they are "checked in," that they are at work in body, mind, and spirit. Make sure they know their purpose and value and how these align with that of the company. By providing a variety of opportunities for employee input, you have engagement.

You can't brush off employees when work is busy and in flux. Be available and accessible. Find neutral areas for meetings. If this is not possible, step out from behind your desk and set up a more conversational space; sitting behind a big desk creates a communication barrier. Provide them with timely information that they want and need on a regular basis. Be as specific as you can, and clear up rumors immediately. For example, your employees should not hear about company news—positive or negative—on the evening news!

Wright

Any special advice for the dreaded performance appraisal?

Traub

That's a tough one. Managers are rarely taught how to coach their staff and set measurable goals. They aren't given the tools or resources to assess or measure performance. In many instances, the manager is not even in the same physical location as the staff he or she manages. Performance appraisals are often done poorly, not in a timely fashion, or not at all. Managers are not coached on how to change the appraisal into a road map for success, which it should be. The process becomes a one-time deal, not an ongoing mutual partnership.

I like to think of a performance review as a high-performance commitment. The appraisal document and meeting are the end products of an ongoing communication and partnership between the manager and employee. The document becomes a road map or blueprint for the year. This document should not be set in stone; during the year, it should change as the company changes and grows.

Wright

Most managers can barely get through the annual process using the standard appraisal form, much less change it throughout the year; any suggestions?

Traub

Use the form as a starting point, a basic tool. Tweak it so it is objective, clear, and up-to-date. Delete any judgment labels (good, fair) and replace them with measurable behavior-based language. Review job descriptions and make sure they are still current. Involve your employees in this process. Set specific goals/results you expect them to accomplish and provide them with guidelines on how to make them happen. Make sure they are held accountable for the goals and that they understand the consequences if they are not met. Use technology with face-to-face meetings; there are several Web-based programs to help keep managers and employees on track.

Employees should be involved in the process year-round. If you don't have a method for reviewing and promoting professional equity, put one in place. Meet with your staff during the year. The meetings should be neutral, productive, and non-defensive. Ask employees what they expect from you and then deliver. Don't discuss pay during these meetings, that's another meeting entirely.

If you have a high trust environment, consider using assessment tools administered by a certified professional. Assessment tools aid in understanding individual differences and uncovering new ways to work and interact with others. There are many accredited and validated assessment instruments available and I am certified to administer several of these assessment instruments.

Wright

There's been a lot of talk about the importance of goal setting, but what if you get the goal wrong? How can you tell if it is an effective goal or not?

Traub

A goal is effective if it accomplishes three things: there is a clear understanding of the goal and performance expectations between the employee and the manager, the goal motivates employees to higher levels of performance than in the past, and allows the employees' goals to be tied to the goals of the department and company.

Wright

Why do so many performance appraisals miss the mark?

Traub

For one thing, I have found that little time and thought are devoted to performance planning; performance appraisals are part of the performance plan, not an isolated event. When appraisals are an isolated event, their significance is reduced for everyone involved, the company, the manager and the employee. Reviews may be filled out routinely, with little or no thought put into them. Another way a performance appraisal can fail is if it focuses on placing blame, rather than evaluating and showing ways for an employee to improve his or her performance. If the manager postpones or cancels appraisal meetings, that may send a signal to employees that the appraisal isn't all that important.

Finally, managers must actually be in a position to accurately assess staff performance. Managers who aren't aware of what their employees have contributed and the issues they have faced cannot complete an appraisal with any competence.

Wright

What do employees actually want from a performance review—besides a high score, of course?

Traub

The performance review is not the time or place for surprises. Successes and improvement areas should have been discussed as they occurred. Employees want specific things from a performance review, and communication is critical to the process. They want clear, specific goals and expectations that are measurable. They expect solid information and feedback and a frank, honest discussion of where they're doing a good job, where they need improvement and what they need to do to take them toward their career goals and toward the companies goals. Naturally, they also want to be paid fairly for their performance.

An effective manager doesn't monopolize the conversation. He or she listens to employees and allows them to discuss the goals they've set for themselves, evaluate their own performance, and provide additional feedback. Eighty percent of the appraisal time should be spent on goal planning for the coming year. Only 20 percent should focus on the past year.

Wright

In summary, you've discussed several ways we can improve our communication skills. Once we've mastered those, what else can we do?

Traub

We are always communicating, so there are always opportunities for improvement. I think it's a matter of continually being aware of and continually striving to improve our skills. There isn't really an event; once you take this class or after you finish reading this chapter, you will know everything there is to know and magically your behavior has changed. After all, we are human and sometimes our emotions override our logic. We fall back into old habits. Just continue to learn, continue to develop your skills on a daily basis, and implement what you've learned on a daily basis. Learn from those errors when you slip back into old habits. Own up to your mistakes, and apologize when necessary. If you do that, these skills and new behaviors will help you in every facet of your life—your professional life, public life, and home life.

Wright

Ellyn, this has been very helpful, and I know we've all seen ourselves in the scenarios you've brought to our attention in this chapter. I must admit, there have been many times I've found myself trying to defend my position and not listening to the other person. I really appreciate the time you've taken today to answer these questions about communication. I know I have learned a lot, and I am sure our readers have too.

Traub

Thank you. It's been my pleasure.

Wright

Today we've been talking with Ellyn S. Traub, Founder and Executive Coach of High Performance Leadership Inc. She brings a wealth of experience to her clients and she delivers knowledge that has immediate real-time and real-world applications. Clients working with her improve their internal relationships, leverage their time more effectively, find better ways to reduce stress, and more importantly, they gain a competitive edge.

Ellyn, thank you so much for being with us today on *Roadmap to Success*.

Traub

Thank you very much, David.

About the Author

ELLYN S. TRAUB is Founder and Executive Coach of High Performance Leadership, Inc. She rescues attorneys, executives, and professionals from frustration and being overwhelmed and helps them gain control of their professional and personal lives. Ellyn shares her wealth of expertise through speaking engagements. As an executive coach and workshop facilitator, she delivers knowledge that results in measurable real-time and real-world application. Clients working with High Performance Leadership improve their internal and external relationships, utilize and leverage their time more effectively, find better ways to reduce stress, and gain a competitive edge. By focusing on critical business and performance issues, leaders produce measurable and significant bottom-line business results. Clients learn how to make a life instead of just making a living. Work is no longer a bad four-letter word.

Ellyn has delivered workshops for The Society of Women Engineers regional and national conferences and has presented for organizations such as eWomennetwork and The Indianapolis Bar Association. She is a member of the International Coach Federation, International Speakers Network, Indiana Health Industry Forum, the Central Indiana American Society for Training and Development, the Society for Human Resource Management, the Carmel Chamber of Commerce, and The Association for Corporate Growth.

To Contact Ellyn S. Traub, MS, CPBA, CPVA...
High Performance Leadership, Inc.
Coaching makes the CRITICAL difference.[sm]
484 E. Carmel Drive, #158
Carmel, IN 46032-2812
317.844.9825
ellyn@hpleadership.com
www.hpleadership.com

ROADMAP *to* SUCCESS 11

An interview with...

Judi Moreo

David Wright (Wright)

Many years ago, Judi Moreo began her journey to success. She has studied, experimented, researched, experienced, traveled, worked, visualized, journaled, and taught for more than twenty-five years. She has unraveled the mystery behind the illusion that only a chosen few are allowed success. Sharing her knowledge with audiences around the world in twenty-six countries on four continents, Judi has become one of the most sought-after speakers in the world at conventions, corporate seminars, and leadership conferences. Today I have asked Judi to discuss that journey.

Judi Moreo, welcome to *Roadmap to Success.*

Moreo

Thank you. It's a pleasure to be here.

Wright

Let's talk about your journey. How did it begin?

Moreo

Have you ever said something that the minute it came out of your mouth, you wished you could take it back? Have you ever said something that changed the course of your life forever . . . only you didn't know it at the time? I have. But I didn't come equipped with a rewind button, so once it was out there, I had to figure out what to do about it.

It was 1970 and I was a fashion coordinator at a local department store. It was my job to put on fashion shows, pose the models for the promotional photos, and teach charm classes to businesswomen, teenagers, and children. The store manager told me to go up to the hardware department and help take inventory. I was supposed to count nuts, bolts, screws, and nails. This was not the first time he had asked me to do things that were not remotely connected to my job as a "fashion coordinator" and I felt he had it in for me. So, out of my mouth came, "That's not in my job description." The minute I said it, I knew it was wrong. He turned a bright shade of red and seemed to swell up twice his size. Then my mouth just kept adding fuel to the fire, "If I have to do that, I quit!"

He was in the right mood to accept that resignation and within an hour, I was packed up and out of a job.

Wright

That would change your life a bit. What did you do next?

Moreo

I only had a total of $2000 in my savings account, but I thought I could do it better than they could if I didn't have the rules and perimeters that job placed on my creative talents. So I took my $2000 and opened my own business. I found a small office to rent, paid a security deposit, and my first and last month's rent. I had a phone installed, bought a typewriter, and a desk to put it on. Okay, it was a long time ago—we didn't have computers back then. But, you get the idea—I got everything I needed to start a business.

After purchasing these bare necessities, I realized I didn't have any money left and was beginning to wonder if it might not have been smarter to have kept my mouth shut and have a regular paycheck. But I was determined to be successful and show them.

That first month was pretty hard. I did everything I knew of to generate business. I personally called on potential clients. I bartered some simple advertising in the local trade paper. I wrote a column for another publication. I made phone call after phone call and sure enough, eventually people responded to my new venture. *But,* two weeks after I opened my business there was a strike in Las Vegas, where I live, and for the first time in history, every light on the Las Vegas Strip was turned off. People were not interested in sending their kids to charm school or hiring models when their livelihood was being threatened.

The first day of the second month came and the rent was due and I knew I was going to be short on cash. Business was coming in, but thirty days is a lot shorter than you think. I had a lot of contracts for future work and some deposits, but I wouldn't collect on those until the work was done. The big payday was still thirty to sixty days out. So, with knots in my stomach, I contacted my landlord to alert him of the pending bad news. I assured him that I was going to make it—that I was committed to succeed, I had a plan and a vision, and more new clients were coming every day. It was going to take a little time to make it all come together and I didn't have the financial reserves I needed to pay the rent on time.

Now, my landlord was one of those old Las Vegas guys who wore his shirt open to the waist, lots of gold chains, and had the kind of hair on his chest that looked like he used his daughter's curling iron. You know the kind of guy I'm talking about—the kind you see in movies like *Casino*. In reality, he was a really good guy and I like to think he believed in me. As I look back, I'm not sure if he *really* believed in me or if he just wanted me to rent his office space.

I explained to him I didn't have the money to pay the next month's rent, but I knew it was coming. I asked him to allow me credit for a month. To my amazement, he looked at me and said, "The man in the business next door bet me you wouldn't last in business six months. I bet him you would. So I tell you what, if you can hang in there for six months, I'll make enough money on the bet to cover your rent. Do you think you can hang in there?"

Are you kidding me! This was the just the break I needed.

Well, I'm happy to say he won his bet and my gamble paid off. My business thrived in his building for the next four years—and I never again had difficulty paying my rent. I moved my business only because I was able to buy my own building when I outgrew his space. He and I remain friends to this day. For seventeen years I ran an extremely well known and profitable modeling school, agency, and convention service business. I even received a Las Vegas Chamber of Commerce Woman of Achievement Award!

Wright

Was there a system, a technique, or a formula you used to acquire success—something that others could use to make themselves successful?

Moreo

There are three simple things that make the difference between living a fully expressed life and just getting by. I call them the ABCs of living:

Attitude—the outer expression of our passions, whatever they may be,

Behavior—how we demonstrate our purpose or the path we take to the achievement of our goals,

Communication—the power that can either gather or repel the people and circumstances that will support our success.

Wright

So, what is attitude?

Moreo

Attitude is an outward expression of your inner feelings. It's your passion—and it is also a *habit!* How you speak and act every day becomes so much a part of you that it is automatic. That's what a habit is—something you do without thinking about it. You know people who come in to work almost every day saying, "I'm just not a morning person"—have you ever noticed these people aren't usually afternoon people either?

Our thoughts are creating our feelings—our passion. Our feelings in turn are driving our behavior. Our behavior brings about the results or lack of results we have in our lives. How we think, what we believe, and the energy, enthusiasm, and passion with which we approach our lives play a major role in our success.

In the average workplace, we hear a minimum of five negative statements every hour. In some places, people hear more than five. It takes approximately fourteen to twenty positive statements made to you to overcome the effects of one negative statement. So when someone says something like, "It won't work. We've never done it that way," you need to say, "Well, let's give it a try and see if *we* can find a way." You should say other positive, encouraging statements at least fourteen times to overcome the original negativity and to stay in a neutral place.

So let's do the numbers. Five negatives an hour in an eight-hour day equal forty negatives a day. There are five days in a week so that makes two hundred. There are four weeks in most months so we are now up to eight hundred negative statements per month that we are hearing just at work. Some of us live with some people who are less than positive, so let's give it another two hundred. That brings us to one thousand negatives we are hearing every month on average. Who do you know who will give you 14,000 to 20,000 positives every month? Probably nobody. Most of us don't have a partner, a boss, or even a best friend who tells us regularly we did a great job on the last project or that we're smart, pretty, talented, creative, or great at being who we are.

So my suggestion is this: *you* put the positives into your passion. That's right—*you* take responsibility to give yourself a positive mental attitude in order to stay motivated and on track to reach your full potential.

Wright

Do we have control over our thoughts?

Moreo

You have control over the kind of messages that are being programmed into your subconscious. Of course, any additional motivation you get from others is great—like icing on the cake—but you should not be dependent on it. *You* are leading the way for your own success. Practice giving yourself praise, compliments, and "atta boys" whenever you can. Every time you think something negative like, "I'm so clumsy" or, "I'm so dumb," *stop* and remind yourself that you are successful, that you can walk down the street without tripping most of the time, and that you are a really great person! Break the habit of telling yourself all the bad things about you. There are plenty of people who are ready and willing to do that for you. Be your own cheerleader—the one person in your life who loves you no matter what! Say to yourself, "I'm powerful. I'm effective. I'm intelligent. I'm good at what I do. People like me. I like them. I'm smart. I look good. I smell good. Yeah, me!"

Make a habit of being your own cheerleader. Every day—throughout the day—find a moment and tell yourself something good! Here's your homework assignment: Never again for the rest of your life will you attach a negative word to the words, "I am." From this day forth, you are to only attach positive words—I am smart. I am intelligent, etc.

If you are to live a life filled with passion, you must take care of yourself; give yourself permission to be you—with all your strengths and all your weaknesses. There's a little voice inside of each of us that sometimes says, "You've been taking care of everyone else, what about me?" You have to take care of yourself if you are to be excited about your life. If you want other people to be excited, you have to be excited first.

Attitude is the outward expression of our inner feeling about ourselves. Our attitude, our thoughts, and our feelings create our behavior.

Wright

You said the B stands for Behavior and that this is how we demonstrate our purpose; what do you mean by that?

Moreo

That can best be answered by telling you a story about two very different people and how their behaviors affected everyone around them.

When I owned Universal Models, we had a convention service division with a full-time staff and approximately one thousand subcontractors. I was doing pretty well—that's when I received the Chamber of Commerce Woman of Achievement Award. Our company furnished the personnel for some of the largest and most prestigious conventions in the world—groups like the Consumers Electronics Show, National Association of Home Builders, and the National Automobile Dealers Association.

I also had a brother, Wayne When he was seventeen, my parents enlisted him in the Navy because that was better than where the local police department wanted to put him. This was in the '50s. Almost immediately he was shipped to Korea to serve in the war.

While in Korea, he discovered tattoos and he came home looking like the illustrated man. When Wayne was discharged, he received a very large check which he immediately put to use purchasing a huge Harley Davidson motorcycle. Remember, in the '60s, a motorcycle was not the status symbol that it is today. Wayne complemented his new machine with a matching black leather ensemble complete with chains holding his wallet in his pocket. He grew his hair to his waist and wore it Willy Nelson style—bandana and all—and he even got a girlfriend who looked like a "Hell's Angels mama." And all those tattoos completed the picture!

One day Wayne was riding his motorcycle down the highway in Brazoria County, Texas, enjoying the day, when suddenly things went terribly wrong. Wayne was way out in the country and came to a crossroad when he saw what we'd probably all call a "redneck truck" with the driver sitting there idling his engine. Apparently the guy didn't like the way Wayne looked, so the driver stomped on the gas and hit Wayne's motorcycle broadside. The impact threw him high in the air and about thirty feet down the road where he was abruptly introduced to the asphalt. My brother said that at the time he was hit, he knew one leg had come off and he wasn't sure about the other one.

We don't know how long he lay on that highway or who called the flight for life helicopter. Here's what I do know: My brother spent five and a half years in the Veterans Hospital. His body was broken, but more than that, his spirit was crushed. He lost his home, his cars, his motorcycle, his girlfriend, his job, his ability to support himself, and his passion for living.

We are a big family—all girls except for Wayne. In our family, we take care of our own, that's what big South Texas families do. So when it was time for him to come out of the hospital, he no longer had a home to go to or the means to take care of himself. My sisters and I got together and decided that one of us must do it, so we took a vote. And guess what—I won!

Wayne came to live with me. Every day I would come home from work and I would be "Sister Sunshine"—Wayne's personal cheerleader, talking positive and bringing motivational tapes and books. I would suggest we attempt to learn to walk on the artificial limbs he had been given. He was less than receptive. Day after day, week after week, month after month I would attempt to get him to buy in to my positive outlook—to no avail.

Then one day, after many months, when I came home, he said, "I have an idea. Why don't I come to work in your office?"

Well, what was I to do? He was my brother, and in our family we take care of our own. So I put him to work.

It took him about a month to tell every member of my staff and the entire contingency of subcontractors what was wrong with them, based on their height, their weight, the color of their hair, the color of their skin, and the way they talked. Do you know what I realized? Donny Osmond knew what he was talking about when he and The Osmond Brothers sang the song, "One Bad Apple." One negative team member is like having a rotten apple in a basket of big shiny red apples—they all begin to rot. I also realized early on that I was losing my best employees, my best clients, and my company was losing money. But what was I to do? He was *my brother* and we take care of our own.

I was very fortunate, however. I had another employee by the name of Robert. I am going to describe Robert to you only so that you can see the contrast of Robert to my brother. Robert was about five feet, nine inches tall and slightly built. Robert wore outfits that consisted of such items as pink pants tucked in magenta suede knee boots, pink shirts, magenta ascots, a lime green silk baseball jacket, pink earrings, and bleached blonde hair with pink tips. I'll bet you can figure out how much my brother liked him.

Every day Robert would go into Wayne's office and say, "Good morning." And every day, Wayne would say something insulting and rude to Robert. I asked Robert, "Why don't you stay out of there and not speak to him? You know he's going to be awful to you."

Robert answered, "Why would I not speak to him? I speak to everyone else. Why would I change my behavior just because he chooses to be negative?"

Wow. What a lesson! How many times have you and I quit speaking to someone or started avoiding someone because of his or her negative attitude? Or how many times have we changed our behavior because of the way someone else acted toward us? You see, Robert was being Wayne's personal cheerleader. It was great!

Then one day, Robert popped into Wayne's office and said, "Good morning. I see you've got your pretty lil' ol' smile on today." My brother started to laugh. He replied, "Robert, don't you ever give up?" Robert said (and these are the words I saw directly affect my brother), "No I never give up—not when someone is worth it. And you are worth it!"

That was the day my brother started to change. Had you met Wayne during any of the last ten years of his life you would have sworn he had never been negative a day in his life.

During his last few months, he was hospitalized back in Texas. Each weekend I would try to get home to sit with him and just be together. We would laugh and talk about all the experiences we had during his recovery. One day he said, "You know, that accident was the best thing that ever happened to me."

Shocked, I replied, "How can you say that? The accident changed all of our lives forever."

"Well," he said, "I learned how smart I was—that I could use my brain instead of my brawn to make a living. I learned it's not what happens to you, but what you do about it that makes a difference. And most of all, I learned to get along with people who were different than me. Robert liked me and believed in me when I didn't like or believe in myself."

Wow! My brother—Mr. Bad Apple—said, "It's not what happens to you, but what you do about it that makes a difference," and that he could learn to get along with people he didn't like or who were different than he was simply because someone believed in him. Wow!

You see, Robert's sticking to his convictions, never changing himself to fit the circumstances, and not letting the negative attitude of another person affect his behavior is one of the best examples of owning one's power that I have ever witnessed. By doing so, Robert made an overwhelming difference in the life of someone else.

When you choose to live anchored in your purpose instead of thinking about your lack and limitations, you will feel more confident and more powerful. You will be better able to think clearly and find solutions to your problems, make the right decisions, and choose the right path for your life instead of running around in a frenzy, grabbing anything and everything that looks like an easy answer. When you have purpose, you will have more control over your life and more power to make things happen.

When you live that purpose with passion, with intent, and with enthusiasm, it cannot be denied. The world steps aside for a purposeful, committed person.

Wright

How will we know that we are helping others change their behaviors and have a more fulfilling and successful life?

Moreo

We don't always know whose life we have changed or how many people we have touched along the way.

I haven't seen Robert in several years. He moved away. I sold the business and we just haven't connected since Wayne's death. Robert probably doesn't even know the true effect he had on Wayne's life, which is exactly my point—you may never know how you've inspired someone, even when you take the time to inspire, to compliment, and to encourage. Don't let that keep you from taking the opportunity to say something positive to someone. You never know when it will change his/her life.

If you see someone doing something well, looking good, or being kind to someone else, compliment him or her. When people are rewarded for their behavior they will repeat that behavior. Remember too, when you say something positive to someone else, you hear it as well. You are raising your own positive statement ratio. It only takes a few seconds to say, "You do your job very well," "You look very good in that color," or, "How nice of you to help that man with his packages." You'll be amazed at how good you feel after you pay a compliment to someone else.

Many people have told me they don't have time to compliment others or they are afraid the other person may think they are strange or forward. If that's true, why is it they have time to find fault with others and complain about them? Why would you care if someone thinks you are strange, especially if you are strange in a good way? Remember, we all need those 14,000 to 20,000 positive reinforcements every month, so make it a habit when you think of it and you are in a place where you can say something positive, pass on a compliment or a kind word.

One day I was conducting a training class in a conference room at a large hotel. I was staying overnight in the same hotel. After class, I took the elevator back to the floor where my room was located and a very good-looking young man got on the elevator. He was dressed as though he was going to model for the cover of *GQ* magazine. I thought to myself, "Wow!"

Then I had a series of thoughts that went like this:

"I should tell him how good he looks."

"No, you're an older woman and he'll think you are hitting on him."

"Well, so what? Tell him."

"No." "Yes." "No." "Yes." "No." "Yes. The floors are going by and if you don't tell him soon, he'll be gone and you will have missed your opportunity."

So I said, "Excuse me. I need to tell you something."

He said, "Yes ma'am, what is it?"

I said, "You are the most gorgeous man I have seen in a long, long time. You really know how to dress."

He said, "Do I know you?"

I said, "No. Would you like to?" At this point, he started pushing the elevator buttons really fast. He wanted out of that elevator. I don't know about him, but it sure made my day. Even now, when I think of it, I smile all over again.

Okay, maybe I went a little over the top in my compliment, but it felt great! Who knows—he may still be talking about that "strange red headed woman who paid him a compliment in the elevator."

Wright

But what if no one does that for us? How will we keep our motivation up to behave in a positive, powerful fashion day in and day out?

Moreo

My dad was a salesman. One day, when I was a teenager, he dropped his appointment notebook on the floor. People didn't have Palm Pilots back then—Dad just used an old spiral notebook for appointments and follow-up. When it fell open, I noticed there were gold stars on many of the pages. I asked him why a grown man would have gold stars pasted in his book. He told me he gave himself a gold star every day just for getting through the day. On the days when he made a sale, he put lots of gold stars on the page. He said it kept him focused on what went right in his life.

On the days things weren't going as well, he'd flip back through the pages and look at his gold stars. They would remind him of what was going right in his life and career. In spite of what was happening that day, he could see he was successful. What my dad was doing back then, though he didn't have a name for it, was "anchoring" his self-esteem.

When you anchor something, you are holding it in place. Just as a ship's anchor keeps it from drifting with the ever-present currents and tides, personal anchoring keeps you from drifting off your course. Every time my dad stuck a gold star on a page, he was telling himself, "I'm okay."

I was sixteen when I got my first job and I started the practice of giving myself stars, just like my dad. I've been doing it ever since. Today there are lots of motivational stickers that you can buy. They say things like "Way to Go!" "You're number one!" "Nice job!" "Awesome!" "Excellent!" "Hooray!" "You're a Superstar!"

So buy some stickers for yourself and when you achieve one of your goals, when you take positive action, or even when you just get through a rough day, put a sticker in your daily diary or your goal achievement journal. You'll be anchoring your own self-esteem. One of my former employees gave me a pair of gold star earrings as a thank-you gift when she left my employ, along with a card that said, "You were the best boss I ever had." I wear those earrings almost every day. When I look in the mirror and see them, it anchors my self-esteem. It tells me I was a great employer and the "best boss" she had ever had.

The Christmas before my life partner passed away, he gave me a necklace with a gold star. On the back of it was engraved, "Until the 12th of Never." The card read, "You are the best wife a man could ever have." The engraved message was his way of telling me he would love me forever.

Reminding ourselves of our achievements, our worth, and our value to others is imperative. Physical reminders help you concentrate on the positive things in your life and recognize that any feelings of inadequacy you may have are carry-overs from your past. So, keep those gold stars handy and reward yourself every time *you* show up for whatever it is you're doing!

Wright

So we've talked about being passionate and having a purpose and being a cheerleader. How do we gain the power that enables us to make a difference?

Moreo

Our power is in the way we communicate with others. I know you've heard it said that "what you are speaks so loudly, others can't hear what you are saying." In other words, our attitudes and our behaviors communicate a message about us.

We all know that our tone of voice, our body language, and our facial expressions give context to the words we speak. I know I have told you several stories, but I have one that will make my point more clearly than all the facts and figures I could give you.

During an international convention where I was a guest speaker, I was seated at the banquet head table next to two other speakers. One was a very successful and well-known car dealer, "Honest Bob." The other was a blind inspirational speaker. I was seated next to the blind man and on the other side of him was the car dealer. The dinner served was prime rib. We've all been to banquets and observed that every cut of prime rib doesn't come out exactly the same. Some are a little more rare. Well, the car dealer was served first, then the blind man, and then I was served. Just as the waiter was putting my plate down, I observed the car dealer switching his plate with the one they had served the blind man. At that point, the blind man turned toward me and said, "I guess he didn't like the way his food was cooked."

This was not only the worst demonstration of bad manners that I have ever seen, it was the best example of how our behavior communicates a message to others. What did this man's behavior communicate about him? I was in the market for a car, and had the money, but I wasn't about to buy a car from a man who would switch his food with a blind person. Can you imagine what kind of a car he might sell you? What he IS spoke louder than anything he could ever say. His behavior communicated so loudly that even a blind man could see it.

Wright

I hear so many people complaining about the way things are. So how do we communicate our purpose, passion, and power?

Moreo

When we live on purpose, when we live with enthusiasm and energy, we communicate our purpose, passion, and power. When we hold the vision of the life we desire for ourselves and others, we have the power to change the world. Our life itself communicates everything anyone needs to know about us.

In 1991, I was attending a banquet given by the *Sowetan,* a South African newspaper. The banquet was to honor women of South Africa who had made a difference to their communities. At this banquet, I sat across the table from a very different man—an elderly grey-haired man with a quiet, soft-spoken manner. He was not dressed in the typical business suit of most of the men there, but in a native shirt traditional of the men of his tribe— surprising for an event of this nature. On him, somehow it was not out of place. Though he wore an air of dignity and quiet intensity; conversation flowed easily and warmly around him. He gave his undivided attention to the story of each of the honorees. His applause was genuine and heartfelt. I watched as he rose to his feet to give a standing ovation to the dozen or so five- and six-year-old girls who had performed a ballet for our entertainment. Then he walked to the front of the stage and shook hands with each of those little girls.

I was so impressed with the manners, the humility, and the graciousness of this man who had endured so much to make a difference in his country and who had touched the lives of so many. There was no trace of bitterness or hatred for having just spent twenty-seven years in prison. There was only a powerful grace that engulfed the room emitting from this man who was soon to become the President of South Africa. I had been sitting across the table from Nelson Mandela.

Later when I read his book, *A Long Walk to Freedom,* I learned the depth of his purpose, the breadth of his passion, and the power of his commitment. He wrote about creative visualization, which he referred to as his vision of the future. He said, "I never seriously considered the possibility that I would not emerge from prison one day. I am fundamentally an optimist. Whether that comes from nature or nurture, I cannot say. Part of being optimistic is keeping one's head pointed toward the sun, one's feet moving forward."

There were many dark moments when his faith in humanity was sorely tested, but he did not give up to despair. He thought continually of the day when he would walk free. Over and over, he fantasized about what he would do.

What did this man know that filled him with determined optimism not experienced by other men? He used the same points we've been talking about today. He had a definite purpose in which he passionately believed. He kept his focus on his purpose, not on his surroundings and circumstances, and put his energy into the pursuit of that purpose, not on complaining or feeling sorry for himself. He never allowed the beliefs or actions of others to keep him from pursuing his goal. His quiet determination communicated loudly to his people, his captors, and the rest of the world who he was and what his intentions were.

During my stay in South Africa, I had two opportunities to visit the cell at Robben Island where Mr. Mandela had been incarcerated. It was three paces wide and six long, with no bathroom facilities. There was just a pot in the corner and a tired, little cot on which to sleep. As I stood in that cell, I wondered if under those circumstances you and I could have maintained a positive outlook and chosen to believe that one day we would make the dream of freedom come true.

I lived in South Africa throughout Mandela's reign as President. I watched and experienced his vision of a peaceful transition become reality. A person with lesser vision would never have been able to make this happen for an entire country.

Wright

But our circumstances are not as extreme as Mandela's.

Moreo

They sure aren't. That's just my point. Certainly, if he could imagine freedom for the people of a nation and have it come true, we should be able to imagine the successful future we desire and make it happen.

Remember in the beginning I asked you if you have ever said or done something that changed your life forever? Ask yourself this question: what am I going to do or say today that will change my life forever?

We all know or have been someone like one or several of the people in the stories I've told here. It is up to us to decide what kind of attitude, behavior, and communication we will demonstrate. Whatever choices you make, you *will* change your world. Will it be for the better?

Wright

So what can we do?

Moreo

Start now. Don't wait until you have the perfect circumstances. Don't underestimate yourself or overestimate others. You have as much ability and brainpower as anyone else. Turn off any negative or doubtful voices in your head. Put all your effort into what you do. Do it so well that others will see the value of doing it with you. Go after your purpose with passion. Take control of your attitude, your behavior, and your communication. Get out there. Do something.

Whether you choose to make a difference in the life of one person, one nation, or one world, when you choose to make a difference in your own life, align your goals with your purpose, and pursue your vision with passion, you will own your power and *know* that you *can't* fail. You have unlimited possibilities.

You are more than enough!

Wright

Judi, thank you for these valuable insights.

Moreo

Thank you. It has been my pleasure.

About the Author

JUDI MOREO is an award-winning speaker, author, and businesswoman. Prior to becoming a full-time professional speaker, Moreo was a successful entrepreneur. She built a virtual empire from a $2,000 investment. In 1986, the Las Vegas Chamber of Commerce honored her as Woman of Achievement—Entrepreneur. In 1992, she became an executive in one of South Africa's most prestigious media groups during the abolition of apartheid. In 2003, the U.S. Business Advisory Council named Moreo the "Nevada Business Person of the Year."

Judi is currently the President of Turning Point International. She has served as past president of the Las Vegas Professional Speakers Association and the International Association of Model Agents. In addition, she has served on the Boards of Directors of the World Modeling Association, Soroptimist International, the Chamber of Commerce Women's Council, and Women in Communication. The American Women in Radio and Television awarded her their "Outstanding Achievement and Community Service Award."

She is the author of seven books including her recent award winning, *You Are More Than Enough: Every Woman's Guide to Purpose, Passion, and Power.*

Her superb talent for customizing programs to meet organizational needs has gained her a prestigious following around the globe. Her passion for living an extraordinary life is mirrored in her zeal for helping others realize their potential and achieve their goals. With her dynamic personality and style, she has become an unforgettable speaker and inspiring motivator.

To Contact Judi Moreo...

Turning Point International
P.O. Box 231360
Las Vegas, Nevada 89105
Phone: 702.8962228
Fax: 702.8968871
judimoreo@yahoo.com

www.judimoreo.com
www.youaremorethanenough.com

ROADMAP *to* SUCCESS 12

An interview with...

Charles Lutz

David Wright (Wright)

Today we're talking with Chip Lutz, Master of Science and Education, CLL. He is the Chief Laughing Officer (CLO) and Founder of Covenant Leadership, LLC, and has had twenty-two years' leadership experience. A retired Navy officer, he has had two command tours and served as the Director of Security for Naval District Washington D.C., during the September 11, 2001, tragedy. He prides himself on keeping it light while getting the job done. A seasoned educator and trainer, he is currently adjunct faculty for two different universities and has taught over twenty different classes in leadership, management, human resource development, and organizational behavior. Chip's ability to relate, respond, and deal with audiences in a humorous, real way has been the key to his success as a leader and an educator.

Chip welcome to *Roadmap to Success!*

Chip Lutz (Lutz)

Thank you very much. I'm happy to be here.

Wright

How would you describe your success in leading and creating positive work environments?

Lutz

I have fun and I serve. No matter where I am or what I am doing, I try to enjoy myself. This isn't a dress rehearsal—it's the only life we have; it's important to make the most of it. I also try to keep an outward focus by serving. I serve those I work with; it's never about me, it's always about the team or the organization or the mission.

Lastly, it's important to remember that emotions are contagious and no one's emotions have more impact than the person leading the team. That is why, as a leader, I face situations optimistically. I couldn't go around like "Chicken Little" yelling, "The sky is falling, the sky is falling!" By remaining focused and positive in my leadership, the organizations I served were able to get things done! That is the example we want to set and how to go about creating an environment that is positive, energetic, and creative!

Wright

You say that tithing is important for leaders. What is tithing and how does it make a difference?

Lutz

Tithing is giving of yourself. It is investing the 10 percent that really matters. It's not that leaders give a 110 percent, but they give that 10 percent of themselves to ensure that the process, procedure, or operation is unequivocally theirs. It shows care, it models what needs to be done, and it is a legacy that lives on. It also builds a covenant of trust—creating a mutual appreciation between leaders and team members.

That's why I have been a success—leaders took the time to tithe and invest in me. I am paying forward the tithe they made to me through my investment in others.

Wright

So how does humor factor into the work equation?

Lutz

Humor is that "sweet spot" where people connect. It breaks down barriers, it is the shortest distance between two people, and it can help ease the most stressful of situations. We've all had times that were trying and we were really stressed. Then, out of nowhere, somebody finds something funny about the situation or you share a laugh with team members. Like magic, all of that anger and all of that stress is gone. It's not about you, it's not about me, it's about us.

For instance, I used to work for a very quiet man who would, when spoken to, sit and reflect on your statements before commenting. He took in everything said to him and always responded very literally. My off-the-cuff remarks would sometimes be taken at face value, which was neither funny nor was it understood. So I found myself feeling very uncomfortable and trying to be something that I wasn't when he was around. In short, I was miserable. I was at a loss as to how to handle myself (or the situation), so I called my previous boss and asked for his advice.

His advice was simple. He said, "Just be yourself. You are your best asset. Hell, I didn't like you at first until I got to know you." I sat and thought about it. He was right. I decided to change it right then. Luckily, that afternoon, the opportunity arose and I went for it. I was standing in the office eating a bag of Utz potato chips. You see, my last name is Lutz, so it's pretty close. While there, the Commodore walked through, pointed at the bag and me and said "Lutz—Utz."

I said, "Sir, did you know that my great-grandmother started the Utz potato chip line in her basement at the turn of the century?"

This caught his attention, he stopped and said, "No," and waited for me to finish.

I continued, "Yes, she started it and they were a huge success. Something about the oil she used. Anyway, as time went on she became concerned about how this new wealth would affect the family. She was, after all, starting to amass a small fortune and it was right around the time of the Lindbergh kidnappings. So, she decided to change the name to protect the family, you know, and she said, *"Get the L out of there."*

He stood there for a minute (reflecting as usual), looked at me, shook his head, chuckled, and then went to his office. It was the only time I ever saw him laugh—even a little bit! That was the turning point in our work relationship.

Humor (even poor attempts at it) breaks down barriers and connects people. It's that connection that matters. People are the most important asset of any organization and adding some fun, humor, and laughter helps bring out the best in people.

Wright

You've made a career of having fun, leading, and now you speak on creating positive work environments. You say that it all starts with a smile; how does that make a difference, and how does that contribute to positive mental attitude?

Lutz

A smile is the catalyst for all the positive emotions: faith, hope, love, creativity. These are all emotions that make us feel good, take the focus off of ourselves, and have more of an outward focus. The best part is that our body doesn't know the difference between a fake smile and a real smile. I would challenge anybody to go out there and spend a day smiling. Not a psychotic smile, but a smile that that is warm and inviting and says, "Hey, I'm happy that you're here, I'm happy that you're providing value to the organization, and I appreciate you as a person!" Spend a day doing that and see what a difference it makes. For your team, yes, but you'll feel better too!

Most of the war, so to speak, is won or fought in our head before it even begins, in that if we have a negative disposition toward something then it will typically turn out that way in the end. If we are pre-disposed to the outcome of something, that's the way it will be. If we're positive toward that disposition, then in the same respect, things will normally go the way that we want them to go. We have to consistently tell ourselves, "Hey, this is what I want." We want to act "as if" it's going to happen. We need to expect that greatness and it will happen, and it all starts with that simple smile.

When I go out and talk to people, I do a little smiling exercise. Even the most stoic of audience members will start laughing and connecting once we have done it. What our brain thinks is where our body goes.

Wright

You've got all kinds of acronyms, what is POB Squared?

Lutz

POB is Positive Organizational Behavior. POB epitomizes an organization that is strong in faith, hope, creativity, and resiliency. In today's society we are constantly in flux. Companies constantly have to adapt and this causes a lot of pressure and stress on people. We need to build organizations that are resilient, can manage change, and that can cope.

In my twenty-two years of leading people, what I've realized is that people are messy, organizations are full of people, ergo, organizations are messy places. If leaders lead with a smile and a positive mental attitude, they're building an organization that is strong in POB. This is a powerful force and much stronger than a normal organization. This organization has what I call POB Squared—it has twice the resilience, twice the faith, twice the confidence, and twice the trust. It's an organization that is productive, creative, and can withstand the changes and the winds that blow.

Wright

What do you mean when you say "the captain is the ship" and what factors go into creating or being "in atmosphere"?

Lutz

In the Navy we've always said that the captain is the ship, meaning that the captain is that organization. I've worked in a lot of different places, and in every place I've worked, the organization takes on the attitude and the personality of the person in charge. As I told you before in my potato chip story, I worked for a man who was very literal, reserved, and the command was very, very reserved. Mid-tour we had a leader who transferred in who was the exact opposite. He was large and in charge. He laughed, had fun, played his radio loud, and connected with people. He did a lot of leadership by walking around, and the command took on that personality—it went from being really, really reserved to an atmosphere of having fun and enjoying what you do, and we were a lot more productive than before. Further, we were a better team because we knew each other as people and not positions.

There are a lot of different factors, what I call "being in atmosphere." Emotions are contagious, and we as leaders need to keep in mind where our emotions are and how we project that to our people. If we're stoic and negative, that will pass on throughout the value chain, down to the lowest person. In the workplace there are two types of atmospheres: there are carriers and there are converters. Carriers are those people who take every negative thing and try to pass it on to the people around them like a disease. If they're having a bad day, they want everybody around them to have just as bad a day as they're having.

What we as leaders need is to be the second type of atmosphere—that of a converter. Converters do just that. They convert the atmosphere from a negative to a positive. For a converter, it doesn't make a difference if they went out to their car and had four flat tires, two feet of snow to shovel, or a slew of other misfortunes; when they get to work they're on and they're there for their people. They meet their team members with a smile, good eye contact, a positive disposition, and a little bit of humor on the ready.

Wright

Leaders have to have the *be*-attitudes—they must *be* in order to do; so what other advice would you give?

Lutz

I have seven key traits for positive living and positive leadership that I call the "Be-attitudes." To create positive behavior in the workplace, leaders at all levels must live it! The *Be-Attitudes* help, through mindful practice, to do just that. To help "operationalize" the attitude, I have an application for each that I call *"Humoration."* That's the application of fun, humor, laughter, and play to whatever you are doing. They are:

1. Be Positive: Happiness and friendliness are derivatives of an outward focus. Leaders keep the glass half full and pass that to their teams. A PMA (Positive Mental Attitude) is contagious and motivational.

   Humoration Leadership Key: Smile today. Meet someone new. Ask yourself (and your team) about some of the challenges you have been facing and fun/playful ways you can work on them. Be prepared—their ideas will blow you away!

2. Be an Atmosphere: Set the pace in having fun in the workplace. The light that you shine will lighten spirits, inspire creativity, and generate good morale.

   Humoration Leadership Key: Be unpredictably predictable. If your work is repetitious, whistle while you work, take a laughter break—celebrate it! Wear a crazy tie, make up new organizational words for processes, or have a weekly fun contest.

3. Be Respectful: The right to swing your fist ends where the other person's face begins. Embrace diversity! Especially the diversity of new thought and new ideas! Welcome resisters—they help to bring depth to the team experience.

   Humoration Leadership Key: Say thank you! Share a laugh with those who oppose change . . . you know who they are. Let those around you know you are human by sharing a funny story about yourself that applies to the situation they are facing.

4. Be a Sponge: Sponges absorb what is being said. Be quick to listen, slow to speak, and *always* slow to anger. Communication is a two-way street—keep both lanes open.

    Humoration Leadership Key: What are the distractions that keep you from listening to people? *Remove them!* Nothing opens up communication like humor. Invest the time in knowing what your team finds humorous and play to that. That investment will pay *huge* dividends in keeping both lanes of the road open.

5. Be a Willow: A willow is firm in its trunk and can sway gently with the breeze. The same applies to creating an atmosphere of flexibility. We remain strong in our core beliefs but can flex as the winds of change (and complications) come.

    Humoration Leadership Key: Where are the areas that you can flex? What can't you flex on? Where are the same areas for your team? How can you have fun in the flexing? Celebrate losses as well as wins.

6. Be a Champion: Know where you are going and let everyone else know too. Stand firm for your team and always remain loyal. Champion fun, creativity, and humor in the workplace.

    Humoration Leadership Key: Allow for your mistakes and allow for other's mistakes too. Take yourself lightly and the work seriously—but have fun doing it.

7. Be Yourself: Combine all of the "Be-Attitudes" into how you act as a leader. Start small, adapt to your own personality and style, and just be. Stay true and stay gold.

    Humoration Leadership Key: Take the advice from Mr. Wizard to Tudor the Turtle: "Be what you is, not what you is not, those that do this is the happiest lot."

We need to combine all of the *be*-attitudes into one package, practice them, and just *be*.

Success is about being yourself. It's about staying true to who we are and it's about being.

Wright

What is your equation for great communication?

Lutz

Let me start out on this with a story about my youngest son, Ben. He loves to sing and from an early age would quickly memorize the words to songs. A little while back, a song from the '80s came on the radio called "Funky Town" (by Lipps, Inc.) and I was surprised to hear him start singing the tune. When the song progressed to the part where they would sing *"talk about it talk about it,"* he started singing "taco body taco body."

I stopped, looked at him very seriously, and asked, "Taco Body?"

He returned my serious look and replied very matter of factly, "Yes, taco body!"

Isn't that what happens a lot in life? We are singing "talk about it" but everyone around us is hearing "taco body!" Why is this?

In communication, we have a sender, receiver, and some sort of "channel" (means of communicating the message) and hopefully, some means of feedback to keep the intended message the same as the perceived message—clarification of the message can be ever so helpful. What can garble all of this is what we call "noise." Noise is any distraction that keeps us from receiving the message. It can be the language we are using, our physical space (or perhaps how we are dressed), gender, actual noise, or what we are doing when we are speaking. In communicating, only 7 percent of what you say is important, 38 percent of the message comes from how you say it, and 55 percent comes from your body language while you say it.

In twenty-two years of leading people in the Navy, I have found that if you want to have everyone around you hear the song you are singing and not misinterpret the words, you should follow this equation:

$$Q2L + S2S + S2A = GR8\ COMMS$$

Quick to Listen + Slow to Speak + Slow to Anger = Great Communication. I keep this equation posted on my desk (or somewhere I can see it) so that I am ever mindful of how I *should* be communicating.

Wright

You were the Director of Security for the Naval District Washington during September 11, 2001. What was that like?

Lutz

I tell you, up until that point I had had a lot of leadership experience and I really thought that I knew what I was about as a leader. I took over as the Director of Security about a year prior to 2001 and I was handed an organization that was forty police officers shy. I was responsible for the safety and security of 25,000 people at nine different naval installations throughout the National Capital Region. When the USS Cole was attacked in August of 2000, we went to enhanced security procedures and quickly realized that we didn't have the training, we didn't have the manpower, and our morale was so low that it was nearly impossible to get the momentum needed to do anything.

It took a *lot* of positive energy and communication, but we set our course to be fully manned, trained, and to strategically place ourselves as the premier law enforcement agency within the National Capital Region. We worked hard and kept our eyes on the horizon.

In a year's time, we were fully manned, trained, and ready for anything that was to come at us—and it did. When the Pentagon was attacked on September 11, we were just two miles down the road and we knew what do to. We had been preparing for it and, not to sound boastful, we *rocked* at putting everything into place. That is the power of positive leadership and how a team can collaborate to meet the goal. It was a *"we"* evolution. The people we protected were stressed and we were stressed, but we were resilient, handling everything as it came while we protected and served.

It was a trying time but spirits were high because we were trained, people knew where they fell in the value chain, and they felt good about what they were doing. I learned a lot about myself as a leader during that time and we were able to get the job done.

Wright

So how does positive leadership get you through times like that?

Lutz

Well, as I said, it helped me connect with the team members I was working along side. That prior year, we had set the vision, we had worked collectively toward reaching it and it wasn't easy. Forty police officers shy is a lot. Most of my officers were working their normal forty hours a week plus maybe another extra twenty to twenty-five with a 9mm strapped to their hip. They were overworked, underpaid, and didn't have any quality of life. They were worn, they were tired, they were haggard, and I tell you, it was just an unsafe environment.

We collectively set our vision. Along the way there were hurdles (and there are always hurdles), but we met each of them with a positive disposition and learned something from each, so all of that positive energy and learning became a part of who we were. We had POB Squared—high levels of trust, confidence, faith (in one another and what we were doing), and we were resilient. At that point in time, we could have collectively conquered anything that came our way.

Wright

Not only are you a retired naval officer, you are also a Navy spouse, and your wife was deployed after our invasion of Iraq, leaving you as a single parent with four children. You say that the movie, *Old School,* saved your life. What's that all about?

Lutz

When my wife was deployed it was in March of 2003. Anybody who knows anything about military families knows that we're a pretty tight-knit group. We have four children (and the reason we have four children is because that way each kid has built-in playmates). When we go someplace, we transfer, and most of the time, it's just us. There are no friends and there are no other family members around—we're starting from scratch.

My wife is my best friend; we've been married for twenty years. She is not only my best friend, she's my confidante, she's my cheerleader, and I'm her cheerleader. We make a really good team. When she was sent overseas I was beside myself. At that time I was in command—I was the commanding officer of the Navy Reserve Center in Wichita, Kansas. I was the only officer stationed there, so I didn't have anybody to talk with about what I was feeling. All I knew was that my best friend was gone. I lost thirty pounds in thirty days. I couldn't eat, I couldn't sleep, and I was depressed.

I spent most of my days sitting in my office with the light off because I had to reserve that energy for when I went home to my kids so I could be "on." When I got home, I needed to be able to function, help with homework, do laundry, do all those things that you need to do, being both a mom and a dad.

Well, after about thirty days, I really was beside myself and I was having a hard time coping. I decided I just needed a mental break. So, I thought, "I'll go see the movie *Old School*,"—I needed to laugh! The movie itself is probably one of the dumbest movies ever made (but I'm a big Will Ferrell fan, so I like all his movies), but I laughed so hard it pulled me out of my depression.

That's when my thoughts on what humor and laughter can do for people cemented for me. You can be faced with the hardest problems in the world, but if you find the humor in what you are facing, take yourself lightly, and laugh, then you can make it through. Humor can be like a helicopter that takes you up above your problems so you can get perspective on what you are facing. That's because it's an impossibility for negative and positive emotions to occupy the same space at the same time in your head. That's not psychobabble, that's neuroscience.

We hardwire our brain in certain ways. If we focus on something, our brain begins to focus on it more and get more proficient at it. If we focus on our woes, we get better at focusing on them. If we learn to cope and heal our woes with humor, our brain develops to handle things that way. As I said before, how we think is where our body goes. This impacts all facets of our life. We aren't segmented to separate work, home, and other facets of life. They are all interrelated and have an affect on each. We have to hardwire ourselves to have the right attitude. That's why I developed my "Be-attitudes"—they are the culmination of all of my experiences with living well and leading well.

Wright

So why do you think it's important that leaders and emerging leaders hear your message?

Lutz

Well, right now we're in a war for talent. Any HR magazine—any workforce magazine—is going to tell you that it's hard to keep good talent. I'm always amazed at the stories I hear from people about what is going on in the world of leadership. By now, one would think that we would have evolved beyond some of the Neanderthal tactics that are used. If we're really serious about retaining talent, if we're really serious about moving ahead, if we're really serious about moving our organization to the next step, then we need to invest ourselves in what is going on. We have to employ positive leadership and incorporate my Be-attitudes into all that we do.

If you want positive out of the organization you have to put some in. It's just like when you squeeze an orange. When squeezed, what do you get? Orange juice. Why? Because that's what's in there, right? The same goes with organizations and with people. When they are squeezed you're going to get whatever's in there. If you're putting negatives into an organization, that's what you're going to get. But if you're infusing positives into an organization, when that organization or that person is squeezed, you're going to get the positives out. You're going to get that resiliency, you're going to get that positive attitude, you're going to get people who are saying, *"We rock!"*

Wright

If you had only one phrase to leave people with what would that be?

Lutz

I would say keep it real—you need to lead from the front, you need to laugh with your people, and you need to connect. That doesn't come from sitting behind a desk. That comes from being out there talking to people, talking about your vision, sharing yourself, your own experiences, sharing a laugh and tithing—giving the 10 percent of yourself.

Wright

Well, what a great conversation, Chip. I really appreciate the time you've spent with me here this morning answering all these questions.

Lutz

Thank you very much.

Wright

Today we've been talking with Chip Lutz. He is the Chief Laughing Officer (CLO) and Founder of Covenant Leadership, LLC. Chip has had twenty-two years of leadership experience. A seasoned educator and trainer, he is currently adjunct faculty for two different universities and has taught over twenty different classes in leadership, management, human resource development, and organizational behavior. As we have found out today, I think he knows what he's talking about.

Chip, thank you so much for being with us today on *Roadmap to Success!*

Lutz

Thank you.

About the Author

CHIP LUTZ is a speaker and trainer who's been there, done that, and has the uniform to prove it!

He is a leader who knows how to have fun and get the job done! Under his command as Commanding Officer of two different naval facilities, both his teams received national recognition for setting new standards of service while maintaining high morale and high retention among team members. He also knows about setting and meeting critical objectives during stressful conditions, having served as the Director of Security for Naval District Washington, D.C., during September 11, 2001, where he was responsible for the safety and security of 25,000 people on nine different naval installations in the National Capital Region.

He is a husband, father of four, visiting professor, author, and friend to his dog, Oliver. He does dishes, cooks, does laundry, but he hates to fold whites.

To Contact Chip Lutz...
4529 Harding Rd STE 120
Kenosha, WI 53142
262.960.2034
czar@funsquadinc.com
www.funsquadinc.com

ROADMAP *to* SUCCESS 13

An interview with...

Martha R. A. Fields

David Wright (Wright)

Today we're talking with Martha R.A. Fields. Martha is president, CEO and founder of Fields Associates Inc. She has served as a management subject matter expert for the Harvard Business School. She is a much sought after keynote speaker. In addition to *Roadmap to Success,* she is the author of three books: *Indispensable Employees: How to Hire Them. How to Keep Them; Love Your Work By Loving Your Life,* and a novel, *Dancing with the Sun.* Her company's mission is to connect human resources with business strategies to make a positive, memorable difference within people, organizations, and the world. Martha is an internationally recognized expert in human resources, healthcare, and diversity/globalization. Her impressive list of clients includes Fortune 500 companies, non-profits, and ivy-league schools. Her clients range from Harvard, Fidelity Investments, NASA, Massachusetts

Medical Society, and the *New England Journal of Medicine* to the US Postal Service, Shell Oil, STAPLES, Harley-Davidson Inc. and MITRE, a seven-time winner of Fortune's 100 Best Companies to Work For. Prior to starting her firm, she served as a Vice President at a Harvard Medical School affiliated teaching hospital.

Martha, welcome to *Roadmap to Success*!

Martha R. A. Fields (Fields)

Thank you David, it's great to be here.

Wright

So, tell our readers and me about your background and what lessons you have learned from life as you've traveled down the road to success.

Fields

My road to success has been unconventional and filled with diversity. I am an African American/Native American woman. In addition, my great-great-grandmother was Caucasian. I grew up in a military family and lived around the world. I spent part of my childhood during the 1960s in Okinawa, an island of Japan. The sixties were a very interesting time to live in Asia. It was there that I learned how to maneuver in an international environment.

My family came back to the United States in 1964, which was the year after President John F. Kennedy was assassinated. Life at first in the United States seemed foreign to me. I was like an immigrant coming into an alien land. In this country, people like me were called "Negro" or "colored," but in Okinawa you weren't black or white, but just American. I had to become acquainted with the distinctions that were made in the United States about people because of the color of their skin. That experience in my youth taught me a simple but valuable lesson about success. I discovered that to be successful in one part of the world does not necessarily translate into success in other areas of the globe.

I went to nine schools in twelve years. In 1971, I moved to Boston, Massachusetts, to attend Boston University. As Baby Boomers, during that time, we went through a lot of social unrest and many of us were looking to change the world. I learned at that stage of my life that success was also about dealing effectively with people from a variety of perspectives and backgrounds. College life certainly exposed me to that element of success, as I lived around people who were into causes like women's liberation and the Black Power Movement and to those, who like Bill Clinton, were smoking but not inhaling.

At age thirty-three, I became a Vice President at a Harvard Medical School affiliated teaching hospital. In the Harvard hospital system, I was a young person dealing with a lot of older people I had to supervise. If you look at organizations today, so many people are successful at a young age and are in charge of people who are old enough to be their grandmas or grandpas. In that venue, I learned that to be successful, you don't always have to be right and win. I got very good at deciphering which battles to fight and from which ones to retreat. Many of the physicians I worked with at that time were like gods to their patients. Individuals, for example, would come from around the world to our hospital to be treated. Many of the physicians were the only doctors in the entire universe for whom some of our patients could look to restore their sight or hearing.

Working in healthcare taught me that success is nothing without your health. I remember once engaging in a lively conversation with a very famous physician who was a Chief of Service. I asked him, given what he knew about people losing their sight or hearing, which one is worse to lose? He didn't want to answer my question. After I probed deeper, he said, "I guess hearing because people seem so isolated when they can't listen to others in the world. You should be very glad every day for your sight and hearing because without your health, success means nothing."

The sweet taste of success soured for me after I fell and broke my ankle in December of 2003 during one of the worst snowstorms in Boston history. After that accident, I faced a year of rehab and had to learn to walk again. The physician who performed my ankle surgery and got me walking on the road to success again was Dr. Lars Richardson. He was a success in his own right and served as the physician to the Boston Bruins hockey team. After months of not walking and experiencing life via an air cast, crutches, and a wheelchair, on a visit to Dr. Richardson's office, he asked me a key question about my recovery. "Martha," he said, "How are you doing?" I replied that I was feeling great and ready to walk again. He praised me and said something very insightful. He told me that I had the power of positive thinking and that I would absolutely walk again and probably ahead of schedule.

The good doctor went on to tell me that while medical research supports the notion that patients who practice the power of positive thinking tend to manage their illnesses better, he didn't need to see any research studies to know the healing power of positive thinking. Dr. Richardson said that from his experience if he asked a patient about how she or he is doing and the reply is, "Awful," and the patient "just knows" he or she is going to die, 100 percent of the time the patient does expire.

A common characteristic of people who achieve lasting success is that they believe and practice the power of positive thinking. Much research has been conducted on the relationship between success and positive thinking. Researchers have demonstrated that success is as much about what you do as about what you think. They have also found that training your brain to look, act, and feel successful is of utmost importance for anyone looking to achieve long-term success.

Motivational gurus explain the power of the brain and a positive attitude in a variety of ways such as:

- You are what you think
- What you give out, you get back
- You attract what you think about

By joining the positive people's club, you can improve your chances both at attracting and sustaining a successful life. The notion of positive thinking and success also extends to how successful people view and treat others in the world. In his book, *Gung Ho*, Ken Blanchard offers some valuable advice to success seekers. He states: "Catch people doing something right, then you'll find magnificence in people."

Wright

You talk a lot about the mistakes people make in their careers as "career bloopers," and I love that term. So what are some of the career bloopers that successful people make?

Fields

I define career bloopers as embarrassing mistakes that prevent success in careers and in life. The value of bloopers is less about the mistakes that people make and more about how and what was learned from them. One of my favorite sayings is "you learn as much, if not more, from the downs as the ups in life."

One major career blooper people make is not planning and preparing for success. Successful people understand that they *must* spend time cultivating their career and life. Unfortunately, people spend more time preparing for a vacation or buying a new pair of shoes, car, coffeemaker, or an outfit for a special occasion than they do in planning their careers. Taking the necessary time to think about where you are going in your life and career is a critical element of success. Many of us may give some thought about our career plans once a year during our performance reviews at work. Given the fast pace of change in the world and workplace, I believe it is necessary to review your career and life plans at least twice a year. I also feel that successful people live by this motto: "if you fail to plan, then you plan to fail."

It is my belief that career and life success come from possessing passion. A career blooper that many people make is to only go for a career that will give them a fat paycheck and financial security, but not to pursue a job or occupation for which they possess passion.

If you don't know what your passion is, try this simple exercise: Take a moment to jot down one or two things that make your heart smile. By that, I mean, what makes you happy, not only when you've had a bad day, but a horrible year. Further, ask what it is that really lifts you up and can make you feel that this is what you were sent on earth to do. Having passion about what you're doing is an essential ingredient for success. Some of us are very lucky and we do find the perfect career. For others, what is a positive career today becomes an unfulfilling one tomorrow. A career blooper some people make is not understanding that you can lose passion for something you are doing and that is okay. What is not all right is to remain stagnant and not move on in life once the passion and thrill are gone.

Another career blooper that people often make is that they don't persevere or persist in the career they truly love and believe in during bad times. I love to read biographies and one common element of successful people is that they persevere during bad times. Throughout history, successful people have proven that failure often leads to success. Legend has it that Walt Disney went bankrupt seven times before he was successful in his endeavors such as Disneyland, which has delighted people for over one hundred years. Berry Gordy worked at the auto factories in Detroit and was a boxer before his life hit a high note when he founded his Motown record label.

Successful people really understand that the road to success is about persevering and persisting during the ups, downs, twists, and turns of life's roadways.

Wright

So what is the key to staying successfully employed?

Fields

You've got to keep on top of your game and stay one step ahead by constantly assessing your career goals in relationship to the road you want your life to travel down. It is also important to take some rest stops on your journey too. Assess where you are in life, but also look at how far you've traveled toward your destination. I often reflect on what happened to many of us and our career journeys after September 11, 2001. Our jobs were one way prior to that date, but after that period of time, many of us had to change what we were doing if we wanted to be successful.

Staying successful is about understanding the world and the marketplace and where I am in relationship to both. It is also about being able to answer these questions even after major earth-shattering and life-changing events like September. 11:

- What must I do to be successful?
- What does the market place want and need?
- How can I be successful in changing the world and workplace?

In addition, life's journey may throw some unexpected detours like a September 11, which are beyond our control.

Wright

So what expert advice would you give people about planning their careers?

Fields

Whether you are sixteen, twenty-six, or sixty-two, take time to record your career and life goals. Experts say those things that are written down get accomplished. You may also want to create a personal action plan that identifies the steps you will take to achieve your goals. This document becomes your road map to success. Your plan should also indicate when you will begin and end each task as well as indentify how you will measure your success. In other words, when you reach the final destination that you have mapped out, what will success look and taste like to you?

I specifically carve out two times during the year to conduct this activity. One time is at the beginning of the year, when I'm doing my New Year's resolutions and during the summertime as I plan for the fall and winter months. There is nothing magical about the time period you select to review your plan. Find a time that works for you. Don't forget to check with others whose opinions you respect about where you are in terms of your road map to success progress. Mentors, loved ones, trusted friends, and colleagues can also help by providing suggestions to help you enjoy your ride toward career and life success. Networking with others can be a powerful way to execute your success strategy and personal action plan.

Wright

Why do you believe that networking is such a powerful ingredient to success?

Fields

One thing I've discovered is that success is about what *and* who you know. I've found this to be the case when I've worked as an executive inside organizations as well as an entrepreneur. Quite honestly, there are a lot of people who have knowledge and expertise, but if they don't have a powerful network of people to help them open doors for business, they're not going to be very successful. Networking is absolutely essential for work *and* life success.

Today our jobs, lives, and everything are so complex and people are time bankrupt. They are not taking the steps to meet people and develop deep and meaningful interpersonal relationships. You can't have a great network if you don't take the time to cultivate and then maintain it. This means staying in touch in a variety of ways—including cyberspace *and* face-to-face interactions. Success today is about making sure that you interact and have people from throughout the world in your address book. Look at how our society has evolved. It's not just about who we know in the United States, but also how we interact with individuals from around the world.

If you are employed, don't forget to network with individuals who are in different departments and disciplines within your organization. For example, if you are in marketing or sales, are you also networking with people in human resources or finances? In addition, make sure that you are getting out to network with people outside of your organization and those from a variety of industries and occupations.

I believe that people who are accomplished at networking don't operate by what I call the WIIFM or What's In It For Me? Instead, they abide by the WIIFYAM—What's In It For You and Me? Effective networking is a give-and-take relationship.

Networking across generations is also important. Whether you like MTV or AARP, it's very important that you network with and get to know people who are much younger or older than you. Why? Currently there are four generations in the workplace and the marketplace. So if I am a Baby Boomer in my fifties and I really don't know how to deal with younger people, I am not going to be successful in years to come. As I mentioned earlier, if I am a young person who is supervising people who are my grandma's or grandpa's age, and I don't really understand that generation, and network with them, I'm not going to be successful at leading and managing that generation if I don't understand how to best motivate them.

Success can be achieved at any age. The lives of Martin Luther King, Jr., President John F. Kennedy, Princess Diana, and Mozart were cut short. Although none of them lived until age forty, the impact of the work they accomplished while on earth is everlasting. People can also obtain or sustain great success during their twilight years. The Rolling Stones, Tina Turner, Paul McCartney, Diana Ross, and Little Richard all continue to rock the world and they are in their sixties. Astronaut-turned-politician, John Glenn, went back up into space when he was a senior citizen.

To be truly successful in our careers, we must practice seeing the world from other people's points of view—preferably a global perspective. Expanding your network with diverse people—individuals around the globe and those who are very different from you—is extremely important. Our perception of reality is colored by our own set of experiences. By putting yourself in the other person's shoes (or moccasins as Native Americans say,) you will expand your horizons and enhance your journey on your road to success. There are billions of people who live in places like China, India, and Africa. If you don't know anyone from these countries, look at how many people you are missing out on knowing and who could potentially help you on your road to success.

The next time you are having a hard time accepting another person's difference of opinion, remember this exercise. I borrowed the image below from Stephen Covey's 1989 bestseller, *The 7 Habits of Highly Effective People.* When you look at  this drawing, do you see a young woman, an old woman or both? The answer is that there is a young *and* old woman in this picture.

Being able to see *both* points of view, a young woman and an old woman, is a skill you'll need to develop. This exercise demonstrates how difficult it can be to see another person's point of view. If the first image you saw was the young woman, your mind will be conditioned to see the young woman again the next time. It may take effort and practice to see the older lady. It is like a right-handed person writing left-handed—it can be done, but it takes concentration.

Likewise, a Baby Boomer female who may have experienced gender bias herself may be more sensitive to issues of discrimination than a Baby Boomer male who may never have encountered the proverbial "Glass Ceiling."

Imagine a multicolored beach ball with bands of white, red, and yellow coloring. Depending on where you stand, you may see a different combination of colors than the person beside you standing at a different angle. Who is right? You both are correct. Remember the drawing of the old and young woman or the beach ball example on your road to success when you need to consider a different point of view.

Wright

Why do you feel that successful people don't just wait for a job or a career to find them?

Fields

Many successful people understand the need to take charge of their career by becoming the CEO of their own destiny. Early in my career I was a human resources executive, and I can't tell you the number of people who would become upset because they had trained people only to see those individuals jump over them and be promoted to higher positions. Many of these people would say, "I don't understand. How is it that they got the job and I didn't?"

I would reply to them, "Did you apply for the job?"

They would respond, "Well, no."

I would then say, "Maybe that's the reason why they got the job and you didn't."

The moral to this story is: next time, go to Human Resources and apply for the job—don't expect that someone is just going to hand the job to you.

If you are simply waiting for a job to come to you, sometimes that will happen, but more than likely that's not the case. You've got to create your own destiny. For some people, this may mean coming to a realization that they will never progress any further in a job or position. In other words, they've hit the proverbial "glass or concrete ceiling." Even successful people reach a point in organizations where they're not going to move into jobs at a senior level, and they're ready to do just that. They may need to adjust to a hard cold reality that the grass may indeed be more lush and beautiful in a new organization. Many of them actually leave their jobs to form their own companies. Unfortunately, the reality is that for some to be successful, it may be necessary to move out in order to advance upward.

Wright

One of your books is titled, *Indispensable Employees: How to Hire Them, How to Keep Them.* Do you really believe that successful people are indispensable?

Fields

Some people do possess skill sets and knowledge that make them indispensable; however, the shelf life for someone who is indispensable is not necessarily guaranteed to last forever. In today's complex world and workplace, individuals can be a hero today and a zero tomorrow. In my book, *Indispensable Employees: How to Hire Them. How to Keep Them*, I looked at what characteristics make people indispensable and successful. People who become successful know how their jobs fit onto the mission, vision, and values of their organizations. They also make sure that those items are in line with their personal values and career and life goals.

When traveling down the road to success, rather than waiting for a job or career opportunity to find you, locate the opportunity and open the door yourself. All too often, people who are not successful in life or in their careers are waiting for others to discover their talents and present them with a promotion or career advancement opportunity that just never materializes.

Indispensable employees are constantly trying to solve organizational problems, and see them as challenges to be conquered. Hard work goes hand-in-hand with success. Perseverance, particularly in the wake of bad times and failure, is very important. In addition, indispensable employees are flexible and are continuous learning sponges. They want to constantly soak up and acquire knowledge around new and different things.

If you're an entrepreneur, I think these things also hold true in regard to your ability to be indispensable to your customers and clients. Clients' wants and needs evolve, so make sure that you're changing to meet your customers' desires. Constantly assessing what you're doing to provide outstanding customer service is very important for success in the business world.

Wright

With so many ups and downs in the world, what other advice do you have about success and persisting and perseverance during bad times?

Fields

Winston Churchill once said, "Success is going from failure to failure without loss of enthusiasm." I think that is so important, but it's also extremely hard to do. One of the key elements of success is to learn to rebound from failure and turn tragedy into triumph. History is full of powerful lessons from people who did not give up, but persevered as they traveled down the road to success.

For example, Michael Jordan did not make it onto his high school basketball team. Imagine basketball without the likes of Michael Jordan. What would have happened if he didn't follow his basketball hoop dream after that rejection? There is a quote from Michael Jordan that explains the importance of learning from failure. He said, "I've missed more than nine thousand shots in my career, I've lost almost three hundred games, and twenty-six times I've been trusted to take the game winning shot and missed. I failed over and over and over again in my life and that is why I have succeeded."

Successful people know that when we break down on our road to success it is important to pull off the road and fix the problem. After that we must pick ourselves up, dust ourselves off, and start all over again. If you truly believe that what you are doing is right and it is your purpose and what you were sent on this earth to do, if you persist, you can overcome adversity and become successful.

When he invented the lightbulb, it has been said that Thomas Edison tried over two thousand experiments before he got the lightbulb to work properly. Someone once asked him why he failed so many times and how did it feel? Edison replied that he never failed once in inventing the lightbulb; it just took him two thousand times to actually make it happen. The lives of Jordan and Edison provide excellent examples of how we can navigate the highways of life if we plan then persevere as we execute our personal road map to success.

Wright

Your last book was titled *Love your Work by Loving your Life*. What exactly does that mean? Do you have to integrate work and life to be successful?

Fields

I truly believe that if people embrace and love what they're doing in terms of their life that they will find happiness and fulfillment in their work. Notice I didn't say "love your life by loving your work." Think about it: almost no one says on their deathbed, "I wish I had put in more time at work." They do, however, often lament that they didn't pay enough attention to their loved ones or spend more time being a better spouse, partner, or friend. Many successful people take the time to examine how to integrate their work with their lives.

Often, people today are feeling time bankrupt, and have pressures to work during off work hours and when at home. If work starts to overshadow your life to a point where you are feeling you don't have a life outside of your job, it is time to ask yourself a hard question: "Is my work driving me down my road to success or hindering me from reaching my destination?"

If after contemplating that tough question, you cannot answer how what you are doing in your work is really contributing to what you were sent on earth to do, then you've got some work to do. This may mean you need to do something to better integrate your work and life and you may need to reverse the direction in which you are driving.

Some people talk about work-life balance. I don't believe in such a thing. I don't think that most of us have lives and work that can be balanced like the scales of justice. I believe it is more about work and life integration— it's more like an act I used to see years ago on the *Ed Sullivan Show.* There was a guy on that television show, who put about five poles on the stage. In his performance, he would put dishes on the five poles, one by one. So he'd place a plate on the first pole and he'd spin it around and once it was going smoothly, he'd put the second dish on the second pole, etc. Eventually, when he got around to the fifth pole, and they were all spinning in sync, he would put his hands out and would say, Tada! Most of our lives are such that not all of our plates are spinning in perfect unison all the time. Every now and then we have one of those Tada! moments where we can put our hands out and are happy that all of our life's plates are spinning well.

In my life, I may be spinning my first plate, which is getting my child ready to go to college next year. Once that plate is spinning, I move to my second spinning plate and continue along my road map to success until I get to my fifth plate where, if I'm lucky, I'll have a brief Tada! moment. Instead of trying to make sure that at all times everything is totally balanced and the scales are equal, I just try to pay attention to keeping each plate spinning along and celebrate and cherish those brief Tada! moments.

Wright

What advice would you have for people about how to obtain lasting success?

Fields

Lasting success is about knowing who you are, what you're about, and understanding why you were sent on this earth. It's also about being clear on what makes your heart smile in the face of adversity. Hollywood stars from Oprah to Dr. Phil and Brad Pitt to Bill Crosby will tell you that even if success came to them early in life, it took years to become an "overnight" sensation.

I read an article in the summer 2007 edition of the *Harvard Business Review*, titled, "Success That Lasts." They actually looked at a number of distinct components for lasting success. They included factors such as:

- *Happiness*
- *Achievement*
- *The significance of what are you doing that positively affects those you care about*
- *Legacy*

I believe people have lasting success when they are able to achieve these four factors.

I feel that legacy is an especially important success factor. At some point, each of us will expire from this earth and what's left behind of your life is your legacy. There's a great poem that sums up what I think about success and what people can do to successfully reach their desired destinations on their road map to success. The poem is attributed to Ralph Waldo Emerson. It goes like this:

Success

To laugh often and much:

To win the respect of intelligent people and the affection of children;

To earn the appreciation of honest critics

and endure the betrayal of false friends;

To find the best in others;

To leave the world a bit better,

Whether by a healthy child, or a garden patch

or a redeemed social condition;

To know even one life has breathed easier because you lived.

That is to have succeeded.

Wright

Well, what a great conversation. I really appreciate all this time you've taken to answer all these questions. I have learned a lot and I think you know what you're talking about.

Fields

Well, thank you so much, David. You interview so many famous people, I am honored by your heart-felt compliment.

Wright

Today we've been talking with Martha R. A. Fields. Martha is President, CEO, and Founder of Fields Associates. She is an internationally recognized expert in human resources, healthcare, and diversity globalization. I believe that you will agree with me, readers, that she does indeed have great ideas and I'm going to listen to her advice.

Thank you so much, Martha, for being with us today on *Roadmap to Success*.

Fields

David, I just love what you and your company are doing. Thank you for letting me be a part of this fabulous project with Stephen Covey and Ken Blanchard. It's been a wonderful experience.

About the Author

MARTHA R.A. FIELDS is president, CEO, and founder of Fields Associates, Inc., which is located in Harvard Square. She is an internationally acclaimed author, motivational speaker, management consultant, and expert on leadership, human resources, diversity, and globalization. She also has served as subject matter expert for Harvard Business School. Martha has been quoted in such publications as *Fortune, Kiplinger,* and the Boston Globe. Prior to starting her firm, she was a healthcare executive and served as a Vice President at a Harvard Medical School affiliated teaching hospital. For six years she chaired the prestigious Linkage Summit on Leading Diversity and worked with such icons as Maya Angelou and the late Coretta Scott King. Martha prides herself as a "corporate cupid," mentor, and strong supporter of social responsibility. A self-described citizen of the world, she has traveled widely to such locations as the Amazon jungle, Jamaica, the Andes Mountains, and has even lived in Okinawa. Utilizing her worldwide experiences and her skills as a mother of a college student, she assists organizations and people to make a memorable positive difference in the world.

To Martha R. A. Fields . . .
124 Mount Auburn Street
Suite 200 North
University Place, Harvard Square
Cambridge, MA 02138
Phone: 617-576-5733

ROADMAP to SUCCESS

14

An interview with...

Vickie Milazzo

David Wright (Wright)

Today we're talking with Vickie L. Milazzo, RN, MSN, JD. Vickie is the founder and owner of Vickie Milazzo Institute. She is credited by *The New York Times* with pioneering a new specialty practice of nursing, legal nurse consulting, in 1982. *Inc.* recognized Vickie as one of the nation's Top 10 Entrepreneurs and named her company one of the Top 5000 Fastest-Growing Private Companies in America. She is a nationally acclaimed keynote speaker and the author of the *Wall Street Journal* best-seller, *Inside Every Woman: Using the 10 Strengths You Didn't Know You Had to Get the Career and Life You Want Now* (currently in its seventh printing).

Vickie, you're an *Inc.* Top 10 Entrepreneur, a *Wall Street Journal* best-selling author plus you're known in the nursing industry as "The Pioneer of

Legal Nurse Consulting." Surely you relied on some experts along the way. So why is your advice contrary to what other experts have been telling us?

Vickie L. Milazzo (Milazzo)

My success, like that of many entrepreneurs, is built on challenging the experts—not relying on them. The whole concept of legal nurse consulting was contrary to what attorneys accepted as an industry standard. Typically, they relied on doctors to try to make sense of medical records. How crazy is that? Doctors don't even *read* the medical records. Physicians' time is way too expensive and attorneys won't often get objective opinions because doctors are way too protective of each other.

In healthcare, the registered nurse (RN) is the only healthcare provider who knows everything that is going on with the patient. Registered nurses are the ones with hands-on information and who have face-to-face, 24/7 contact with patients; they are the only healthcare providers who ever read the entire medical record. RNs not only have the expertise to uncover vital facts and key pieces of information that can make or break an attorney's case, they're cost-effective too.

Shortly after I began consulting with attorneys on the medical issues in their cases, I recognized this widespread need that nurses could fill in the legal arena, so I began training other nurses on how to consult with attorneys. Soon I expanded my training to include audio and video formats to reach those nurses who couldn't travel to my seminar locations. The response was overwhelming.

Seven years later I realized the need for not only the standardized education I was providing, but also for levels of competency and quality evaluation. So I revamped my educational program and created the first national certification program that trains RNs to become Certified Legal Nurse Consultants[CM]. Since then I've trained thousands of nurses, many who quickly ratcheted their $40,000-a-year nursing salary into a high six-figure income. Some have even created $1,000,000 businesses! My success is their success.

Wright

So you took a big idea, ran with it, and it paid off. Would you advise others to act on their big ideas?

Milazzo

Big ideas, small ideas—the key word is "act." America wasn't built by experts. Our Founding Fathers weren't expert politicians. Our captains of industry weren't experts in their fields. Our best inventors weren't experts. America and almost all of our achievements here in the United States were built by a nation of amateurs, tinkerers, and inventors constantly poking, prodding, testing, and discarding what didn't work.

Contrary to what most people believe, it doesn't take an Einstein to spawn brilliant ideas, and even Einstein wasn't born an expert. Experts and extraordinary people can and do wake up with dumb ideas while ordinary people can and do wake up with extraordinary ideas.

The reality is that there are very few Einsteins out there and a lot more ordinary people like you and me. As I said, ordinary people wake up with ideas every day; some are brilliant ideas, some are ordinary ideas and some are just plain dumb. But even a small, ordinary idea can pay off huge when you have the courage to own it and take action.

Every woman hates panty lines, but only one woman acted on that little idea to create a multimillion-dollar business. Spanx is a great example of someone having an ordinary idea and acting on it to make it big.

In my company, I encourage everyone in every department to speak up when they have a new concept and to verbalize their objections when they think something isn't working. As individuals, you'll advance your career faster by being an idea person than by being a nose-to-the-grindstone, head-in-the-sand grunt. As a CEO I appreciate my hard workers, but I appreciate even more the hard workers who generate million-dollar ideas that keep us all working hard. If a $50,000-per-year employee brings me a $1,000,000 idea, I'm not sweating her salary.

We constantly triage ideas—tossing up the hottest, edgiest, most financially promising and time-sensitive ideas first. We have to. If we acted on every excellent idea we generated, we'd be juggling so many balls in the air that we'd need catcher's mitts to keep them moving. Instead, we throw them around and get everyone's opinion, which can get messy. Business, like life, is messy. If it's too sterile, if people tiptoe around an idea, oohing and aahing instead of kicking its tires a little, the business goes static. I always know I'm onto a truly innovative idea when the majority of my staff is freaking out over it.

We also destroy ideas on a regular basis. What seemed hot and financially promising at first toss can suddenly turn cold and costly when examined from all angles. We've yanked more than one project off the drawing board or out of production after recognizing it would not be the moneymaker we initially expected. An important part of being successful is being willing to ditch a bad idea, even if it was yours.

Wright

It's easy for you to try out ideas and ditch them because your company has the budget to fund it. Don't you agree that "it takes money to make money"?

Milazzo

People think they have to invest a lot of money to make it in business or get to the top of their career. And that stops them from doing anything. Of course, money is relevant, but the best investment is the one you make in yourself first. The best investment isn't always in a product, office space lease, or a computer. It's not what you invest in, but how you manage your total investment—time, money, and resources—that counts.

I started my business with $100 in my savings account. I worked out of my one-bedroom condo. I didn't lease office space or buy office furniture or a computer. Instead, every evening, after pulling a ten-hour shift at the hospital, I set up shop and ran my business. Every night I cleared it all away. Only after I had earned my first million dollars did I take on the overhead of leased office space. As I made profits, I used a portion of that money to get to the next level. Now it's a $17 million education business.

A Harvard student invests nearly $200,000 in an education, and that investment will pay off. But so will an education from your state university, if you actively use it. I attended a small, private university in Houston and yet I earn more than most ivy-league graduates. Why? Because I believe that *taking action* makes money. By taking the right action steps you can usually advance a good idea without putting your banker in a new Ferrari. Notice that I qualified this statement: you must take the "right" action steps. In business or career success, you have to put adequate focus into each action step you take and those you choose not to take.

Wright

How do you know which action steps to take?

Milazzo

That's where your road map—your business plan—comes in. You have to chalk your walk. You have to visualize your destination and plan at least the first important steps that will take you into that future. You also have to record the steps you make so that you can look back at where you made the right choices and where you missed. No road is ever without a few bumps, and no road map can prepare you for every detour you'll encounter; but even the most crudely drawn plan is better than running ahead blindly or not going for the run at all. You also have to access your ability to detach—to honestly and brutally assess when something is not working and ditch it immediately.

Wright

Ah ha, then you agree with other experts who say that "if you fail to plan, you plan to fail."

Milazzo

Some experts would have you perfecting the plan...perfecting the plan...perfecting the plan until your idea is as dead as last month's bouquet, or worse, someone else had the same good idea and has already pounced on it. Many of my students get so bogged down in planning that they never get their business off the ground. Don't continuously revise and rethink. In the beginning of any new venture the reality is that it doesn't really matter what you do—it just matters that you do something every day. Plan your major actions and the specific initial steps that take you forward, then ditch perfectionism and get moving. Plan your career path, but even if you don't have all the answers, start taking action. You have to set out on the path before you can clearly see your next steps.

Avoid following a rigidly drafted plan that will take you right past some of the places you would most want to explore. Inject flexibility into your plan. Look around and assess where you are. Contrary to what many experts believe, deviating from a plan can sometimes get you where you want to go faster, smarter, and with more spectacular results.

My first business plan was handwritten on a single page. Now it's sixty-three pages. As your business or career develops, you'll have roads going in many directions and more complex decisions to make. Don't expect to predict today in agonizing detail where your working idea will take you. How can you know explicitly what opportunities will pop up tomorrow or who you'll meet who can influence your progress?

Wright

That brings up another adage, "It's not *what* you know, it's *who* you know." You must have known quite a few lawyers when you started.

Milazzo

I didn't know any attorneys! I didn't live in their neighborhoods or get invited to their parties. I didn't even think I knew anyone who knew an attorney. That *false-ism* is a leftover from the 1980s, when "networking" was the buzzword among out-of-work professionals vying for consulting or other business. They gathered at events to eat, drink, pass out business cards, and ask for referrals. While referral and word-of-mouth promotion are still the strongest and most cost-effective ways of building a career or a client base, networking events often do little more than waste your time. That's when networking is *not* working.

Contrary to what people who wrote the books on networking say, a better use of your time is to examine "what you know" or "what you can do well" and find an employer or client willing to pay for that knowledge. One example is technology. Company executives are far too busy to keep up with changes in hardware, software, telecommunications, multimedia, wireless applications, or online storage. Conversely, the "geek squad" is often clueless concerning softer skills such as writing, graphic design, personal communications, and human resources. What you know that others don't know and what you can do well that others can't will create opportunities for you. That's not to say that "*who* you know" isn't a valuable resource. Once you package your knowledge and expertise for a niche market, you can rap on the right doors and sell it.

Wright

Did I hear you right—networking is *not* working?

Milazzo

Networking is overrated. I've seen people spend countless hours in meaningless conversation with people they really don't want to spend time with while trying to build a business or a career. The best way to network is to spend time with potential prospects. If your prospects are attorneys, hang out at the courthouse. If your prospects are your managers and CEO, hang out around the office after hours when you may have an opportunity to "bump" into them and share an idea. Target your networking to where it will make the most impact.

Be cautious also with established networking groups such as associations and with how much power you give them over your success. Sometimes when you're within a network, and your ideas don't align with that network, people can try to persuade you to their side. Or even worse, the network will try to eliminate you or blackball you in your industry. Your idea, your career plan, your business model has to be strong enough to stand alone without network support. That's the entrepreneurial secret that has helped to build this country.

Even after pioneering the industry of legal nurse consulting, I took a grand departure from what others believed our industry needed. I believed we needed a standardized certification program. They disagreed. So what did I do? I ticked some people off by creating what became the first and most widely recognized certification for legal nurse consultants. The less approval is important to you, the freer you are to succeed. I believe in inviting my staff to disagree with me and they are quite comfortable doing so. My ideas often get shot down. We are a stronger company for that.

As I started to achieve success, I began to realize that my position would be stronger if I didn't rely on a network to advance my company, but instead built a strong company of free-thinkers. Don't let association groupthink dictate what is accepted or appropriate for your future. Taking a grand departure from conventional wisdom can be a powerful career builder.

Wright

So networks are a "go along" type of situation, and when it comes to career building, you don't believe that a person has to "go along to get along"?

Milazzo

Did Madonna "go along" to skyrocket her career? Does Donald Trump "go along" with *anybody*? Is Richard Branson "going along" as he promotes one crazy, successful venture after another?

You have to be willing to take a stand. Audaciously successful people often stand contrary to what the world believes is right and proper, and they don't care if their ideas upset people. Your goal, of course, is not to upset people but to express your ideas and opinions, uncensored, in your truest voice. Neutrality is a death sentence. You'll never please everybody, so don't kill your career—and your earning potential—by trying. As we say in Texas, "There's nothing in the middle of the road except yellow stripes and dead armadillos."

Dramatic success comes from taking a stance, even if it's contrary to the expected. Stir things up. Stand out. Be willing to tick off a few people. Let your competitors "go along" and have their middle-of-the-road, mediocre successes.

Wright

Taking a contrary stance may have worked for you in responding to networking naysayers, but how do you apply that theory to interacting with a supervisor or with your own customers? Isn't the customer always right?

Milazzo

In business, you can't please all your customers. The sooner you accept that fact, the better off you'll be. Contrary to what they say, you don't have to please every customer to be successful. In fact, probably no matter what you do—and I'm a believer in jumping through hoops for customers—10 percent of buyers are never satisfied with anything they buy. The question (and it's a difficult one) is when is it worth your while to cater to a disgruntled few? The most successful people seem to know when it's right to change a policy or pricing structure to fit a prospect's or client's narrow idea of what's appropriate. Likewise, they know when not to change what they believe is smart and right just to please a few squeaky wheels.

Our company is not interested in attracting every buyer. There are some people we don't want as customers—the wrong attitude, the wrong energy—and *we* reject *them*. We can tell that they are not right for our product. We're actually glad when our competitors scoop them up. I've even referred people to competitors because I know they're not someone I want buying my product and I would rather a competitor who deserves the headaches get them.

In building a career, you'll have many opportunities to do what others believe is best for you—family, friends, well-meaning employers. And their expectations of you might differ. You can't always please them all and please yourself. If an opportunity works into your action plan, fine, but don't take an offer that clearly diverts you from your chosen success path, no matter whom it pleases.

But what's also true is that even impossible-to-please customers (this includes friends and family members) may have the ear of a thousand other prospects. It's amazing how a little respect and understanding—along with the willingness to accept that your product or idea might not be right for this person—can reform an individual's attitude. Unhappy customers, if mishandled, have the ability to spread ill will about your company. They can also spread goodwill when handled properly. While you can't please all the people all the time, you can train yourself and your customer relations staff to interact with prospects and buyers in such a way that even bad news makes them smile. Excellent customer service is paramount to growing a successful business and building career success. When our clients tell us we charge "too little," I know we're doing things right. And that it's time to increase prices.

If you're employed, your CEO, supervisors, and directors are your customers—and they certainly aren't always right. The key to advancing—rather than getting fired—is learning how to present contrary ideas and opinions respectfully but persistently so people want to listen and hear more. You may feel they're stupid, stubborn, wrong, or worse—but no one likes a negatron, so pick your battles wisely. Your CEO may not be right, but your CEO does sign your paycheck. Your job is to figure out how to walk that fine line between pertinent but contrary contribution and downright insubordination. Any time you position a thing contrary to what others are seeing, point out how it will help further the company's goals, the department's goals, or your manager's goals.

Wright

Okay, but what if your ideas and opinions are rejected or ignored? Not everyone is born with the thick skin necessary to take rejection.

Milazzo

Contrary to what they say, *nobody* is born with thick skin. Have you ever felt a baby's skin? If you want career success, you have to develop thick skin, so just buck up. Rejection is part of life. The stronger you get at moving past rejection, the more successful you'll be at everything you want in life—making sales, pitching your ideas, getting a raise or a promotion, or building a business.

Wright

So you have to be thick-skinned enough to keep pushing an idea forward even if most people around you think it's wrong?

Milazzo

Conflict is healthy. Conflict triggers fresh ideas and solutions. I'm not talking about shouting or banging a shoe on the conference table, I'm talking about civilized conflict. Sometimes my managers will be so agreeable with one another that they're smiling and nodding their heads in agreement to what are actually very bad ideas.

My solution to this is to hire a "hit man," so that you're not as easily influenced by the group. Every company needs at least one person who sees things from a contrary viewpoint and is willing to shoot holes in popular concepts, established policies, or any otherwise unopposed positions—even if those positions are yours. A good hit man isn't a naysayer, doesn't disagree just to be argumentative, and knows how to equably state a conflicting opinion. You may be glad you developed that thick skin when the conflicting opinion is aimed at your pet project, but the resulting changes are usually worth any temporary discomfort.

As an individual, your hit man may be a friend or family member who will honestly point out where your ideas have holes or are being skewed by your own desires and expectations. Listen and be willing to reassess, rework, and, if necessary, abandon an idea that doesn't measure up. In the end, you have to decide what works for you, but a well-meaning dissenting voice is a valuable asset. Plus, if things really go south the hit man makes a good scapegoat. (Just kidding!)

The ultimate responsibility is still yours. And at the end of the day, you alone have to shoulder the responsibility for making a final decision.

Running a business or a department is not a democracy—in my company we joke that it's more of a benevolent dictatorship. I laugh (sometimes). Consensus does not and should not rule. Consensus, if it goes unchecked, can be devastating. Someone once said there are no statues of committees; there's a reason for that just like there are no statues of focus groups or polling groups. There are only statues of thick-skinned leaders who believed passionately in their contrary viewpoint or cause.

Wright

Would you say that time is money?

Milazzo

Not if you plan on striking it rich. You'll never be audaciously successful while watching a time clock. I realized in working with attorneys (at an hourly fee five times what I had made at the hospital) that people who get paid by the hour, including salaried executives, will always be limited in what they can earn. That's also true of consultants. Their income is capped by how many hours they can work in a day, a week, or a month. That's a pretty bleak outlook in my opinion. It was only after I started conceiving and creating products that were not dependent on someone's time that my company's earning potential became limitless.

Wright

So, as an entrepreneur, do you agree that "product is king?" And if you "build a better mousetrap," the world really will beat a path to your door?

Milazzo

Constantly improving an already excellent product won't guarantee success. But it can and will deplete your resources.

This is as true in individual career building as it is in entrepreneurship. People can be extremely smart and well educated yet be limited in people skills or work ethic. No matter how much they pile on the advanced education, they may not succeed as expected because improving the already excellent intellectual "product" wasn't where they needed to direct their resources. Nothing is worse than wasted talent, and in my opinion, one of the largest wastes of talent is to keep improving it without using it.

Everything is marketing. A good product will succeed if you present it in the right package to the right market at the right time.

Product is not king. *Presentation* of an excellent product is king. We know we have the best product, and we also know we could spend every day of the week improving it to make it better. Our continued success comes not from polishing and buffing our already shiny product, but from spinning off new ideas, auxiliary products, and more elaborate versions of our base product so that our customers can build on what they already have. This is similar to Microsoft, but in an Apple kind of way.

Wright

In that respect then, are employees a company's most valuable asset?

Milazzo

Employees are a company's most volatile asset. Some can be all smiles and enthusiasm one day, then inexplicably dull and lazy as time goes by. For a small business, one employee with a bad attitude can do more damage than all the company's advertising and public relations can undo. Yet, even at our favorite stores, don't we frequently encounter surly clerks and rude managers?

My staff is small—twenty-nine employees and a handful of consultants—and I personally interviewed every one of them. Most of them have proved to be a pleasure to work with and a treasure to the business. But a few former employees have disappointed me. Being small, we expect everyone, from directors to shipping staff, to give 100 percent of their energy and enthusiasm to their jobs. We expect the same commitment from our contractors and consultants. It's funny to say, but for a bad employee there is safety in numbers. A large company can tolerate a bad apple or two. But a small company simply cannot absorb the discord and expense that a bad employee generates, so a successful entrepreneur learns to trim out the deadwood.

As a business owner, I sometimes joke that I have twenty-nine kids because that's how it can feel at times. But they are not my children. They're all adults. I have to be strong enough to set rules and boundaries, and they have to be strong enough and smart enough to abide by them. They all know that while I graciously and sometimes not so graciously tolerate mistakes, I won't tolerate a bad attitude. Anyone who "cops an attitude" has crossed my boundaries, and they're out the door. I've been known to call someone on their attitude while in a meeting. When it comes to attitude, I won't pull punches.

Entrepreneurs who are diligent about hiring the best person available for the job, then equally diligent about expecting excellence and rewarding outstanding results, can find themselves surrounded by star-quality people. In those instances, employees are certainly a company's most valuable asset. And an individual who strives for star-quality performance will undoubtedly succeed at continuingly higher levels while the others will eventually gravitate right out the bottom.

Wright

Many business experts say that it's hard to keep good people today—that loyalty is out the window.

Milazzo

It's true that people don't enter a job with the idea of putting in a quick twenty-five years and retiring any more, but it's easy to keep good people if you give them reasons to stay. If employees can walk down the street and get the same benefits with less work, it's easy to think "why wouldn't they?" Our company consciously offers employees incentives that pretty much guarantee they want to stay on board—even the X and Y generations. Some obvious benefits are tuition reimbursement, profit sharing, good health benefits, hefty bonuses, and bonus days off. More important, we offer them a fun, exciting, and challenging work environment; we also encourage them to be creative and to grow in their job positions. One staffer completely rewrote her job description. It changes so often, I can't even keep up with it.

The only people who leave us are those we want to see go out the door. People will be loyal if they perceive that you're loyal to them and promote their advancement. The lesson here for individuals is: before you leave a company that treats you right, and trot down the street to make a few more dollars or gain a few extra perks, think carefully. We have an employee who came to us from Enron—need I say more?

Wright

Vickie, is it lonely at the top?

Milazzo

It sure can't be any lonelier at the top than it is at the bottom. At least at the top you can afford good wine for your friends and never have anything on layaway at the dollar store. My point is that if you're going to be lonely, you're going to be lonely whether or not you're successful. Why deprive yourself of success out of fear that you'll be lonely? One of the ways you avoid loneliness at the top is to work with a team you enjoy. Loneliness is a choice that has nothing to do with being rich or successful. This is one of those false-isms created by less successful people to justify why they're still mucking around at the bottom.

Like money and conflict, loneliness is relative. I have fun with my staff. We have a relaxed dress code and we laugh often during a day's work. But I tell them not to confuse my relaxed state about dress code and having fun with having relaxed standards.

Someone has to set an example of excellence, so I shoulder that load; and I expect my directors to pass it along. In an eight-hour day, I expect eight hours of prime time. We cook in prime time. We create, we confer, we sell, we ship, and we tally the results and we laugh while we're doing it. When the cooking's done, we even laugh as we wash dishes. Fear of loneliness can cause smart people to do dumb things like going along to get along.

In building a career, you'll see fellow employees who skim by exerting minimum effort with one eye on the clock, and you may wonder why you should be any different. You both knock down the same salary, so what's the gain? I saw that in the hospital and it's one of the reasons I started my own business. Too many people were rewarded for simply turning up, not for turning on. I want employees and coworkers who are as fired up as I am and hopefully they want the same.

If you have ambition beyond where you are right now, you'll pace yourself against the employee who's recognized for getting results. You'll look ahead to where you want to go, evaluate the person who's in that position now and what it took to get there, and compose your work ethic accordingly. You may be abandoned by your minimum-effort friends, you may even be lonely at times, but you'll be noticed by those who can influence your career success.

Wright

I've heard you state that the only real option for women who want career success is entrepreneurship. Why is that?

Milazzo

Contrary to what the corporate world wants us to believe, women still earn 23 to 54 percent less than men. The most recent census shows that the median annual salary for men is $38,000 and for women it is $26,000. And among physicians and surgeons—the highest-paid occupation for men and for women—the female median is $88,000 while the male median is $140,000. That's 63 percent less.

Every seriously career-oriented woman—and man too—should start his or her own business. There's no ceiling except the one you set yourself. A business is your hedge fund, your personal lottery, your jackpot. Only you control how much you earn.

In the corporate world, your salary is dictated by the guidelines and restrictions of an enormous system that starts with minimum wage and ends with the select few who knock down seven-figure incomes. How long it takes to move from one level to another depends on where you enter the game and how many contenders you encounter at each level.

As your own boss, you can strategize to skip those income levels completely, moving your business as fast as your energy and other resources allow. The only limits you'll encounter are those you set yourself.

Wright

But owning a business is risky, isn't it? Don't most businesses fail?

Milazzo

It's riskier to work for a company that can downsize you, take away your pension, or take away your voice. With no business training, I didn't exactly have "Entrepreneur" written on my forehead, and when I started my business I knew it had the potential for failure—but I also knew I could always go back to traditional nursing. What did I have to lose? I was working ten-hour shifts in a $28,000-a-year job.

My initial entrepreneurial idea was a "patient information" business. In healthcare, patients are often uninformed about their situation, and busy healthcare providers are not always the best educators. The idea was sound. The market was good—there's never a shortage of ill or injured patients. But I soon learned that insurance companies wouldn't pay for patient education, so the profit potential was low, and the first fixed rule of business is "create profit." Fortunately, I didn't jump in headfirst. Instead I created a completely new business idea that had the potential to be profitable. We owe it to everyone—ourselves, our families, our employees, and our clients—to succeed *big*.

Wright

In a corporation, there is usually a chain of command and a board of directors to spread the power around, while an entrepreneur is more like a dictator. What does that do to the individual when it's said that "power corrupts; absolute power corrupts absolutely?"

Milazzo

Some people are intimidated by or afraid of power, and that's just silly. Some people think that power is evil, and that's also silly. Maybe they're afraid of being "corrupted," as you say. To succeed on a high level you must possess a strong sense of self. You must trust yourself. Personal power leads to success, emotional well-being, and an enormous sense of freedom. When you get in touch with your own personal power you have more to offer, more to gain, more to share.

From actress Jennifer Hudson to financial guru Suze Orman to billionaire cofounder of The Gap, Doris Fisher, their power is sexy, fun, provocative, thrilling, dangerous, seductive, uplifting, and ennobling. Only when we can appreciate power in others can we reinforce it in ourselves and use it effectively.

If you choose to don the entrepreneurial mantle, you must strip your mind-body energy to its primitive essence and run naked into power. Accept that you are not perfect. In this acceptance, you realize the real power within. Expecting yourself to be perfect often keeps you inside your mental-emotional house with a fear of leaving the house because you're not perfect.

An entrepreneur can choose to be powerfully humble. For accountability and responsibility, the buck stops with you. If you choose power, you are equipped to seize each moment. If you choose to be powerless, your life and each moment in it will reflect that choice. You can exercise your power muscles and integrate that power into your entire life. How you use your power is a heady decision, but power doesn't corrupt. It's wrong thinking on any level that corrupts.

Wright

Don't entrepreneurs often say, "You don't own the business, the business owns you"?

Milazzo

It doesn't have to be that way. People who let their job or their business take over their lives are not good organizers or they're letting themselves get sucked into the myth. Every year, I take twelve weeks of vacation, and at least 50 percent of that time, I have no communication with my staff at all. I recently traveled to Antarctica where I had no communication with my employees for twenty-six days. As soon as I publish my vacation schedule my managers are already shining up the party glasses and lining up the Jell-O shots for their staff meetings (a tradition I proudly started). Sure, I own all the gadgets designed to stay in touch, but I don't take them along. It means less baggage, and no temptation. If you're in touch every day, you're not vacationing—you're just changing the view from your office. That's not for me—when I'm gone, I'm off the grid until I resurface.

Cutting myself off occasionally is healthy not only for me but also for the staff. When I'm around, people naturally consult with me. When I'm gone, they have to make critical decisions without me, and having that responsibility helps them become more independent in their job positions, which in turn builds their confidence for the next decision. I don't always like the decisions they make, but it's usually too late to unmake them (and they really like that).

Many individuals who work for corporations feel that their job owns them, even when they're not there. The best way to assure that you can leave work at the end of the day is to pack your workday with meaningful action or, as we say, "more sack and less yak." For some people, work hours are leached away into projects or conversations that don't specifically relate to their own workload or are taken away from someone else's. Contrast that typical situation with how much you get done on the day before you leave for vacation. If you approach every day with that same level of intensity, you will be able to feel proud and secure about walking away at the end of the day.

When you leave, be just as intense and protective of your off time. Just because you own a BlackBerry® doesn't mean you have to turn it on over the weekend or check it compulsively every time you sit down. We often see high-tech business "experts" glued to their communication devices like music lovers glue their ears to their iPods and television lovers glue their bottoms to their recliners. On your road map to success, these devices are the quicksand. They'll suck you in, suck your brain empty, and suck all the living out of your life.

While staying in touch with your world is important to career and business building, staying in touch with yourself is even more important. While I'm on vacation—cut off from just about everything—my mind and body are renewed, refreshed, and readied for action. The ideas start popping, the juice starts flowing, and I can't wait to get back into a high-speed lane headed for my next big success.

Wright

This has been interesting, illuminating, and even a little disturbing. Now I'm convinced that most of my true-isms are really false-isms. Do you have any last words for your readers?

Milazzo

Just two: No matter what you are doing *have fun*. Success means hard work but it doesn't have to be simply hard. We consciously have a lot of fun, and when things get dull one of my staffers is great at reminding us by saying, "Let's get this party started!" Remember to laugh, remember to take your job seriously and not to take yourself too seriously, and if you forget, just ask your spouse or best friend—they'll be happy to remind you.

About the Author

VICKIE L. MILAZZO, RN, MSN, JD has appeared on television and over two hundred national and local radio stations as an expert on legal nurse consulting, entrepreneurship, and career advancement. She was a contributor to the National Public Radio program, *This I Believe*.

Milazzo has been featured or profiled in numerous publications, including *The New York Times, Entrepreneur,* and *Investor's Business Daily.* Her work has been published everywhere from *USA Today* to *Seventeen* to *PINK* magazine.

Milazzo's many honors include the following:

- *Wall Street Journal* best-selling author
- *Inc.* Top 10 Entrepreneur—one of the top entrepreneurs in the nation
- *Inc.* Top 5000 Fastest-Growing Private Company in America
- Stevie* Award for Women Entrepreneurs—Mentor of the Year
- *NurseWeek* Nursing Excellence Award for Advancing the Profession
- Most Innovative Small Business—Pitney Bowes

To Contact Vickie L. Milazzo, RN, MSN, JD ...
Vickie Milazzo Institute
5615 Kirby Drive, Suite 425
Houston, Texas 77005-2448
800.880.0944
mail@LegalNurse.com
LegalNurse.com
InsideEveryWoman.com

ROADMAP to SUCCESS

15

An interview with...

Glenn & Barbara Smyly

David Wright (Wright)

Today we're talking with Glenn and Barbara Smyly. The Smylys are international professional speakers, master facilitators, and premier philosophers. They have dedicated their lives to helping people heal themselves physically, mentally, spiritually, emotionally, and financially through their unique brand of self-healing known as Careapy˚. For three decades, Glenn and Barbara have been blessed to help tens of thousands of people who have participated in their seminars, workshops, retreats, and personal consultations. From parenting to leadership and success, from money to spirituality, Glenn's and Barbara's inspiring courses and books give participants the power to change their attitudes and their lives.

Glenn and Barbara, welcome to *Roadmap to Success.*

Glenn and Barbara Smyly (Smyly)

Thank you for including us in this important project, David. We are honored to be asked to share a synopsis of what we have learned on our journey in the self-help, or rather, help yourself field.

Wright

After facilitating success and leadership programs for both corporate clients and personal clients internationally for twenty-six years, how would you define success?

Barbara

When our clients first asked us to develop our "Success Seminar," we would ask the participants coming in to start the Seminar what success was to them. There were always answers like money, prosperity, health, or family. Everyone had their own ideas about success, but we could never find an answer any better than the one Napoleon Hill defines in his book, *Think and Grow Rich:* "Success is the progressive realization of a worthwhile, predetermined goal."

The moment we set a goal and begin moving toward it, we are a success. Failure is only when we give up and quit going for it.

Wright

Glenn, you speak about how important role models are to those learning about success. Who are some of the most influential people in your success as a professional speaker and facilitator? What made you decide to devote your life to sharing and teaching others the tools to being successful?

Glenn

One of the most influential people in my life was my granddad, Edgar Bowen. He lived in Jacksonville, Florida, and was a chief executive of the Standard Oil Company.

In my family there were seven children—four boys and three girls—and two adults living in a three-bedroom, one-bathroom home. My brothers and I had the front bedroom, our sisters had the middle bedroom, and Mom and Dad had the back bedroom. We didn't live in poverty because Mom and Dad worked to make just enough money to pay all the bills, provide clothes for us all, and put food on the table.

When I was fourteen years old Granddad Bowen came to visit and invited me to spend the summer with him in Jacksonville. He owned a brand new 1956 Buick and started driving us north on the Florida State Turnpike to Jacksonville. After two hours of driving he pulled over to the side of the road and said, "Okay, it's your turn to drive." I told him I had never driven a car before and this was a brand new one. He laughed and said, "It's easy. There is the gas pedal, that is the brake, and this is the steering wheel." He then climbed into the passenger seat, leaned back, closed his eyes and went to sleep. I drove for the next four hours at speeds up to sixty-five miles an hour as king of the road in that brand new Buick. My self-esteem grew three sizes that day just knowing that for perhaps the first time in my life someone believed me capable of succeeding at something I had never done before. And succeed I did. By the time we got to St. Augustine I could drive a car!

My granddad was very wealthy in all aspects of the word. He lived in the penthouse of a large hotel with maid service, fine dining, and the best of everything, which I saw him generously sharing with everyone he met. Whether it was a kind word or a dollar, he always gave. He bought me all new clothes and treated me as though I was someone deserving of his special treatment and attention, just as he did to all he met. This shifted my view of my own self-worth. If my granddad thought I was worth something, maybe I was.

In only a few days I went from living on the edge of poverty to living a rich lifestyle. I soon discovered how the "wealthy people" live. Being financially and emotionally capable of giving whatever was wanted or needed to whomever I pleased was a new goal for me. To my fourteen-year-old brain, this was success. It inspired me to study successful people and attain that level of success myself. My very first goal in life was well established by the end of our visit. I would be a success in my life! I just didn't know how. The more I was around him the more I noticed what success was and how it felt to be successful. Just being around him interacting with others made me feel successful. That summer with Granddad planted seeds that would guide me through the rest of my life.

Some of the people I studied with along my journey to becoming successful were Napoleon Hill *(Think and Grow Rich)*, Zig Ziglar, Jose Silva, Werner Erhardt, and Leonard Orr. Each one contributed to my knowing myself better, and guided me on the path to success.

Wright

Glenn, how did your brand of self-improvement, Careapy, come about?

Glenn

I reached a critical stage in my life in 1978, after being married for twelve years, when I realized I was "doing marriage and family" exactly the way my parents did it—surviving but not thriving. I was working hard at every level of my being but going nowhere fast and unintentionally hurting those I loved in the meantime.

Having limited tools and resources available, I ended the marriage—I quit. I failed. The thought of myself as a failure—as letting down so many people I loved—rocked my world. Beginning life anew, as a failure, I was determined to be successful financially, mentally, emotionally, and spiritually. I began researching and working to heal myself—to become a better man and father.

For three years I traveled the United States leading other successful people's seminars and gradually, through sharing in others' healing I began developing some philosophical ideas of my own that I began incorporating into my own life and sharing with my clients.

I met Barbara in late 1981 and shared with her my philosophy. Barbara was supervising a private, twenty-eight-bed home for abused, abandoned, and neglected children and had her own experiences and philosophy of how to encourage children to begin to heal themselves of past experiences. We combined my philosophy with adults with her philosophy of children and developed a weekend retreat we called, "Alivening." Word-of-mouth and client referrals began filling these retreats.

As people continued participating in the Alivening Weekend Retreats and having so many powerful results in their lives and relationships, they started sharing about the Weekend with their friends, families, and loved ones. Soon more and more people began calling to enroll in the next available Weekend until today we have thousands of successful graduates of the program.

The participants of the Weekend wanted ongoing support, so we soon developed our "One Day Seminar" program. We would meet one Sunday each month from 9:00 am until 6:00 pm. Everyone would bring a favorite dish, so we shared a delicious meal together as well. We would focus on a different topic of discussion each month as an extension of what was taught in the Weekend. We developed a new daylong course each month.

Barbara and I were married in 1985 and soon after we were asked to write a book about the Weekend so people could refresh what we shared with them and give it to their family and friends to help them understand themselves also. Our book, *All in the Name of Love,* went into its second printing in 1986.

There came a time when clients wanted more specific growth, so we developed more programs. Our retreats included an "Alivening Week-long" program in Florida, a "Couples Only Retreat" in the Poconos, and a "Singles Only Retreat." We developed a six-month "Leadership Course" and a ten-day "Commitment" course. We also held "Positive Parenting" seminars, "Success Seminars," and "Money Makeover" seminars. We trained others to facilitate our Alivening Weekends and continued writing and creating new courses addressing specific issues.

As we continued facilitating these various, powerful, intimate retreats, courses, and programs, we began discovering, revealing, and noticing "common truths" that helped people heal significant physical, mental, spiritual, and emotional problems in their life. This information—this body of knowledge gained from our experiences—was developed into an educational curriculum we decided to brand as Careapy.

Wright

What is the difference between Careapy and therapy?

Barbara

To us, therapy is a place for those who are suffering intense emotional or psychological traumas. For those whose lives are consumed by self-talk that is destructive, paralyzing, or downright emotionally painful, therapists can save their lives and their sanity.

Careapy is for "healthy people with healthy concerns." Our goal is to educate clients in the "how-to" realms of mental, emotional, spiritual, physical, and financial health. Many times, when therapists and their clients have completed their treatments, the therapist recommends Careapy to help his or her clients move forward into their new ways of viewing the world and managing their self-talk so they can continue to boost their self-expectations and self-esteem. Careapy is a tool that can help clients redefine and rewrite that self-talk for the future. The tools of Careapy are easily learned and can be used daily to re-inspire ourselves and those around us.

In Careapy we take people back through their life to examine original causes of current circumstances. When they get to the cause of the circumstances they can see how they are responsible for causing them to be exactly the way they are and exactly the way they aren't and they are empowered to heal them. The first step in responsibility is to disengage from the blame game.

The moment we take responsibility for our circumstances, based on what we said about ourselves at that time—to be the way they are and the way they aren't—we get our power back to heal and readdress how it will be for us in our future.

Most of us put a band-aid on past events and don't recognize that past decisions about ourselves become self-talk throughout our lives. Without addressing—and yes, changing—our mind about our value in this world and our unique special-ness we continue to surrender to current circumstances as being "just the way it is for me" in this life, which produces a defeatist attitude all around.

Careapy is based on two basic fundamental ideas:

We are each 100 percent responsible for the circumstances and events that are happening in our life. They are happening the way they are to make us right about our own self-talk—our own expectations of what we deserve or don't deserve. In saying we are responsible, we're saying that we are at cause in the matter, we are accountable for the circumstances, we are the source of the circumstances being exactly the way they are, and exactly the way they aren't, based on what we tell ourselves. We are the author, producer, director, and actor (or actress) in our own drama. This is an exciting concept since it means we have the power to directly change our circumstances, or at least change how we react to those circumstances.

It is important to understand that responsibility has nothing to do with blame or guilt. Blame is our attempt to make someone else be responsible so we can be a victim of the circumstances. Guilt is the energy we use to punish ourselves before someone else can. When we reject blame and guilt, we have the ability to forgive ourselves or others and move strongly into our future.

So the first foundational idea is that we are each 100 percent *responsible* for the circumstances in our life being exactly the way they are. We are however, *not responsible* for what other people do. We do not have power over other people and their behavior. Now, if we are in an abusive relationship, it is *irresponsible* if we do not take some kind of corrective measures to remove ourselves from that abuse. It becomes important to make these distinctions when examining the past with the intention of empowering ourselves for the future.

The second foundational idea is that in the beginning, at conception, in the womb before we were born, at child birth, based on the circumstances of our birth and what happened there, or during early childhood, in the midst of a very emotionally, upsetting circumstance or event, we took a stand, we gave our word, and we said how our life was going to be. This becomes the foundation of a lifetime of self-talk. The circumstances and events that are happening in our life are happening the way they are to make us right about that stand. It has become a self-fulfilling prophesy. That's why these circumstances keep recurring over and over and over—to make us right about that original decision. Not only do they recur but they do so in a timely fashion.

If that stand was, "I am an unlovable person," anytime someone showed up loving us, it would make us very uncomfortable. We would have to push people who loved us away so we could be right that we were unlovable. It would always look like they were leaving us, but in truth, we were pushing them away so we could be right. If our stand was, "I'm not good enough," we would continually find evidence to show us we were right—we were not good enough. We would create breakdowns so that we would not be successful, so we could be right that we were not good enough. There are those we know who get right on the edge of having success, only to have it fall through at the last possible moment. These are CEOs who build a company from scratch only to have the Board of Directors take it away from them just prior to financial success.

One way to know if your stand is "I'm not good enough" is to notice when people acknowledge you for doing a great job. When people acknowledge you for doing a great job, do you feel awkward and fidgety or get embarrassed? If that happens then you know your stand is, "I'm not good enough." You're saying, "I am not good enough and they are saying I am good enough so either I'm lying about my stand—I'm not good enough—or they're lying that I am good enough. I'm not going to be liar, I'm going to be right."

Would you rather be right or alive and in love? If you would just stop for a minute and listen to what you are saying to yourself daily you could see that your thoughts are not always conducive to success. Successful people take responsibility for what they listen to and from whom they hear it, especially their own self-talk.

Wright

Glenn, what is the largest barrier people have to being successful and how does Careapy help people overcome that barrier?

Glenn

We have found that the moment you make a commitment to do something or achieve a goal, everything shows up to make it look impossible.

At fourteen I had a goal to be successful like Granddad Bowen but I just didn't know in what. When I went back to my "real" life, it looked utterly impossible.

Successful people know you have to be committed. You can't be committed sometimes; you have to be 100 percent committed all of the time to producing the results—your goals. You have to be committed, but the moment you make a commitment, everything shows up around you making it look impossible. You can talk to friends about what you're doing and they'll tell you, "Oh that won't work," because they tried, somebody else did it, it won't work, etc. They may even try to present their evidence of why they are right that it is impossible. Again, everything shows up to make it look impossible, highly risky, or even downright fiscally irresponsible.

Now, if you keep on going for your goal and going for it, what shows up next is, well, maybe—maybe you can reach that result, maybe you can reach that goal. Then, as you keep going for it and going for it, you achieve the goal. When you do achieve the results, those other people who said it was impossible in the beginning will come back and say, "Oh, I knew you could do it all along." This is why it is so important to have people around you who believe in your ability to be successful. They already know you to be a success and they'll encourage you along the way to enjoy the journey.

Most people stop when it looks impossible, and that's the barrier that keeps them from being successful. In Careapy it's imperative that we persist even when it looks impossible. We encourage our participants to celebrate when somebody tells them it's impossible because they know they're getting close to succeeding.

Changing our own expectations about ourselves and our capabilities is what Careapy affects. The self-talk, doubts, and fear of failure, being made to look like a fool, so to speak, can stop even the most courageous from stepping out of daily rituals to reach for their goal. Careapy addresses and helps people to transform this self-talk and gives them tools of self-empowerment so they can keep going and growing.

Wright

Barbara, what role does leadership play in success or failure?

Barbara

The most important thing about leadership is that leaders have a vision. They can look ahead and see how they want things to be. They move forward where there is no road map; they are pioneers.

When Bill Gates was starting out in computers, he did not try to become rich and famous. His goal—his vision—was to have a computer on every desk in the country, and he hasn't reached that goal yet, but I have no doubt he will. He has come a long way toward achieving it by surrounding himself with creative managers who share his vision. He has become very wealthy in every sense of the word because he is a leader with a vision.

Again, leaders have a vision. That vision is what makes them excited to get up in the morning. They're passionate about it, and they would do it whether they made any money or not. They have to be involved in what their vision is because in a way, it fulfills their ideals and dreams about themselves. Leaders know everything that doesn't work and what will. Leaders will take what others deem failure and put in corrections until they find the solution that will work. Leaders recognize that for every problem there is a solution and the challenge to solve that problem can become a team effort. Leaders surround themselves with people of like mind who become their managers.

Our definition of failure is when we quit. The only time we've ever failed is when we've quit on a vision and yes, we have failed. We have consciously chosen to put aside visions that we couldn't get behind 100 percent. In these endeavors we failed. Our road map to success is to keep going, to persist through uncertainty until certainty is achieved.

As long as we are moving forward in our vision of Careapy—to educate "healthy people with healthy concerns"—we are successful. This has been our vision for twenty-six years and we are successful in this vision. You know it is a vision when you look forward to taking a month vacation and are asked to speak at a seminar instead and find yourself saying, "Sure, I'd love to."

Wright

What do you think the difference is between a leader and a manager? Is it just vision?

Barbara

A leader has the vision. The overall responsibility of bringing it forward as a reality lies with the leader. A manager knows what the leader's vision is and is committed to produce that result. A manager uses all of his or her talents and abilities to bring forth the results that the leader's vision is. Now, a leader can be a manager too, because the leader can put all the particles together and bring all the people together to make it happen. A manager is a partner in producing the vision and can add brilliance and insight to enhancing and bringing the vision of the leader to reality.

Wright

If your mission in life, in all probability, comes from your vision, how does Careapy help people discover their mission in life?

Glenn

We help people identify what they love to do in life the most. In our Careapy work we use guided imagery meditations that take people back through their life to find out what they really love to do the most, not what is available to them or what is practical to achieve; but rather, what is their dream? If they truly could contribute to their world, what would they contribute? Careapy helps free people to dream again. Once they've identified that arena, we support them in putting together a mission statement to support them in bringing forth their vision.

The mission statement is developed by writing down everything they love to do. Then they list all of the qualities they have and what they bring to the table. We teach people how to write a mission statement by combining those two lists into a strong powerful statement. For example, my mission statement is: "I bring my ability to communicate, my integrity, and my sensitivity to help people be more healthy, happy, alive, and in love."

My mission started when I was twelve years old. At twelve years old I would go to the corner drug store at night, buy a pint of ice cream, and continue down to the schoolyard. I would sit on the swings and talk to God. I would say, "God, there's got to be more to life than what I am seeing going on in my family. My mom and dad are not happy. They are working all the time; they're not having fun. I want to know the truth about life. God, please show me the truth about life."

I did that for most of the summer. As many nights as I could get out of the house, I would go down there, eat ice cream, and talk to God. Then I went on about my life with a sense of internal peace. My granddad came to show me a new way to view life two summers later and I had my answer: life is to be lived, enjoyed, and shared, regardless of current circumstances.

Working so intimately with people, at the very core of their lives for so many years, we have rediscovered how important it is to our own well being as humans to know that we make an imprint on those we interact with. Our character does count. Our behavior does impact our self-worth and esteem. We knew this as small children, but we have forgotten.

A personal mission statement is a constant reminder to us to never give up on our own personal integrity. This is why we teach about the *"ity"* family.

Wright

I have heard you speak so much of the *"Ity"* family. What in the world is the "Ity" family?

Glenn

The "Ity" family is a group of issues that most inspiring leaders and successful people embody:

1. *Integrity*—It is imperative that people have integrity in their life. If they operate from integrity in their life everything runs smoothly. What we have found is that when our integrity is out—if we lie, cheat, steal, or have an affair—within seventy-two hours, we punish ourselves. The punishments come in the form of receiving a bad check or somebody will rip the radio out of our car, we'll stub our toe, or we'll get sick. When we tell the truth and clean it up, the problems will be resolved within seventy-two hours. This can be difficult because not many of us want to acknowledge temporarily losing integrity. But, the truth is, sometimes we do.

2. *Responsibility*—We spoke about this earlier—being the cause in the matter. Successful people take responsibility for all aspects of their lives. They set their priorities to include all aspects of their lives, not just their work.

3. *Sensitivity*—Successful people are sensitive to what's going on with the people in their life, the people they're working with, the people they are supporting, their family, and their friends. They are attentive to what is happening.

4. *Perseverity*—It's important that we persevere—that we keep going, even when it doesn't meet our picture. I have taught seminar after seminar in my life where it cost me money to actually teach because the groups were so small. The people, however, would get the value and the healing. The mental, spiritual, and emotional healing was phenomenal. So you just keep going for it because you have to do it. When you're in touch with your vision and it is your purpose in life, you have to do it whether you get paid to do it or not; it doesn't matter, you still have to do it and do it well. Then you go back to the drawing board and find out what didn't work and put in the correction. So you do make money doing what you love.

5. *Connectivity*—You have to connect with the people you're working with in your career, in your vision, and your mission. The most successful people remember and recognize those who helped make them successful along the way.

6. *Reliability*—People have to be able to count on you. You have to give your word and keep it. Again, it has to do with integrity, but it's also being reliable, dependable, and flexible.

7. *Creativity*—We have to be able to open up our creative channels, see things differently, and tap into the idea bank that's all around us to find solutions for the problems that we're looking at. This requires a plan for stress management. A mind that is filled is not open to new ideas.

8. *Spirituality*—It's imperative that successful people have some kind of connection with God. Whether it's a religion or it's their own personal relationship with God, it's important that they have a spiritual pathway they follow that allows them to tap into a higher energy greater than they are, and helps them to be successful and centered in serving their mission.

9. *Relationship-ability*—We have to be relationship-able; would we want to be in a relationship with us? So the way that we can help be in a relationship with people is to serve them, to find out what they want, and need, and do our best to provide it for them. When we can provide them with what they want and need, they'll provide us with what we want and need. A little appreciation goes a long way.

10. *Morality*—This is an issue of personal integrity. Defining what is and is not acceptable becomes extremely important as success begins pouring in. This is what keeps our ego and priorities in check.

Wright

So what do you want our readers to know about success?

Barbara

We would like people to know that if they have a set of worthwhile, predetermined goals and are moving toward them, they are successful. If they are excited and passionate and love what they're doing, they are successful. When they set the goal and begin taking action to achieve that goal, they are successful. People want to be around happy, successful people. Enthusiasm is infectious.

But what is a goal? We have worked with so many people and helped them in their goal-setting that we have come to the following definition of a goal:

"A goal is a commitment we make to produce a specific result within a specified time-frame with no evidence that it can be achieved."

When President Kennedy said, "We will put a man on the moon in this decade and bring him home safely," that was a goal. He spoke out with emotion, with commitment, with intensity. If you have ever seen him give that speech, you can see how intense he was about achieving that goal. Then what happened? Everybody thought it was impossible—America could not go to the moon. Instead of stopping at the impossible, NASA kept going for it and going for it. Then it was, well, maybe we can do it. They kept going and going for it until it was achieved.

Now, very often what a goal is today becomes a "to-do" for tomorrow. Once we went to the moon, then we made another trip to the moon—we could do it again. But then it became a "to do"—it was no longer a goal. If I have to pick up my laundry because I need my suit for the seminar tonight, I have got to have it—it's a goal—I have to fit it in and I have to make it happen today. Normally just picking up the laundry would be a "to-do."

So perhaps an immediate goal (or for some a "to-do") is for just one day to listen to how you speak to and about yourself and begin to reject any self-sabotage, perhaps your world would be a happier, more successful and productive place. Success begins as a state of mind and it is incumbent on us all to remember that we each have a unique contribution to make to this world, and we all need to get about making it.

Wright

What a great conversation, Glenn and Barbara. I really appreciate all the time you've taken with me today to answer these questions. I've learned a lot and I'm sure that our readers will.

Glenn

Thank you for inviting us to be a part of this worthwhile project. It is our hope that your readers embrace and investigate what has been shared in these few pages and realize that success is one dream away and thought is creative. Tapping into that creativity is the goal of our Careapy programs.

Wright

Today we've been talking with Glenn and Barbara Smyly. They are two of those rare people who have dedicated their lives to serving everyone sent to them for support. For more than three decades they have helped thousands of people who have participated in their seminars, workshops, retreats, and personal consultations. Their patience, compassion, intuition, and integrity have generated a safe, loving environment for people to confront their deepest concerns and heal themselves.

Glenn and Barbara, thank you so much for being with us today on *Roadmap to Success.*

Barbara

It has been our honor. Thank you!

About the Author

BARBARA & GLENN SMYLY founded the Alivening Project Inc. in 1982, with the vision of empowering people to create relationships that are more alive, happy, healthy, and in love. As a result of their combined strengths, personalities, love, and talents, tens of thousands of people have benefited from their seminars, workshops, consultations, retreats, books, and home study courses.

Their commitment to helping people has been so strong that during the past twenty-six years, they have held many successful weekend seminars each year, in addition to week-long Living Relationship training sessions, six month Leadership Trainings, Success Seminars, and monthly one-day seminars on different topics. The Alivening list of educational programs, conducted throughout the United States, also consists of couples' weekends, singles' weekends, Character Education Programs, childbirth and parenting training, as well as stress management, money makeover seminars and developing prosperity consciousness.

Both Barbara and Glenn are members of the American Seminar Leaders Association and provide workshops that are extremely powerful and productive in public, private and corporate sectors.

It is a gift to spend time with Barbara and Glenn. They bring to all their work a high level of energy, intelligence, compassion, a depth of caring, and a strong desire to support people in making significant changes in their lives.

To Contact Glenn and Barbara Smyly...
P.O. Box 1368
Land O Lakes, FL 34639
813.996.3659
www.careapy.com
glenn@careapy.com